"A page-turning tale of personal obsession to solve a great historical mystery frozen in time. Rachel Lance dives deep into an era during the Civil War when combatants took almost unimaginable risks, then uses a thrilling combination of creativity, ingenuity, and curiosity to answer questions long thought lost beneath the waves. A wonderful adventure told by that rarest of breeds—a scientist who writes beautifully and won't relent until she knows."

—Robert Kurson, *New York Times* bestselling author of
Shadow Divers and *Rocket Men*

"*In the Waves* draws the reader deep into a layered mystery, rich with explosive experimentation, Civil War history, and the engaging personal narrative of a young scientist. As persuasive as she is passionate, Rachel Lance expertly unravels the tragedy of the *Hunley*, complete with its scientific and historical context. Yet Lance's book reveals more than torpedo blasts and shock waves: it is an inspiring look at what is possible when devotion and science are joined."

—Nathalia Holt, *New York Times* bestselling author of *Rise of the Rocket Girls: The Women Who Propelled Us, from Missiles to the Moon to Mars*

"*In the Waves* is a thrilling expedition into one of the great unsolved mysteries of the Civil War. Harnessing the revelatory wonders of the digital age and her own undersea expertise—along with gritty determination and persuasive powers—Rachel Lance has delivered a mesmerizing tale of science, history, tragedy, and adventure!"

—Liza Mundy, author of *Code Girls*

"Lance deftly blends historical narrative and the unraveling of this scientific puzzle in a thoroughly accessible and entertaining style. . . . This engaging investigative work will intrigue readers of Civil War and naval histories and sleuths of scientific puzzles."

"Ever since the Confederate submarine *HL Hunley* was brought up from the ocean floor in 2000, with the skeletons of its eight crewmen still at their posts inside the intact hull, conservationists and historians have speculated about their fate. Were they drowned by water pouring in from damage by the torpedo explosion that sank their target, the USS *Housatonic*? Were they asphyxiated by lack of oxygen and carbon dioxide poisoning? Or did they die from some other cause? In this enthralling account based on extensive research and testing, the US Navy blast-injury specialist Rachel Lance solves the mystery in convincing fashion and offers an important contribution to Civil War literature."

—James M. McPherson, Princeton University, author of the
Pulitzer Prize–winning *Battle Cry of Freedom: The Civil War Era*

"They were the first crew of a submarine to sink an enemy ship, but did they ever have a hope of coming home? To find out, Rachel Lance brings together an unlikely mix of old-style weaponry, modern science, and people who love to make things go bang. This is her determined search to uncover the truth about an impossible mission. It is a great read!"
—Sherry Sontag, co-author of *Blind Man's Bluff*

"Rachel Lance's *In the Waves* is a captivating magic trick of a book: part detective story, part scientific mystery, and part personal essay on the challenges—and triumphs—of researching stubborn history. Lance weaves these threads with astonishing aplomb, and the devastating denouement will haunt you long after you've turned the final page."

—Karen Abbott, *New York Times* bestselling author of
The Ghosts of Eden Park

"[Lance] has a firm command of both the scientific and historical subject matter and writes with flair. Her richly detailed account appears to definitively solve this Civil War–era mystery." —*Publishers Weekly*

"Anyone who enjoys reading outstanding narrative nonfiction will absolutely love Rachel Lance's *In the Waves*. Reading it is like watching Sherlock Holmes investigate a murder mystery—if 'Sherlock' were an exquisite writer, a woman, and had to solve the mystery while battling petty academic jealousies. Lance unravels the science and medical hypotheses with engaging observations, venturing from Kurt Vonnegut and the allied bombing of Dresden to Senator Strom Thurmond. And this storytelling 'Sherlock' also packs a genuine sense of humor."

—Gary Kinder, author of *Ship of Gold in the Deep Blue Sea*

"*In the Waves*—a perfect title for Rachel Lance's captivating tale documenting her obsession with solving the Civil War mystery about a tiny Confederate submarine that successfully blasted apart a Union ship in the Charleston harbor and then disappeared without a trace for 131 years. With determination and a knack for storytelling, Dr. Lance recreates the daring mission of the *HL Hunley* and her demise, using precision-based bio-medical expertise to solve the mystery of how her eight-man crew died."

— Ann Blackman, author of *Wild Rose: The True Story of a Civil War Spy*

"When we brought the *Hunley* up in 2000, we were shattered with exhaustion and had put everything we had into prying the *Hunley* from the mud of Charleston harbor, but the recovery team assumed that the scientists and researchers who came after us would bring the same passion to the science and the story of *Hunley* as we had. We were not wrong. Dr. Lance brings a razor-sharp mind and an equally sharp wit to the greatest remaining mystery of the Civil War—how and why did *Hunley* sink? [Lance's] rigorous and highly accessible science, leavened with more than a few lovingly described characters and wry observations of graduate student life, makes *In the Waves* a compelling explanation and a rollicking good read!"

—David L. Conlin, PhD, *Hunley* recovery team field director, chief archaeologist, National Park Service

"Lively . . . An entertaining account of research that solved a historical mystery." —*Kirkus Reviews*

"This solid, engaging mystery recounts Lance's quest to solve the mystery of the crew of the Confederate submersible *Hunley* . . . in a lively, entertaining, novelistic style that carries the reader along with all the verve of an Agatha Christie whodunit." —*Booklist*

"Important, timely, and deeply entertaining . . . *In the Waves* is many things, all of them entertaining to read: a scientific documentary woven with thriller-novel intrigue, a serious history accented with gentle snark, and a rapidly paced recounting of the dogged pursuit of scientific truth and a PhD. But *In the Waves* is also an accessible and important exploration of the injury deeply affecting the current generation of America's service members." —*Garden & Gun*

IN THE WAVES

My Quest to Solve the Mystery of
a Civil War Submarine

RACHEL LANCE

DUTTON

DUTTON

An imprint of Penguin Random House LLC
penguinrandomhouse.com

Previously published in a Dutton hardcover edition in April 2020

First Dutton trade paperback printing: April 2021

LIBRARY OF CONGRESS CATALOGING-IN-PUBLICATION DATA
has been applied for.

Dutton trade paperback ISBN: 9781524744175

Printed in the United States of America
10 9 8 7 6 5 4 3 2 1

BOOK DESIGN BY LAURA K. CORLESS

To my brothers Jeff & Kevin,
Because I think we all made each other
into engineers

CONTENTS

The Ocean has its silent caves,
Deep, quiet, and alone;
Though there be fury on the waves,
Beneath them there is none.

The awful spirits of the deep
Hold their communion there;
And there are those for whom we weep,
The young, the bright, the fair.

Calmly the wearied seamen rest
Beneath their own blue sea.
The ocean solitudes are blest,
For there is purity.

The earth has guilt, the earth has care,
Unquiet are its graves;
But peaceful sleep is ever there,
Beneath the dark blue waves.

"THE OCEAN"
—Nathaniel Hawthorne

PROLOGUE

The dark hull of the submarine rose a few inches above the waterline, belying the impressive metal body submerged below. Pale moonlight glinted off the quiet ocean as small waves lapped rhythmically against the hull. The submarine was 40 feet long, cylindrical down most of her slim length, but with a tapered, wedge-shaped bow and stern that hinted at how quickly she could slice through the water. Two narrow, oval conning towers rose above the peak of the rounded hull, and a double row of small, glass deadlights punctuated the surface between them. The deadlights, with their thick, imperfect, handmade glass, provided the only means for the moonlight to pierce the submarine's bulk, and the only sign that there might be a crew within.

The *HL Hunley* was lying in wait to the east of Charleston Harbor, off the coast of South Carolina. The submarine had been there for months, practicing for her crucial mission and waiting patiently for flat seas.

Her bow carried the true source of her threat. A spar made of wood and metal was bolted securely to a pivot on the bottom corner of the boat's leading edge, and at the far end of this spar was a copper cylinder the size of a keg: the boat's torpedo. The torpedoes of the time were simple stationary bombs, very different from the modern, independent devices that can propel themselves through the water from a great distance. To complete her mission the *Hunley* would need to approach her target closely, then use this spar to press the charge directly against the side of her enemy's hull. As the submarine bobbed slowly in the waves, the lethal orange cylinder bobbed with it.

The propeller on the long submarine began to spin into motion. Its three arced blades cut through the cold February water and accelerated the sub in the direction of the open ocean. The tide was beginning to turn, and the outgoing current would further speed the *Hunley* toward her target.

On the deck of the Union ship USS *Housatonic*, the sailors gazed out over the flat seas of the Atlantic. Confederate torpedoes, later renamed "mines" by a future generation of warriors, lay peppered throughout the waters of Charleston's harbor, drifting idly on weighted tethers anchoring them to the ocean floor. The *Housatonic* had reached an uneasy détente with these hidden underwater bombs by staying in the shallows outside the harbor's mouth, but the Confederates were always trying new ways to attack. There had been reports of small, stealthy boats armed with charges on spars, and even some reports of mysterious boats that could supposedly travel completely under the water. The *Housatonic* was just one of many Union ships that had been prowling the waters outside Charleston for months, and tonight, like every other night, the cool air was punctuated by the sounds of Union artillery gradually chipping away at that city's stately stone buildings. She tugged gently against her anchor as the tidal currents shifted and pulled her seaward. The *Hunley* swam closer.

It took hours to reach the ship.

The *Hunley* approached the hulking wooden mass of the *Housatonic*, and the comparatively tiny submarine began to pick up speed. A sailor on watch spotted the narrow sliver of the dark metal hull exposed above the surface of the water and alerted the other sailors on board, but submarines were new technology and the men did not yet understand the deadly shape in the water. For a few brief minutes speculation ran wild among the crew, and the sailors did nothing as they comforted themselves that the dark shape was merely a porpoise coming to play near the ship. They realized the approaching danger too late, and the crew scrambled for firepower, any firepower, that could be trained to hit the oncoming object. The submarine remained undeterred.

HL Hunley pressed her torpedo snugly against the *Housatonic*'s side. One of the three thin metal rods protruding from the leading face of the bomb depressed slightly against the wooden hull. The fragile wire holding the rod precariously in place snapped, freeing the coiled and waiting energy of the compressed spring that was firmly wrapped around its body. As the spring rapidly expanded to its natural shape, the metal rod leapt backward in response and smashed against the thin wall of the compartment that was nestled in the back of the trigger. Inside the compartment were two small caps filled with mercury fulminate. The simple, elegant chemical was inherently unstable, dying for the slight nudge that would propel it into a cascade of cathartic release.

Any fire is a release of energy. Chemicals and materials in one state leap to a more stable, lower-energy state, like a rock rolling down to a lower-energy state at the bottom of a hill. The energy released from the reaction takes the forms of heat, sound, and light. An explosion is a similar reaction but pushed into higher speed.

The rod impacted the thin compartment wall directly opposite one of the unstable mercury fulminate caps, and the boulder was shoved violently off a massive cliff.

Electrons began to transfer. The nitrogen, oxygen, and carbon of the fulminate rearranged, and the potent chemical reaction inside the caps released fiery heat and energy into the surrounding black powder. The powder caught next, each small granule beginning to burn, release heat, and pass the explosion to its neighbors like trees in a dense forest caught in the tempest of a wildfire. The granules of black powder converted one at a time into a mass of extraordinarily heated gas, trapped in the thick copper casing of the tightly sealed torpedo until enough fiery, pressurized gas accumulated to muster the power to tear and destroy the metal.

The copper ripped open, sending jagged shards peeled backward over the *Hunley*'s spar, and releasing the fearsome pressures of the powder into the water and against the wooden hull of the *Housatonic*.

A spray of shattered wood planks burst upward from the deck of the ship. The submarine had hit her target, triggering her massive black powder payload directly against the stern and punching a lethal blow through its underbelly. The force of the blast rippled through the entire ship, and even the sailors at the bow nearly 200 feet away instantly understood that their vessel would soon be on the ocean floor.

As the crew scattered to save themselves, the metal hull of the submarine silently disappeared from concern. Those in Charleston awaiting the return of the *Hunley*, hoping to celebrate her successful mission, never saw her again.

One hundred and thirty-six years later, in 2000, in a massive custom-built water tank with a cathedral-like crown of metal support joists, archaeologists clad in protective coveralls and wearing respirators sorted patiently and painstakingly through the muck and silt that had slowly filled the hull of the submarine as it had lain waiting on the bottom of the ocean floor. Hunched over the curved surface of the boat and removing silt one small scoop or chunk at a time, they revealed bone after bone.

Accounts of the *Hunley*'s sinking had assumed horrific scenes of the men trying to claw their way through the thick iron hatches, or huddled in the fetal position beneath the crew bench in their agony. Sinkings of modern submarines always resulted in the discovery of the dead clustered near the exits in their desperate efforts to escape their cold metal coffins, because to sit silently and await one's own demise simply defies human nature.

The crew of the *Hunley*, however, looked quite different. Each man was still seated peacefully at his station.

The lost crewmen of the *HL Hunley* are often painted as gilded martyrs, noble and titanic warrior-champions who squeezed voluntarily into a narrow tomb for the patriotic reasons of home and country. No other explanation is ever offered, or even made to seem necessary, to explain their presence in the doomed submarine. In reality, however, the simple mechanical device was the product of the cumulative effort of many people working together to accomplish their own varied and disparate goals, and something far more complex than pure nobility motivated these men to volunteer themselves. The final mission took place even after two crews had already been killed by the vessel, and at first everything seemed to go according to plan: the mechanical beast of the submarine behaved exactly as she was designed to behave, they reached their target, the bomb exploded. Yet somehow the victorious little boat also profoundly failed, because every man of the crew died without a single external sign of struggle.

For decades since her recovery people have wondered about the final mission of the *Hunley*, how the crew died, how they ended up trapped in a silent grave buried beneath the sea. For decades people have wondered, in a question imbued with more than one layer of meaning: *How did these men get here?*

About one-quarter of the world's countries now boast a military submarine fleet. Hundreds of the vessels of this "silent service" continuously prowl the world's oceans under the cover of salted waves. They carry untold thousands of sun-deprived sailors for months at a time, and transport without detection a portion of the world's nuclear arsenals.

And it all started with the *Hunley*.

CHAPTER 1

WHAT ABOUT THE *HUNLEY*

Being a scientist is like being an explorer. You have this immense curiosity, this stubbornness, this resolute will that you will go forward no matter what other people say.

—Sara Seager, planetary scientist

I stood on the deck of the slightly rolling ship and looked down at the sea below. A faint breeze across the Gulf of Mexico was not enough to make the day comfortable. I had rolled out of bed at 0330, or less specifically oh-dark-thirty, as the smaller numbers of the morning are sometimes called by the men and women of the United States Navy. That had left me just enough time to rouse myself to a state of consciousness sufficient for driving, get to base, and get safely on board the specialized military diving vessel before she got under way. We had been waiting for good weather to undertake this mission, and the calm waters off the starboard gunwale looked bleary through my tired eyes. I had been working toward the next moments for the last year and a half.

My job as a civilian engineer in Panama City, Florida, had been to get us to this point: to find a new underwater breathing system, prove it was safe, and get the navy to let us test dive it in the open ocean. It was a seemingly straightforward task, but one that had required plenty of sweat, creativity, and math. By the time the divers emerged from the ocean, I knew that the new system worked.

We cast celebratory fishing lines off the stern and trolled for dinner on the way home. The success of this project meant that the navy would want me to lead projects myself, to submit proposals for new technologies. They had even offered me the chance to go back to school and get a PhD in biomedical engineering so I could do it.

A few months later, I was assigned a seat at a curved desk with pale faux-wood veneer in the far corner of a narrow office on the Duke University campus. Wedged to the left of my desk was a battered black filing cabinet containing hundreds of meticulously labeled manila folders, shoved full of papers by a compulsive graduate student who had long ago studied cardiac function from my chair. The filing cabinet blocked my view of the lone, slitlike window on the wall opposite the doorway, and I had recycled the papers in the bottom drawer to make room for a small stockpile of individual-serving bags of potato chips— stolen booty from the catering tables at lectures on campus.

Unlike undergraduate students, who pay the costs of their own tuition, engineering PhD students are paid a stipend to perform their work and are often given the job title of "research assistants." However, these students are still different from normal employees because from the first day they arrive at their new labs they are already hoping to leave as quickly as possible. Graduation with a PhD is not guaranteed by completing certain classes; rather, the degree is granted only when, and if, a student's adviser declares the student to be finished. It's tacitly forbidden to ask the senior students when they will graduate because they are likely asking themselves the same question every day.

As students finish and move on, they often leave behind objects like relics of their time there, and new students moving into these borrowed spaces shift around the layers of abandoned artifacts to clear themselves an area. I had claimed my secret snack drawer but moved almost nothing else since I had first been placed into that office when I arrived at Duke in August 2011.

My research adviser was Cameron R. Bass, known as Dale to everyone who had ever spoken with him. He was an associate research professor of biomedical engineering and the director of Duke's Injury Biomechanics Laboratory. Dale believed in efficiency above all else. His white hair and facial stubble were all trimmed to the same short-cropped length, a process his wife could do for him at home without wasting time at a barber. Every day he wore the same type of black polo shirt, with black or gray cargo hiking pants that zipped off at the knee, and the same heavy black lace-up combat boots. This daily uniform saved time shopping or picking out clothes. The students in Dale's lab researched injury biomechanics: the various mechanisms by which human beings got injured and killed. About half the students worked on car crashes, and the other half, including me, focused on explosions.

For several months I had been working through medical case reports from underwater explosions. Scientists have long had a fairly clear idea of how well human beings can tolerate blasts in air, but not as much is known about human tolerance to blasts that occur underwater. Injured people and shrapnel chunks tend to stay where they fall when explosions occur on dry land, leaving a scene that can be safely examined later, whereas the waves and currents of the ocean quickly destroy all clues. The underwater science, therefore, had received much less attention.

But cases with eyewitness testimony, with survivors to describe the details of what had happened and where, were still useful. My first goal had been to compile as many cases of human exposures to underwater explosions as I could find. Then, I would use a complex piece of navy modeling software, called Dynamic System Advanced Simulation (DYSMAS), to calculate how strong of a blast each person experienced. The DYSMAS software could accept crucial information like the size of the charge and the depth at which it detonated, then model the resulting explosion. The output from the software about the strength of the shock wave could then be combined with the medical report describing how badly each person was hurt. These cases, examined together as a group, would allow me to find the blast levels at which humans in the water get injured or killed. The hope, at least at that time, was to turn the project into my PhD dissertation.

Most of my cases were from World War II. I had been spending long days sorting through testimonies of human wreckage, seventy years after the fact, hoping to convert them into something useful. I combed through dozens of reports a day, looking for those where a sailor's physicians reported enough information to let me model his case. The stories were usually the same: feeling of a sharp kick to the groin, with a stabbing pain in the gut. Sometimes they would immediately vomit blood, sometimes they would have sudden and uncontrollable bloody diarrhea. Both are signs of severe trauma to the intestinal tract. Sometimes they would start coughing blood, a sign of damage to the lungs. Sometimes they watched a nearby friend sink silently beneath the waves.

The doctors in World War II were weirdly obsessed with food. They seemed to think there was some relationship between injury severity and the victim's most recent meal. The case reports are riddled with statements like "Case 47 had a sandwich three hours before the blast, but Case 48 had only coffee. . . ." I would find a case that reported distance from the charge, plug it into the navy's software, and then stare vapidly at the blank beige wall above my desk, munching on stolen potato chips while the code ran, wondering what was in Case 47's last sandwich. Were there pickles? I wondered what it was like to be moments from death, screaming in agony, with a large intestine split open along its length by a bomb, and then to have your doctor ask you about your sandwiches.

It was during one of these depressing reveries that I was glad for a distraction.

In graduate school, you learn to sense when your adviser is coming for you. Dale in particular had a distinct way of walking down a hallway. Point A and Point B were never close enough together, and the time spent between them was time he could have used more beneficially for research. His office was at the west end of the hallway and the lab's grad students, myself included, worked in the shared offices scattered down the line between him and most useful destinations. We all knew the rapid staccato *thunk* of his ever-present combat boots coming down the hall.

Each of us would listen for the boots to pass our door. If they kept going, we kept working uninterrupted. But sometimes the boots stopped a few steps past a door, paused, and then reversed. This interruption in their rhythm meant Dale had an idea. This day, a few years after my arrival at Duke, the boots stopped for me. Dale pulled a tattered blue office chair out of the corner, sat down, and looked at me expectantly.

"What about the *Hunley*." The words were delivered as a statement. There seemed to be no question mark in his tone. I had no idea what he was talking about, and the expression on my face probably told him so.

"What about the *Hunley*," he repeated. Dale often spoke in the clipped, truncated pattern I was familiar with from working on the navy base and talking to military operators. Minimal adjectives. Pleasantries are an inefficient use of time. Make your point and move on. My need for the repetition must have irked him, but still I had no idea what he was talking about.

"Can your fancy software model it?" he asked.

"Sure," I responded, still without any idea what he was asking. "I don't see why not." In grad school, unless you already have a damn good reason locked and loaded, the correct answer is always yes. Besides, DYSMAS was designed to assess ship damage. Whatever he was talking about, assuming it was a boat of some kind, the navy's software could probably model it.

The boots proceeded back on their mission down the hall.

Once Dale was safely out of earshot, I pulled up a new browser window on my computer and began to investigate the *Hunley* and what I had signed up for.

Being a blast-trauma expert requires a certain degree of mental immunity to death. Every project is started because someone died, or because there is a good chance someone could die. Even in the early days of blast research, long before the Nazis and the Nuremberg Trials made patient and test-subject protections a global concern, doctors shared a common tendency to obscure the details of cases that would make the victims human and identifiable. Papers often contain detailed drawings of torn and perforated intestines, but almost never are there external views of stiff or distended abdomens. There are illustrations showing blast lung, but fractured skulls are limited to text descriptions. This hesitation is not because researchers do not want to think of victims as people; it is because, in order to function in our jobs, we simply cannot. The emotional toll of processing dozens of deaths per day in a normal fashion is not sustainable. Thinking of the case reports as only patchy blast lung or an isolated perforated bowel is a necessary defense mechanism. The alternative, at least for me, would have been spending every evening getting drunk in the bathtub.

But still, there were unavoidable moments. Like with the sandwiches. Victimless descriptions of gut trauma don't eat sandwiches. I could tell immediately that the *Hunley* would be one of those cases. The mystery of that night, without its human element, is not actually that interesting: tiny submarine sets off large bomb; tiny submarine sinks. But when the human element is introduced, the story becomes haunting and inescapable, like mental quicksand.

The afternoon passed quickly as I became absorbed in *Hunley* search results. The blast software finished its current project, and the large desktop computer I used for the DYSMAS computational modeling sat whirring softly, awaiting its next instruction. But I sat totally engrossed, reading piece after piece of the *Hunley*'s story.

The little handmade submarine had been constructed during the American Civil War, and on the evening of February 17, 1864, the crew of the submersible boat decided the conditions were right to attempt her mission. The *Hunley* departed from near the city of Charleston, South Carolina, one of the last-standing Southern ports in the waning years of the war. She set out to try to break the Union blockade that prevented supply ships from bringing food and munitions to Charleston's battered citizens and weary troops. Her target had been the USS *Housatonic*, which she destroyed with what seemed like ease to become "the first successful submarine to sink an enemy ship during time of war." This victory was the *Hunley*'s claim to fame, and almost the exact phrase was repeated in every reference. It was the reason she was remembered when so many earlier attempts at submarine technology had been long forgotten.

The small sub disappeared after her mission, and the relative lack of information meant that the internet was filled with countless speculative theories from professional and armchair historians. The modern public interest was resuscitated in spectacular fashion in 1995 when bestselling author Clive Cussler and his organization, the National Underwater Marine Agency (NUMA), announced they had found the wreck of the long-lost submarine. By 2000, a plan for raising the *Hunley* and an agreement for her preservation had been formalized, and in exchange, Cussler and NUMA released the coordinates of her resting place. The US Navy would own her, as she was sunk in combat and therefore considered the spoils of war, but the submarine would be on permanent loan to the city of Charleston, South Carolina. The nonprofit group Friends of the *Hunley* would be the public face of the collaborative "*Hunley* Project" to enable her conservation, and they would work in partnership with the South Carolina *Hunley* Commission, the Naval History and Heritage Command, and the Charleston Naval Complex Redevelopment Authority. Clemson University would also be part of the collaboration, and the university's Restoration Institute would employ the archaeologists and conservators who performed the conservation and preservation of the artifact. With the paperwork finalized, the *Hunley* was brought home to Charleston to see if her recovered hulk might reveal to the world why she disappeared that night so long ago.

In her custom water tank at her new home in Charleston, the archaeologists and conservationists from Clemson assembled into a team and got to work.

When the team cracked open the hull of the vessel, they discovered that the silt of the ocean floor had completely filled the interior cabin, but not until long after she sank. Based on the pattern of the layering in the sediment, they could tell that the hull had been intact when she first went down and for an extended period afterward, except for a small hole in the fore conning tower that occurred during or shortly after her sinking.

They painstakingly removed the layers of silt in blocks to allow careful mapping of the remains within. All eight men inside were found resting at their battle stations. None showed any signs of skeletal trauma. None appeared to have made any attempt to escape the vessel. There was no crowding near the exits or clambering on top of one another. There was no evidence of panicked attempts to claw out of the sunken wreckage, or even to unlock the firmly secured hatch of the rear conning tower. The pilot of the submarine had been seated directly below the first point of intrusion of the silt, the fore conning tower. The early trickles of sediment through the tower locked much of his skeleton in place before it had time to decay and crumble into the bilge. His head had tumbled from his spine before the sediment levels built to that height, but his limbs still sat poised on his small bench, ankles lightly crossed, one hand rested casually on his knee. He had slumped docilely onto his seat.

The bilge pumps were not set to pump out water, so the boat hadn't been filling slowly while the crew was conscious. Even the heavy lead weights along the keel remained firmly attached, with no efforts to turn the bolts inside the hull that would set the weights free and rocket the submarine to the surface. Furthermore, stalactites of concretion dripped

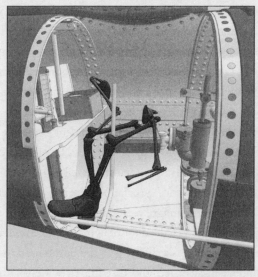

Positions of the arms and legs of the pilot.

from the roof of the interior. These slim, icicle-like formations can form only in gas, not in water, which means a large gas bubble remained inside the hull for a long time after she sank. It looked as if all eight men simply sat back, relaxed, and died.

People are born with the instinct to fight against their own death, to struggle with their last breath against even the most unavoidable and uncompromising ends. That universal instinct is why the *Hunley* case fascinates. It would be simple to think that the crew members saw no logical option and chose to spend their last moments nobly, in peace, but it would defy human nature. Something killed these men. Something that left no trace on the boat or the bones.

If people near a bomb die, I always suspect the bomb first. The explosive used at the time would have been black powder, which is made by the careful and often deadly practice of grinding the ingredients together into a material with the consistency of coarse sand. It is the earliest known explosive, and the gritty, volatile substance was the monogamous darling of militaries everywhere until it was discovered around the turn of the century that trinitrotoluene (more commonly known as TNT) could build a stronger, safer bomb. During the Civil War, black powder was used for everything: for firing musket balls, for firing cannons, and for building torpedoes.

As I searched for information on the *Hunley*'s explosive charge, one image in particular kept appearing: a yellowed, faded scan of a cylinder, with painstakingly hand-drawn lines and circles describing the details of its shape. "Singer's torpedo," proclaimed the large, old-fashioned calligraphy at the top of the image, with the more crucial information in a slightly smaller font below: "used for blowing up the *Housatonic*." These words implied that this was a drawing of the bomb used by the *Hunley*. The image had been scanned and distributed widely online since its original release from the National Archives in Washington, DC, which meant it was available for me immediately in Durham, North Carolina. And better yet, the script on the page contained the bomb's specifications.

According to this drawing, the *Hunley*'s charge contained 135 pounds of black powder. One hundred and thirty-five pounds is a lot of powder. It's a lot of any kind of explosive. The charge would have been about the size of a beer keg.

Eventually I found the second detail that I had been looking for. The spar, attached to the bottom corner of the *Hunley*'s bow, had recently been conserved. What had initially seemed to be voluminous concretion, the accumulated crud of thirteen decades underwater, had turned out to contain the peeled-back shards of the torpedo casing itself. I sat staring at photos of the beautiful, shiny copper ribbons. The strips of metal from the torpedo casing had been opened and peeled backward over the end of the spar like the carnage of a prank cigar in a cartoon. The bomb had to have been firmly attached to the end of the spar for those strips to have been peeled back so cleanly, and the spar was 16 feet long. Sixteen feet was therefore the distance between the boat and the bomb.

I leaned back in my rickety chair to think and opened yet another potato-chip bag from my secret drawer of inappropriate starches. This project was possible. At least, it seemed that way. The DYSMAS software could do the math, or so I thought at the time. I had a distance, and I had a charge size. I was sure I could get the measurements of the submarine somehow. Modeling the blast would take a lot of extra work—more than the few months Dale had estimated—and I didn't know if it would be worth the extra hours in the lab.

The very idea of a new side project was exhausting. Still, the publicly favored theory of the *Hunley*'s crew's demise was intriguing: Most assumed the crew suffocated. The idea was that they were either knocked unconscious by a bucking motion of the submarine or that they simply fell asleep during a break, unaware of their dwindling oxygen supply. This particular question seemed to have a lot of scientific parallels with my previous work for the navy, which often involved calculating the amount of oxygen needed by military divers as they performed physically laborious tasks underwater.

As I propped my feet up on the desk to think, I caught a glimpse of the window around the corner of the tall black filing cabinet. At some point, the sun had set, and I realized I was destroying my potato-chip cache because I was starving. I closed my laptop, leaving open the browser windows so I could continue to stare at the pictures and articles later from home, over a burrito. This project would be complex. Historical projects always are, and there was nothing modern I could use as a starting point. Chances were this work would never affect anyone ever again, a concept that is usually the kiss of death for a scientific investigation. Graduate students need to make their mark on science, to contribute, in order to be considered employable. I made my way out of the building, past the doors of open offices filled with other students still working well into the night. But as I swung my leg over my black

Suzuki motorcycle parked on the sidewalk outside the lab, I decided I could spare a few weeks to calculate the crew's oxygen supply and determine whether suffocation was a realistic theory.

I have never in my life so drastically underestimated a problem.

———

The next day I had the browser windows still open on my laptop, ready and waiting for Dale's inevitable appearance in my office. As predicted, the warning rhythm of his boots only slightly preceded his materialization in the old blue chair.

"Well?" he asked. I angled the laptop screen toward him.

"This is the charge. One hundred thirty-five pounds of black powder." I flipped to a second window. "This is the end of the spar. The charge was made of copper. It was still attached. The spar was sixteen feet long."

A third browser window. "These are the remains." The image showed a neat, color-coded row of skeletons inside the narrow hull of the submarine. Each color represented the remains of one individual, and each individual's remains were crumpled in place at his battle station inside the boat.

"Nobody tried to escape. They died where they sat." A slow, broad grin spread across Dale's face, and he let out a small chuckle. I smiled too.

The submarine had a thin metal hull. Blasts can transmit through certain surfaces, around corners, and echo down hallways. One of Dale's previous experiments had even shown blasts transmitting to the inside of the protective "bomb suits" worn by military Explosive Ordnance Disposal (EOD) personnel. Nobody had suspected blast trauma for the *Hunley*'s crew because, thanks to decades of action movies with exaggerated special effects, most people assume a blast would propel bodies in all kinds of crazy trajectories, causing broken bones and piles of smashed skeletons.

My first inclination was to call the Friends of the *Hunley* and loudly and proudly declare, "I KNOW WHAT HAPPENED." But Dale talked me into a more reasonable approach. We didn't know this organization, he pointed out. They had a high-profile historical artifact, and they had spent every working day for the past fifteen years poring over it with dental tools. For us to declare we knew the answer—and they did not—would have made us come across as arrogant fanboys, even with Duke's academic credibility attached. Worse, they could have taken our theory and proved it without us. They had more money and more manpower.

I decided to tone down my email, instead describing my enthusiasm for history and carefully listing what I could offer to their project. To get started, I needed their drawings and dimensions of the submarine so that I could calculate the gas supply, and I wanted to make it clear that I was willing to share my knowledge of explosions and injury biomechanics in return.

"I am a blast researcher with an injury biomechanics lab at Duke University," I wrote to the Friends of the *Hunley*, "and I would really like to look at some of the details of the sinking of the *Hunley* from an injury biomechanics perspective. Would it be possible to get copies of these drawings, with dimensions?"

Silence. Hitting the Refresh button repeatedly on my inbox did not help. However, the Lances are not a people known for being easily dissuaded. A few days later on February 17, 2014, exactly 150 years after the sinking of the submarine, I woke up to find that the unsolved mystery of the *Hunley* was the lead story on CNN's website. Determined to get a response from Clemson and the Friends, I wrote again.

"I am extremely interested in historical research and think I can contribute a valuable perspective with my expertise in both air and underwater blast exposure. Please let me know, I am very eager to learn more about the structure of the ship itself. I am willing to make the trip to Charleston if it would help." I was hesitant to say even that much. I thought that openly stating my field of study would serve as a giant red arrow, a highway sign declaring that I recognized this as a blast injury. When I forwarded the email to Dale, he agreed with my suspicions, laughingly pointing out during our next meeting that if the archaeologists searched for his name and saw his publications on air blast they might be able to figure out our theory. It was over, I thought. I have tipped them off. But I was hopeful that maybe they would still let me help with the project.

A few days later, a response arrived in my inbox. After some helpful forwarding of my contact information by personnel within the *Hunley* organizations, Michael Scafuri, one of the lead Clemson archaeologists on the project, wrote to me. My initial, giddy excitement on seeing the email quickly faded when I realized his email was a rejection—a polite rejection, but a rejection nonetheless.

"As you can imagine, we are focused on supporting our existing research partners in these [other] studies, and wish to see them through to completion." In other words, thanks for caring, but we've already got this handled. Maybe someday we can collaborate, but not today. "We would also be more than willing to give you a tour of our facility and the submarine should you be in the Charleston area," he wrote. On some level, I understood; they probably had plenty of people wanting to collaborate with them. I shrugged off the email and decided to study the boat anyway. The famous artifact was publicly owned, after all.

Dale was, as I expected, fully on board. He had already written in his characteristically brief fashion, "Wonder if there are existing pubs on *Hunley* with measurements. Bet there are." In other words: charge on. I began accumulating files and references on the *Hunley* so that I could slowly chip away at the problem.

One evening, many months later, I looked out my office window at the artificial lights struggling to illuminate the green patch of campus grass and contemplated going home. There was no point, I thought to myself. What would I do once I got there? The honest answer was that

I would keep working, so I might as well keep working on campus. I persevered, processing data until my hunger finally drove me out the office door close to midnight.

On the ride home, the chill of the fall air pierced the open gap between my helmet and heavy armored jacket, freezing the skin of my neck. The dimly lit roads of Durham were empty. I was cold and alone.

By the time I traveled the short distance home, I had made a decision: I needed to change my routine. The repetitive cycle of working late and sleeping all weekend was not the life I wanted. I needed a reason to leave the office at the end of the day.

Several months' worth of uncomfortable dates later, a tall, handsome man in a maroon V-neck sweater sat with his hand awkwardly cupped over the white dry-erase panel that had been crafted into an otherwise wooden bar.

"What did you create?" I asked, taking my seat beside him after returning from the bathroom. He removed his hand with a dramatic flourish.

"It's us!" he declared with excitement. "And I gave us cowboy hats to make it more festive." The stick-figure male and female cartoons he had drawn sported colorful cowboy hats, and the smiling male figure had a word bubble proudly declaring that tall people should date other tall people.

This was Nick, and I liked him. He did in fact stand even higher than my six-foot self, but, more important, he had already made me laugh several times since I first recognized him earlier that night from his online picture. With very little persuading he talked me into a second date.

I quickly realized that Nick would be around for a while. My parents, frequently bored with retirement, asked if they could drive down to North Carolina from their home in Michigan to meet him, but I had a better idea. I still hadn't found a funding sponsor to finish my project examining blasts to unprotected swimmers in the water, and I had been thinking about that damn submarine again a lot lately. I couldn't forget the offer from Michael Scafuri of a tour if I ever happened to be in Charleston, even though I was not sure if the offer was genuine. With that obvious ulterior motive, I suggested that my parents drive to Charleston instead and that Nick and I would meet them there.

———————

I thought going to see the *Hunley* would be like going to any other museum, with some emphasis on serving casual tourists. However, I questioned whether my GPS was leading me astray as the quaint downtown buildings of Charleston gave way to the high chain-link fences of a shipyard. The submarine is housed in what looks like a repurposed warehouse tucked toward the back. As I pulled into the empty parking lot, I breathed a sigh of relief. High on the warehouse were gigantic banners that said HUNLEY and SOLVE THE MYSTERY in a large, proud font, clear signs that I had arrived at the correct place. Rounding another corner revealed simple letters with the official title of the facility: Warren Lasch Conservation Center. The blank white facade of this building was all that guarded the fabled submarine.

Dale had decided to meet me in Charleston to talk to the archaeologists. As we knocked on the small door at the end of the long, sloping approach ramp, I was reminded of Dorothy trying to gain access to see the Wizard. Once inside, we were led down a window-paneled hallway to a conference room that, while clean and pleasant, disappointingly contained zero submarines. Michael Scafuri and a second archaeologist, Brent Fortenberry, walked over to the far side of the conference room table, while Dale and I selected chairs near the door.

My nervousness stemmed from more than the fact that I had left Nick alone with my parents. I had become increasingly interested in this project. I had studied modern soldiers with traumatic brain injuries, World War II soldiers with underwater blast injuries, and World War I soldiers with shell shock. We had learned something about our human bodies from the patterns of their traumas, and I wanted to learn from this trauma too.

Dale and I had decided to keep our theory to ourselves until the Clemson archaeologists agreed to collaborate. Their publications contained very little detailed information about the submarine or her measurements, I had observed, and I assumed this paucity was intentional. Even the drawing of the torpedo was always ambiguously cited simply as "from the National Archives," with no further information to pinpoint it within the archives' prodigious catacombs of file folders. Now that I was in a room with them, I asked.

"Yeah," Scafuri responded, confirming my suspicions. "Things are finally getting so that we can publish more openly. For a while we weren't releasing anything." Dale shot me a glance. In the academic world, the number of publications is the primary yardstick by which most researchers are measured; academics don't decline to publish without a good reason. Such a response meant that they might be withholding the information to limit the ability of other researchers to study the sub. I decided to change tactics and talk about something I could contribute to their work.

"I've been reading a lot about the theory of suffocation," I mentioned. "Have you guys studied this more? Is this one of the things you'll be publishing on soon?" In science there is often a long delay between a researcher's moment of epiphany and when a publication on the breakthrough is released. It was possible they had already done the math on the gas supply inside the hull, in which case I was less useful to them.

"No, not really," Scafuri replied, causing a release of tension in my brain so massive it may well have been externally audible. He explained that they had originally been collaborating with Chatham University in Pittsburgh, Pennsylvania, to look at gas supply, but those researchers had unfortunately left the project.

"We're looking forward to studying the theory of suffocation more, though," Scafuri continued, "because we're about to get to the conservation of the crank. Once we have the crank conserved, we can start to measure things like the coefficient of friction as they turned it against the brackets, and then use that to see how much oxygen the crew would have used." I stared blankly at the two archaeologists across the table and tried to transform my pure nerd excitement into a more professional-looking countenance. I fidgeted with the pale-green graph-paper lab notebook I had brought to take notes before saying quietly, "I can do that for you. That math used to be my entire job."

The fact that the archaeologists were focusing on the friction of the crank indirectly provided me an important piece of information: They didn't have a physiologist on their team. A physiologist would have told them that the coefficient of friction did not matter. This problem had already been studied, and studied to death.

Ergometers are devices used to measure the work a person is performing during exercise. They most often take the form of stationary bicycles with adjustable resistance levels, but sometimes scientists use ergometers that measure the work done by cranking hand pedals. With one pedal in each hand, test subjects rotate the crank at different speeds and resistances, almost exactly like the crank of the *Hunley*. Often these tests include measurement of how much oxygen is being consumed by the test subject. Science had already tested this problem many times and had already measured the oxygen consumption of every size and shape of human being, working at every possible combination of pedal speed and resistance.

Human beings are restricted by their hearts and lungs, not by the precise details of the activity they are doing. The amount of oxygen they consume will follow the same predictable rules and will actually be dependent on the level of effort, not on the specific nature of the work. If someone is working moderately hard, they will consume about the same amount of oxygen whether they achieve that moderate work rate through swimming, jogging, or biking. Whether they are turning an easy crank rapidly or turning a difficult crank slowly does not matter.

I attempted to explain this to the archaeologists sitting before me.

For years I had been using the information from scientists who preceded me when I built rebreathing systems for the navy. I could use the same information about oxygen consumption to do the math for the *Hunley*.

When most people picture scuba equipment, they think of the simple open-circuit devices invented by Jacques Cousteau. In these devices, pressurized gas from a metal tank passes through the stages of a mechanical regulator, each stage lowering the pressure until it can be easily inhaled by the diver. When the diver is ready to exhale, the gas leaves as bubbles, floating quickly and wastefully up to the surface. In any given breath, only 5 percent of the inhaled gas is consumed, and the rest is discarded. In the specialized piece of dive equipment known as a rebreather, all of the exhaled gas is trapped by a second hose. The diver's lungs push the gas back into this closed circuit instead of out into the ocean. A granular material chemically reacts with the carbon dioxide produced by the diver, removing it from their exhaled breath as it passes by. Sensors measure the oxygen levels and inject more to ensure that when the diver inhales again they get exactly the cleaned and replenished gas mixture they need. The remaining 95 percent of the exhaled gas is saved—no bubbles, no waste.

Building and testing these devices requires careful measurement of the volumes inside to understand how much gas is available to the diver. I used to spend a lot of time taking apart rebreathers, filling their individual parts with water, and then pouring that water into a beaker to measure the volume. The volume of the water told me the volume inside the part. All the parts together added up to the volume of gas inside the rebreather. The volume inside the rebreather affected how quickly the oxygen levels would drop, and how quickly the carbon dioxide would build up.

The *Hunley*, to me, was one big rebreather problem. The crewmen opened the hatches to the night sky, letting in air to ventilate the submarine. They would start out breathing air, consuming oxygen and producing carbon dioxide as they cranked. If I could get the exact volume of the inside of the boat, I would know the exact amount of fresh air available to the crew.

I looked up at Scafuri and Fortenberry. They seemed unimpressed by my explanation.

"We're already working with some navy people," Scafuri explained. "We're collaborating with some blast experts out of the base in Carderock."

"Oh, who is it?" I asked, genuinely curious. The scientific blast world is fairly small and it was entirely possible I already knew their collaborators. I thought this might be my window of opportunity. Maybe the Carderock scientists in Maryland would help encourage the Clemson group to include Dale and me.

"I think we need to check with them before discussing that with you."

If someone is not willing to share even the names of their collaborators with you, the refusal is typically not a preamble to them incorporating you smoothly and happily into their group. As we stood to leave, rejected, Scafuri offered us a chance at a glimpse of what had brought us there.

"Do you want to see her before you go?" he asked.

"Absolutely," replied Dale with booming emphasis, and we walked together toward the large open room where she lounged in her custom chemical pool.

As we climbed the metal stairs to the industrial-looking viewing walkway above the *Hunley*'s pool, our small group fell silent. Broad, clear protective panels formed a wall along the length of the grate of the viewing platform, guarding the edge of the pool from overzealous tourists. Only the top edge of the *Hunley* was visible in the water below, but her conning towers and cutwaters rose distinctly and unmistakably above the upper curve of her rounded hull. Patches of concretion still blemished the smooth texture of the metal submarine, and her long, cylindrical body looked so much larger than I had imagined. She was always described in the written accounts as small, a David to the *Housatonic*'s Goliath, and in my head I had made her a toy. As I looked down, it felt right to view her for the first time in the water. The gently moving surface of the liquid reflected patches of the overhead lights and made it harder to see her details, but underwater was where she belonged.

As Dale and I walked out of the building and back down the long, sloping ramp I looked over and saw a smile expand across his face while he walked. I started to speak, but he silenced me with hushed words.

"They don't know," he said quietly. "But we'll talk in Durham." A few steps later, he added, "They don't have a physiologist on the team." He had reached the same conclusion I had, and I began to grin too because I knew what he really meant: that we were going to do this project anyway. "See you back in Durham," he said, then got into his small red Volkswagen. The conservation center was otherwise closed, and mine was one of the last vehicles in the expansive parking lot. I sat in my car for a moment, looking out at the concrete and chain-link fences of the shipyard, trying to appreciate what Dale had just indirectly given me permission to do. This boat's story was a key piece of American history, and she was not the private possession of one closed group. I looked back up at the sign urging me to help "solve the mystery," and I knew exactly what I could contribute.

———

The next day I returned to the conservation center as a regular tourist, having recruited my parents and Nick to aid me in my mission. Our group of four stood on the viewing platform, looking down at the submarine with our faces and hands pressed against the protective panels. We wandered through the museum, reading and photographing all the displays that I thought might be useful.

Forensic experts had performed facial reconstructions using the skulls of the crew, and the pale, waxen models of their heads transfixed me. Four of the eight men smoked pipes, and the stains and damage to their teeth had survived the ravages of the ocean. Their habit had been so strong that they had carried their pipes with them on board the tiny submarine, and I wondered if they actually smoked while enclosed in such a confined space. I stared at the deep, sad-looking eyes of Crewman Lumpkin, first name unknown, who held his pipe firmly between his teeth, and willed him to tell me about his final moments. His eyes stayed fixed stubbornly, silently forward, the features of his face better known than his identity.

Several buttons stamped US NAVY were found near crewman James Wicks, a sign that someone had carried a Union pea coat on board. The famously thick, warm coat would have been an asset. While pressed against the conductive metal hull the crew would have had no protection from the frigid February temperatures of the water aside from the clothes they carried into the vessel. As I traced my finger across the display of buttons, I looked at their tarnish and thought about the cold that would drive a proud Confederate soldier to wrap himself in a Union coat for his most important mission.

On entry to the museum, each person is given a golden-colored plastic token. HUNLEY MYSTERY ONE VOTE it reads along the edge, with FRIENDS OF THE HUNLEY stamped in the center. Friends of the *Hunley* was the organization dedicated to fund-raising for the conservation of the federally owned boat, and as I would soon learn, they considered themselves its guardians. The tokens are meant as replicas of the gold coin found with the remains of Lt. George Dixon, the pilot of the submarine on her fatal mission. Visitors carry their coins through the museum with them as they view the exhibits, stare at the submarine, and read all the known facts of the evening of February 17, 1864. Near the exit of the museum, the true purpose of the coins becomes evident. Four clear plastic cylinders adorn a wall with the words "Solving the Mystery" in large, bold print. Each cylinder represents one theory: (1) that the torpedo damaged the hull and sank the boat, (2) that the crew was somehow trapped inside and asphyxiated, (3) that the submarine collided with another object and sank, or (4) that a lucky shot from the crew of the USS *Housatonic* somehow sank the boat. The coins of visitors indicated the popular vote on this day was that somehow the torpedo had breached the hull and caused the *Hunley* to sink.

My dad stood and looked at the display. Always sarcastic, he couldn't help but joke. "Hey, they don't have your theory up here," he jabbed at me. "Guess that means they disagree. Which one ya gonna vote for?"

Smiling back at him, I gripped my gold coin between my thumb and forefinger and held it up near his face.

"I'm keeping this," I said, "for when they have to put up a fifth cylinder on that wall." I slipped the coin into my purse. As we left the museum, Nick and my parents handed me their coins too.

CHAPTER 2

SUFFOCATION

The question of air supply was at one time one of the most difficult problems to solve on paper with which early experimenters with submarines had to contend.

—Submarine pioneer Simon Lake, 1918

Once back in the scientific toy store that was Duke, I tore off a small strip of Scotch tape and attached the gold plastic coin to the black edge of my computer monitor as motivation. *Work, Rachel*, it seemed to say, *solve the mystery*. It was time to get started.

After an avalanche, a buried skier has only minutes left to live. They commonly survive the initial tumble and burial in snow but, unable to move, are then smothered in the white powder. Some air can move through the snow and provide them with oxygen if their bodies strain to inhale, but the breath they exhale nonetheless becomes their undoing. It first melts the snow and causes a gas pocket lined with ice to form over their nose and mouth. Unable to pull in fresh air through this shield of ice, they then breathe and rebreathe the same gas inside the small space. The oxygen levels slowly decline, but what often gets forgotten is the odorless, colorless carbon dioxide.

Rebreathers can carry people hundreds of feet beneath the surface of the ocean only because of the chemical reaction that "scrubs" out the carbon dioxide. The scrubber material looks disturbingly like kitty litter, and when the devices are used without it, people often tear the breathing loop out of their mouths after a few minutes, aware that something is very wrong with the gas within.

I was already reasonably certain that suffocation, a term that specifically describes lack of oxygen or cessation of breathing, would not have caused the deaths of the crew of the *Hunley*. Instead, like a skier in an avalanche or a diver with no scrubber, they would have been susceptible to the effects of high carbon dioxide, or CO_2, before they lost consciousness from low oxygen. However, the timeline was key: After they first felt the noticeable symptoms of CO_2 buildup, if they did not have sufficient warning time to open the hatches or try to escape, then asphyxiation—a more general term that can include inhalation of CO_2— was still plausible. I needed the dimensions of the interior volume of the boat to calculate how long it would take for lethal CO_2 to build up, and to determine the crew's precise oxygen supply.

Sitting in my dimly lit office at Duke, I opened my laptop and began sorting through the digital pile of *Hunley* references I had accumulated. As I flipped slowly through the photographs, I noted the measurement stadia. Almost every photograph contained at least one stadia—a checkered plastic bar with black-and-white squares used to indicate the exact size of the neighboring objects. Leaping up to riffle through the graduate-student detritus on the cluttered bookshelf behind me, I managed to uncover an ancient and battered but still-functional clear plastic ruler. Digitally zooming in on the image file, I pressed the ruler up to the screen of my laptop. I measured one square on the stadia, and then the thickness of the hull. Comparing the two, I concluded the hull was ⅜ inches thick, which matched the published values from the Friends of the *Hunley*. I had correctly calculated the exact thickness.

The lines and angles of the *Hunley* emerged from the ocean on August 8, 2000, to a cacophony of wild cheers and honks. History buffs had surrounded the recovery site with hundreds of personal boats of all shapes and sizes and were jubilantly celebrating their first glimpses of the submarine. She was just over 40 feet long, and the sleek, smooth taper of her bow and stern were evident even beneath the thick layer of concretion that obscured many of her finer details. As salt water dripped off the rough encrustations that coated her hull, the sideways slant of her vertical axis looked misleadingly unintentional. Yellow slings cradled her securely inside a large, custom metal scaffolding to avoid jumbling the internal crime scene that would soon be uncovered.

The National Park Service provides many of the dimensions of the *Hunley* in their carefully performed, publicly available assessment of the submarine's site prior to its recovery. These dimensions made my improvised method of measurement happily unnecessary for the most critical numbers and allowed me to start immediately building a 3-D rendered model.

The binding of my paper copy of the white-jacketed National Park Service report had cracked after remaining open nonstop on my desk for weeks, and it was covered with multicolored sticky notes marking the pages with dimensions. Holding the report pages flat with my left hand and dragging my mouse arrow across the screen of my computer with my right, I drew an oblong cross-section and then extruded it to form a hollow pseudo-cylinder in the engineering software that I previously used to design equipment parts for the navy. If I could find measurements and fill in the rest of the details, I would be able to calculate the internal gas volume. My digital *Hunley* was beginning to take shape.

During missions, seven of the crewmen crouched inside and between the internal ribs of the vessel, seated along a single white-painted pine bench that ran along much of the port side of the crew compartment. The long wooden bench, 2 inches shy of 18 feet, provided each man only 2.5 feet of width to contain their muscled shoulders and perform their duties. As they hunched over within the narrow tube, all their energies were focused on the crank.

The behemoth crank itself consumed much of the starboard side of the crew compartment. Each man had a station and a handle, and each handle was offset from the others to ensure smooth, continuous cranking without pause, just like the oversized crankshaft of a modern car. When the crewmen worked together in their rhythm, they would have listened to the familiar throaty roar of metal turning against metal.

I held my right arm out straight and measured the distance from the grip of my palm to my shoulder: 25 inches. Retracting my arm fully back toward my chest, I performed the same measurement: 5 inches. Each handle was offset 10 inches from the center of the crank, so if I were cranking I would have to extend and retract my arm to its maximum with each stroke. Bobbing up and down at my desk to try it out, I decided: it was one seriously awkward workout. The twisted crank tracked gracefully toward the stern of the boat, where it met its end at two gears and a flywheel, the boat's rudimentary transmission, powering the propeller outside.

The conning towers, oval-shaped protrusions sticking 14 inches above the top curvature of the hull, served as the only means of entry—and of exit—from the crew compartment. They were 12 inches wide and 21 inches long, and each mission began with a wriggle as the men squeezed through these narrow passages like oysters through a straw. The hatches on top of the towers sealed with thick rubber gaskets and locked from the inside.

The *Hunley*'s eighth man was the lucky pilot of the craft, the only one exempt from the interminable cranking. He got his own tiny bench, a small wooden block positioned beneath the fore conning tower that allowed him to stand up quickly and look out the glass windows while still pulling on the long rods that would steer the boat. The deadlights along the rest of the hull could all be covered tightly to prevent light escaping and giving away the position of the submarine, but the small round windows on the front of the conning tower were the only way for the pilot to navigate.

Behind the fore conning tower was the snorkel. The rectangular snorkel box had two hollow pipes jutting out the sides that could be angled up to reach above the surface of the water or laid flat against the hull for stealth and speed. Inside the boat, reportedly attached to the side of the crew compartment, was a bellows pump connected to the snorkel tubes. However, the snorkel system was largely discounted in all descriptions. The historical reports that describe it mention mainly that it never worked properly, and most accounts simply omit its existence. Publications by Friends of the *Hunley* also display skepticism that it would work but fail to elaborate as to why.

The fore conning tower and snorkel box were the first identifying features uncovered by the National Park Service dive teams. The divers dropped through the murky, cloudy water to land on the site, carefully scraped off enough soggy ocean silt to recognize the *Hunley*, and then reburied the distinctive features to protect her from scavenging treasure hunters. In the National Park Service report, both the rounded tower and the angular snorkel box are described in great detail. The meticulous descriptions are doubtlessly the result of loving and careful hands repeatedly pressing tape measures against their various unusual features (while exhaling endless streams of bubbles).

After more than a month of going cross-eyed measuring details, I digitally spun the 3-D rendered submarine model around on my screen. The engineering software I had used to build the model could calculate the weights and volumes of each of the parts, allowing me to add them all together to calculate the gas volume within. However, there were still pieces I was missing. Rubbing my eyes in frustration, I once again turned to the internet, where I stumbled upon the VernianEra.com website run by Michael Crisafulli.

Michael's website was the public platform for his hobby: He takes ancient and historic descriptions of ships and fantastic vessels and turns them into gorgeous, textured, three-dimensional renderings that visually bring the old vessels back to life. He is one of those people whose passions can flourish because of the internet, which allows him to connect via his site with the handful of other enthusiasts around the world who are fascinated by the same niche intersections of history, science fiction, and engineering. One of his models, the one I was most interested in, was of my favorite submarine.

Michael and I had a shared love for the curves of the *Hunley*, and he quickly responded to my email. I was overjoyed to talk to another human being about this submarine and my frustrations, instead of simply muttering expletives at my potato chips and my battered ruler. To this day I have no idea what Michael looks like in real life; we have never met or even talked on the phone despite our frequent correspondence. But in my imagination he sits wearing a sweater, ensconced in an overstuffed cozy leather chair in a pleasantly dark, book-filled home library.

You can have everything, he said. Michael had been watching the boat carefully from the day it was raised in 2000. The Friends of the *Hunley* had placed webcams above her conservation tank, allowing members of the organization to log in and watch the archaeologists and conservation experts at work. Michael had spent hours watching these webcams, preserving innumerable screen shots and pulling measurements the same way I had been pulling them from the published photographs. He had crafted a beautiful, artistic model for his website that presented a terrifyingly realistic image of what it would have been like to be inside the submarine.

He also had every piece of data I had been unable to find. With our photo sets combined, I pieced together my complete model. Overlaying

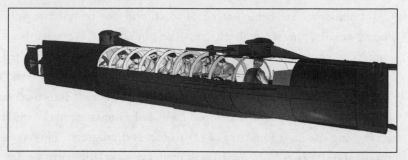

The *HL Hunley* and her crew.

the outline of my model with the images of a laser scan of the recovered *Hunley* showed that I had to nudge the position of the rear conning tower forward by a few inches. Otherwise, the two were an exact match. Victory on the first try is rare in science, and I relaxed enough to allow myself a brief mental celebration.

Still, something nagged at me. The long metal panels that lined the bottom of the submarine's keel were there to provide her with the negative buoyancy she needed to sink below the surface. I had been obsessing over the exact shape of the irregular weights in the name of calculating their precise mass, because that could affect the amount of ballast water the submarine would have needed to carry. I had a published value for the dimensions of these panels in addition to measurements from multiple photographs, but nothing is more satisfying than precision, so I wanted another confirmation to be sure. On a whim I emailed Michael Scafuri, the Clemson archaeologist.

"Are you willing to release the exact weight of the keel ballast removed from the outside of the hull? I have approximated it using reconstructive modeling, but it would be helpful to know the exact value," I wrote simply. My efforts to follow up with him since our meeting had been met so far with silence, but for some reason, on this day, this short email caught his attention.

"I apologize for being so out of touch and not replying to your recent emails," he wrote back later the same day. "We have been concerned about conflicting research due to our already established partners." He went on to offer to "start the conversation over as it were." But then, he stated that he would not be able to "release information [about the *Hunley*] without a signed non-disclosure agreement" while also asking me for a summary of my project and progress. "How does this sound? Thanks." The email was signed congenially with his first name only: Mike.

The nondisclosure agreement appeared to be a standard form used by the Friends of the *Hunley*, and it had some odd terms. Among them, any scientific publication I ever wrote would be subject to the inarguable ability of the Friends of the *Hunley* to edit or even reject the publication before it could see the light of day. In addition, I would never be able to write, publish, or express through interpretive dance, smoke sculpture, or traditional medieval ballad any nonacademic anything about the *Hunley* without their express permission and unrestricted editing.

OK . . . so the dance, sculpture, and ballad bits were not an explicitly written part of that clause, but it was so restrictive they may as well have been.

I rocked back in my chair and took a gulp. Dreams of a science-themed contemporary dance routine aside, my palms began to sweat as I entertained exaggerated and melodramatic daydreams of an archaeologist printing out a research paper I had labored over for months, only to hold the sheets of paper up and light them on fire while cackling loudly. This clause meant that I could write a complete doctoral dissertation and the Friends could reject my ability to publish it. Notably, without a published, *publicly available* dissertation, Duke would not allow a student to graduate.

Duke's rule was nonnegotiable. This rule was the reason graduate students were not permitted to work on classified projects for the government; if their work was not public, it could not be used to receive a degree. Otherwise, the institution had no proof to show the degree was deserved. Previous students whose work could not be published were forced to start over again, with new projects, having torched years of their youth in mind-warping, back-breaking pursuits that were doomed to die the quiet, slow death from obsolescence reserved for science that has been packaged up and hidden from the world. It was not common, but it was also not urban legend; I had witnessed it. When it happened, the students who had to begin afresh were whispered about in hallways, were checked on by friends at night, were asked relentlessly by concerned colleagues about their states of mind.

I could not sign this document.

"Unfortunately that's not really an option for me because of the expectation for frequent publication within Duke's environment," I replied. "It would be very difficult for me to justify working on a project that would require external approval prior to publication. Perhaps something else will come up for collaboration in the future." I was crushed. No scientist works alone, but I would have to find a way to finish my project through other means and without the Friends' direct data or help.

Brushing off the second rejection, I still wanted to determine if the crew might have asphyxiated. Prior to measuring my computer screen repeatedly like a nut job with a weird penchant for dimensions, I had performed what engineers call a SWAG, a scientific wild-ass guess, and I had roughly estimated the internal volume of the boat as 8 cubic meters to allow for some preliminary calculations. Now that I had spent months carefully measuring, reading about the average weights of Civil War soldiers to account for the volumes of the crew, papering the walls of my office with printed submarine photos, and examining the submarine's buoyancy characteristics to calculate the amount of ballast water, I could finally plug in the decisively more accurate, yet oddly close, value of 7.61 cubic meters at which I had painstakingly arrived.

Knowing the internal gas volume, I could confidently calculate the rates at which oxygen and carbon dioxide would fall and build inside the boat. I had already determined which rates of oxygen consumption were most reasonable by capitalizing on the glut of hand-pedaled ergometer test data available. At the lower end, I decided to use 1.5 liters of oxygen consumed per minute by each person. This value was how much oxygen a male would consume doing a moderate amount of work at a level of exertion he could theoretically continue for several hours— for example, walking briskly or swimming at a mild and not-too-strenuous pace. On the upper end of the exertion scale, I picked a value around the maximum level any person could physiologically maintain for more than a few minutes, a consumption rate right in the middle of the range the US Navy characterized as "severe work," or as I called it more technically, "cranking really darn hard." This value was 3.2 liters per minute of oxygen for each person. Lt. George Dixon, sitting alone on his tiny special officer's bench and working the levers to steer, probably wasn't sharing in the physical exhaustion of the less-privileged crewmen at the crank, so I assigned him at the "moderate work" consumption rate of 1.5 liters per minute. He still had to work, but he was an officer, so not as much.

Air is made up of about 21 percent oxygen, with the balance being almost all nitrogen. The *Hunley* had an internal gas volume of 7.61 cubic meters, according to my shiny new model. Therefore, at the moment they closed the hatches, the eight men inside had access to 1.60 cubic meters of sweet, sweet oxygen to keep themselves alive, equal to 1,600 liters. With the gas consumption rates I had determined, that 1,600 liters of oxygen was being depleted at a total in the range of 12 to 23.9 liters per minute. Basic division provides a very rough first estimate of the time before the oxygen supply would be completely consumed down to zero: somewhere between 67 and 133 minutes, depending on how hard the crew worked at the crank.

However, this was not equal to the amount of time until the men lost consciousness. That would occur somewhere above 0 percent oxygen, well before they had completely depleted their supply. But where?

And there was still the problem of the skier in the avalanche . . . how long did they have before feeling the unpleasant presence of carbon dioxide? For the answers to these questions, I needed to travel to my favorite place on Duke's campus: the hyperbaric chamber.

————

Duke's was not my first hyperbaric chamber. Years before graduate school I had once stood with my hand on a large red valve, staring at the needle on a pressure gauge and waiting for the moment when I would need to give the valve a twitch. A young boy next to me looked through a porthole at his father, who was trapped inside the huge metal hyperbaric chamber by the immense internal air pressure that forced the door tightly shut. The man and his two attendants were under air pressure equal to 165 feet of seawater while still located somewhat safely within the enormous gray hangar building on Catalina Island. If I messed up, released the gas, and brought them straight to the surface, they would probably all die of decompression sickness. The nitrogen that had been forced into the tissues of their bodies by the 165 feet of pressure would escape back out as the pressure was removed. It would release back into their bloodstreams as bubbles, blocking circulation and causing the equivalent of a million tiny strokes throughout all parts of their bodies.

The man was here for medical treatment for an arterial gas embolism, an often-fatal type of lung injury that he incurred by holding his breath and ascending through the water while scuba diving. As he had rocketed toward the surface, trachea clamped shut, the reduction in water pressure nonetheless caused the gas inside his lungs to expand. With his throat tightly closed the gas had no pathway for escape except to rupture his lungs and send a massive bubble careening somewhere into his body. He had been rushed to our chamber on a stretcher, his skin a mottled gray and blue, the bubble in his body blocking the flow of oxygen-rich blood to one or more of the critical organs inside. He needed recompression in the high pressures of the hyperbaric chamber to shrink the bubble so that his blood could flow again. His son, who had thankfully remembered to exhale safely on his way to the surface, was visibly nervous for his father.

"Don't worry, Dad, I won't tell Mom," the boy whispered cautiously into the heavy black phone handset. Communication to the chamber was by sound-powered phones, which could still be operated in case of total electrical failure. The phones used sturdy black receivers that would have appeared at home on a movie set in the 1950s, and the receiver looked comically large in the child's hands as he tried to reassure his father. He stared at his father through the small glass window.

My job was to turn the valve wheels and drive the chamber, delivering or venting gas at the correct times to change or maintain the simulated ocean depth. Everything on this chamber was manual, old-school, analog, just like the sound-powered phones. It was designed to keep functioning no matter what natural cataclysm hit the island.

Treatments were not frequent, which was fine with me. It's difficult to see people that damaged, to see human skin that shade of blue. But at a hyperbaric chamber when you turn a knob, the hiss of gas sounds, the needle on the dial moves, and the man gets better. The bubbles in his body compress under the pressure, like balloons brought to the bottom of a swimming pool, and the blood can flow past them once again to deliver life-saving oxygen to his organs and all other tissues. His lungs, capable of handling smaller bubbles, gradually process the compressed gas and let it leak into each exhalation until the bubbles are gone and it is safe to bring the chamber slowly back up to surface pressure.

The machine is simple and beautiful, and it works. The man and his son got to go home together, shaken but happy and whole.

It's satisfying to be able to use pneumatics and engineering to manipulate and heal a human body, to manipulate something positive out of our weird physiological responses to pressures. This love of undersea medicine was what inspired me to go work for the US Navy, and the hunt for this satisfaction was what propelled me to Duke. Their hyperbaric medicine department was legend, and when the navy asked me to go back to graduate school, Duke University was the only place I bothered to apply.

A stray IV stand was jammed next to the studded burgundy leather couch in the small office in the hyperbarics department, and I sat looking expectantly across anesthesiologist Richard Moon's desk at him, in his meticulous white physician's coat. The medical doctor's office was tucked behind the chambers, and the view out his window was of the doors and portholes of the part of the complex used for clinical treatments. Moon had long been one of my heroes in the field of dive medicine, and his lauded career gave him the kind of immediate respect that lets him effortlessly and without arrogance control an entire room while also wearing a Mickey Mouse necktie. He was smiling at me, the subtle folds around his kind eyes revealing it was a facial expression he made often. I had just finished recounting to him the tale of the *Hunley*, and the theory of suffocation, as best I could in my stammering enginerdy excitement.

Dr. Moon and I met when I had wandered uninvited into the hyperbarics department and volunteered myself as a human test subject for their science. With a grace and efficiency that suggested I was not their first stray graduate student, Moon and his staff warmly welcomed me as a data point and began inviting me to participate as a two-legged guinea pig in their experiments. Eventually they had even permitted me to start up a collaborative project using their chamber for my own research idea—a small but personally important theory I was testing on the side of my PhD studies. Normally my role in this department was to breathe weird gas mixtures and patiently allow myself to be jabbed with large needles, but today I was here to talk.

With a depth of baritone that is unexpected for someone of such a normal stature, Moon, flanked by a floor-to-ceiling wall of well-worn textbooks about respiratory physiology, stated simply: "Well, this sounds fun."

————

Human beings live longer when they have access to oxygen. However, what's less commonly known is that the successful oxygenation of the human body depends not just on the percentage of oxygen in the gas that is inhaled, but also on the overall pressure of that gas. For example, air contains about 21 percent oxygen. That seemingly low percentage works just fine because we are operating underneath one full atmosphere's worth of pressure (1 "atm"), and the collective weight of planet Earth's shroud of gases helps to press that oxygen into our lungs.

However, if that overall pressure gets reduced, the same 21 percent can start to feel dramatically insufficient. Citizens of Denver, Colorado, have adapted to live at 0.82 atmospheres, and this reduction is enough to start people panting if they are visiting from closer to sea level. On top of Mount Everest, with only 0.33 atm of external pressure, the same 21 percent is not enough to live on without giving the human body time to adapt and acclimate on the ascent.

For this reason, physiologists typically use the concept of "partial pressure" rather than percentage alone to describe breathing gases. Partial pressure is the product of both the percentage of oxygen in the air and the air pressure. Think of 21 percent oxygen as the decimal number 0.21. If you multiply 0.21 by the 1 atmosphere of pressure present at sea level, the so-called partial pressure is 0.21 atm of oxygen. However, in mile-high Denver, that same 0.21 percentage of oxygen in the air is multiplied by only 0.82 of an atmosphere of total pressure. People in Denver therefore live with only 0.17 atm of oxygen. Trekkers on Everest are gasping to inhale a meager 0.07 atm, even though they are still breathing the same

21 percent. Helpfully, the human response to a certain partial pressure is the same regardless of how that partial pressure is achieved. Astronauts breathing 100 percent oxygen in their low-pressure space suits are just as happy and functional as Earthlings breathing 21 percent oxygen at full pressure back home. This response is critical to many aspects of hyperbaric medicine, and it would be critical to determining the responses of the *Hunley*'s crew to variations in the gas inside their boat.

Moon shifted his gaze to his computer monitor and began to click the mouse.

"I'm sending you some references," he said. His encyclopedic knowledge of respiratory physiology was an inestimably powerful tool, and as I unlocked my phone I saw his email arrive, replete with attachments. He was famous for this; other researchers in the department often joked about his ability to instantly recall not just the scientific contents but the year of publication, facility, and shoe size of the authors for every paper in his field. These documents contained all the information I would need to assess the partial pressures where the crew of the *Hunley* would lose consciousness from lack of oxygen.

The references Moon sent me were select chunks of data from hundreds of military tests on aviators. The men (they were almost exclusively men in the decades before 1990) had been artificially taken up to high altitudes in low-pressure chambers and then removed from supplemental oxygen. The field of aviation obviously has interest in knowing the exact partial pressures where their pilots might pass out. Some planes can fly themselves, but none are great at landing themselves.

The data were defined in terms of "time of useful consciousness," meaning not just the length of time someone could sit physically upright, but the length of time someone could cognitively function, take actions, and try to save themselves. Unlike an exhausted graduate student who can still empty a beaker, a drooling, mentally vacant pilot is not useful even if they are technically awake. Same with the pilot of a submarine. Nobody passed out above oxygen levels of 0.10 atm; therefore this was my upper limit for risk of loss of consciousness. Pilots remained functional for about two minutes at 0.063 atm. Even though pilots had about two minutes of functionality at this level, I decided to use it as my lower cutoff. My goal with this choice was to try to err on the side of being conservative and to account for the fact that the oxygen levels were lowering gradually in the *Hunley* instead of suddenly like the rapid drops in the aviator experiments.

At the 43,000-foot cruising altitude of a standard Boeing 777, depressurization of the passenger cabin would result in exposure to air with 21 percent oxygen at 0.16 atmospheres of total pressure, for an oxygen partial pressure of a physiologically insufficient 0.03 atm. Once wearing a mask and breathing 100 percent oxygen, passengers are immediately brought back up to a comfortable and functional 0.16 atm despite the loss in cabin pressure. However, without additional oxygen, the passengers of the plane would have at most ten to fifteen seconds of useful consciousness before they crumple into limp, unresponsive messes. The flight attendants aren't kidding when they advise people to put on their own oxygen masks first.

With Moon's benediction, these were my cutoff levels for lack of oxygen. However, there was still the problem of carbon dioxide. Luckily for me, the submariners and their physicians have studied carbon dioxide even longer than the aviators and their physicians have cared to study oxygen. Unluckily for them, some submariners had become real-life case studies . . . like the crew of the HMS *Thetis*.

Thetis, the Greek goddess of water, is also a famed failure as a protector of warriors. She tried to use the sacred liquid flowing in the river Styx to render her son Achilles impervious to the wounds of battle but failed to dip his heel. Therefore, to give her name to a submarine, a vessel designed to move through the water while protecting the warriors within, seems a natural but ill-omened choice.

In June 1939, the newly constructed *Thetis* ventured out on her first sea trial. World War II was looming for Europe, and submarine construction was part of the wary United Kingdom's preparations for her defense. Submarine technology had taken a massive leap in the generations since the *Hunley* had proved how useful the devices could be. The now-massive vessels were considered a crucial component of warfare, especially to nations surrounded by water.

It was supposed to be a short trip: a routine dive to prove seaworthiness followed by a celebratory buffet served by the two chefs on board for the occasion. The vessel was packed with 103 men—double her rated capacity—to accommodate the many excited sailors and engineers who were eager to be part of her maiden voyage.

Inexplicably, despite the weight of her excess human cargo, the submarine was too buoyant to dive. In an attempt to add more ballast, one of the officers on board decided to allow a small amount of water in through the torpedo tubes so the vessel could sink beneath the surface and the trial could still be declared a success. But a speck of the paint used on the shiny new boat had dried inside the test cock of the torpedo tube, blocking the telltale flow of water that should have alerted the crew to the fact that the external tube door was wide open to the sea. When the inner door was opened, the ocean rushed in unimpeded, swamping the submarine by the bow and sinking her within minutes. At low tide her stern could be seen protruding above the surface of the waves, marking the location where the men suffered inside.

Archival documents would later reveal the choice made by the admiralty to preserve the submarine at the expense of her crew. Rather than cut ventilation holes through the hull, the precious submarine was left intact for the looming war—sentencing the men to death. Four of the crew managed to escape using their specially designed underwater breathing apparatuses, but the panicked premature release of an escape-hatch door rendered the hatch useless. The remaining ninety-nine were sealed inside. Days later, long after the last sounds of tapping on the hull had faded and stopped, British scientists would wonder if the men could have even survived an escape attempt.

To answer the question, a few weeks after the accident, the physician scientists Haldane, Alexander, Duff, Ives, and Renton hunched over and slid into a metal chamber, sealing the airtight door behind them. All five had experienced the effects of carbon dioxide before in their experiments for the silent service, but John BS Haldane especially was aware of the discomfort and pain he was about to inflict upon himself. An old veteran of self-experimentation, he had spent the past decades using his own body to test the human tolerance to the odorless gas. His father had begun the experiments, often breathing within enclosed spaces until the CO_2 levels reached a disconcerting 5 percent and his body forced his respiratory rate to double from an insuppressible hunger for fresh air. The younger Haldane had been helping his father in these experiments with carbon dioxide since 1905 at the age of twelve. In that year, he and Haldane the elder had conducted tests inside submarines to try to find chemical materials that would absorb the noxious CO_2 from the enclosed boats' atmospheres, just as the public was becoming aware that such undersea vessels even existed. As an adult he took his legendary father's legacy to the extreme.

On that day these men were trying to establish whether the remaining crew of the sunken submarine *Thetis* had even had a chance at escape. Haldane himself always vomited after tests above 6.5 percent carbon dioxide. He wanted to know if the crew could have made it out of the submarine without expelling the contents of their stomachs into their underwater breathing apparatuses, which needed to stay vomit-free to deliver people safely to the surface. The last escaping survivor of the *Thetis* reported the CO_2 level was at 6 percent at the time of his exit.

The hiss of gas echoed through the small space as the doctors filled their hyperbaric chamber to begin the test.

I stood on the metal platform that served as a floor in the center of the bright-blue spherical hyperbaric chamber at Duke, officially designated Delta Chamber. With both arms outstretched, my fingertips brushed against the various instruments, masks, and gauges that dangled from brackets on the sloping walls and ceiling. This sphere was 3.2 meters in diameter, giving it a small internal volume of about 17,000 liters, which then got further reduced by the need for a flat floor to stand on and the pneumatic tubes and assorted equipment required to sustain the lives of the people inside. During testing, I had always thought its confines to be impractically tiny, its diminutive size to be one of the obstacles we had to plan around in order to fit the three people and the bicycle ergometer we needed to shove inside in the name of science.

To see if the crew of the *Thetis* had any chance of survival, the five British scientists had jammed themselves into an airtight steel hyperbaric chamber one-third this volume, a mere 5,800 liters. It was a horizontal cylinder, but otherwise a smaller version of the blue golf ball in which I stood, and it was only 2 meters long by 2 meters in diameter. With the tips of my fingers already grazing the hoses and breathing masks on the walls in the chamber at Duke, I tried to imagine which life-sustaining medical gear I would choose to remove if given an even smaller test space. With five men inside, their tubelike chamber resembled the cramped crew compartment of the *Hunley*. The math supported my visceral impression: My measurements showed that the *Hunley* contained 952 liters of gas per crew member, and the scientists had given themselves only 1,160 liters apiece.

After half an hour of inhaling the expired breath of their colleagues, the crew of five felt compelled to add fresh air to the chamber to slow the accumulation of CO_2 that was causing them headaches and hyperventilation. By the end of the first hour, despite the temporary relief of the air purge, all five were panting and gulping for breath, with Duff "in considerable distress" and fighting a severe headache. After leaving the chamber they tried to use the submarine escape apparatuses, but two of the doctors had to tear the mouthpieces instantly from their own mouths as the withdrawal-like effects of breathing high CO_2 then suddenly switching back to normal air forced them to vomit repeatedly and violently.

Like good scientists, they kept a log of their experiences. The final partial pressure of carbon dioxide in the chamber was 0.067 atm, equivalent to an oppressive 6.7 percent at surface pressure. The oxygen stayed in safe ranges, with no risk of loss of consciousness or suffocation at any point, above 0.17 atm the whole time.

The extensive experiments of the father-and-son Haldanes outlined a clear set of expectations for the progression of physical symptoms from carbon dioxide inhalation. By 0.039 atm, headache and nausea would begin. By 0.040 atm, the shortness of breath and other symptoms were noticeable to almost all test subjects, described by many as a sensation of "choking" on one's own breath. At 0.058 atm, all participants were experiencing an inescapable mixture of panting, headaches, sensitivity to light, and nausea. By 0.100 atm, or 10 percent CO_2 on the surface, the physical distress would become so severe that it would "make it impossible to continue the experiment."

The medical literature contains fatal case studies of people asphyxiating in high-carbon dioxide environments, but these are cases where the victim entered suddenly and unexpectedly into an environment that already contained a massively high dose of CO_2. In one notable case a woman triggered a carbon dioxide–based fire suppression system to set off an alarm because she had been trapped in a bank vault. These unfortunate victims lose consciousness almost immediately, and because the CO_2 has also displaced all of the air that could provide oxygen to the fallen victim, they do not survive. However, in these fatal cases the carbon dioxide level jumps suddenly; in one breath the person is happily breathing normal air, and in the next they are inhaling CO_2 levels potentially upward of 30 to 60 percent. The crew of the *Hunley*, in contrast, slowly exhaled their own carbon dioxide. The levels rose gradually, and therefore before they lost consciousness they would have had to endure the intense, prolonged discomfort created by the slow increase.

Carbon dioxide flows through the bloodstream not as a gas but in a few different, slightly altered forms. The majority of CO_2 in the body combines with water, H_2O, through a series of chemical reactions and jumbles the alphabet soup to make two new molecules: bicarbonate, written as HCO_3^-, and one lonely free-floating hydrogen ion, a single little H with a positive charge, written as H+. This little H is the reactive part of any acid. The power of an acid is measured by its eagerness to expel such an H+ off itself and thrust it onto a nearby chemical. Accepting the H+ forces the other chemical to change its very nature to accommodate the new element, and the mandatory rearrangement of molecules often leads to complete breakdown or dissolution of the material itself: This is an acid burn. The hydrochloric acid contained inside my stomach, for example, is written HCl, and it is more than happy to donate an H+ to help disrupt and dissolve the molecules of chocolate cake.

Carbon dioxide is normally a tiny 0.04 percent of each breath that we inhale. As the percentage starts to climb, more and more CO_2 is driven into the bloodstream, leading to more and more H+ traveling to all of the tissues in the body. The blood itself literally becomes more acidic.

Receptors in the brain sense the increase in acidity and try to counteract it. The blood vessels on the surface of the brain dilate and widen in an attempt to transport the acidity away from the sensitive neurons; this dilation causes the headache. The brain increases the breathing rate and the heart rate and expands all the blood vessels, trying desperately to increase the amount of blood being pumped past the lungs so they can process and eliminate the deadly gas (hence, the panting). However, when the carbon dioxide is being inhaled from the air outside, these efforts are useless. In the end stages of carbon dioxide exposure, acidic blood in the veins, replete with far more loose and wild H+ than normal, begins to chemically break down the myriad enzymes and proteins that control bodily functions on a cellular level.

Experiments by Haldane's counterparts in the US Navy would similarly test the effects of high CO_2 on hard-hat divers. After only three minutes of breathing a gas mixture with 0.05 atm of CO_2, equal to 5 percent on the surface, divers experienced what they chose to label "distracting discomfort," characterized by mental depression, headache, dizziness, nausea, and "air hunger." At 7 percent concentrations, divers experienced the symptoms of "distracting discomfort" immediately. Other scientific studies have shown that after seven minutes of breathing 7 percent CO_2, a person's pulse increases by about 50 percent. Their breathing rate almost quintuples. That is a bigger increase in breathing rate than when I go from sitting still to a dead sprint.

Modern psychiatrists use carbon dioxide to induce panic attacks, both in patients with panic disorders but also in test subjects who have no history of anxiety. People without disorders begin to feel an induced anxiety above 5 percent CO_2, and about half can be expected to experience a full panic attack by 7.5 percent despite having no other biological predilection.

Eden Creamery founder Justin Woolverton told his own story of hypercapnia in an interview, relating what happened to him as the dry ice keeping his ice cream cold slowly filled his vehicle with CO_2: "His breath got shallower; his heart began pounding; his head started to spin. He tried to remain calm, but by the time he reached West Hollywood, he was hyperventilating, on the verge of fainting."

The *Hunley*, operating on the surface, would have been at 1 atm of pressure. I drew two simple lines on my graph of the *Hunley*'s crew's breathing gas: 5 percent CO_2 and 7 percent CO_2. They should have known by 5 percent, but it was implausible that they stayed peaceful and quiet at their stations beyond 7 percent. Even if they had tried to push themselves beyond these levels during practice, each time they re-opened the hatches some of them would have expelled their digesting suppers into the bilge.

Using these values, the crew would have had a thirty- to sixty-minute-long window of warning time, depending on their level of phys-ical exertion, between the time when they first reached a noticeable 5 percent CO_2 but before they reached the dangerous low-oxygen level of 6.3 percent. Even assuming my dimensions on the keel weights were wrong, that the internal ballast tanks would need to be full to the brim and therefore gas volume was at a bare possible minimum, the time windows barely shift to provide a range of twenty-six to fifty-one min-utes of warning time.

The calculations for the worst-case scenario, with completely full ballast tanks and therefore the minimum possible gas volume, the crew cranking at their absolute physiological utmost to consume oxygen as quickly as possible, and using 7 percent CO_2 and 10 percent oxygen as the cutoff values for noticeable symptoms and suffocation, show that the crew still had at least ten minutes of warning time to open the hatch doors and refresh their air supply.

The snorkel system, if it worked, would have increased these warn-ing times further still. The bellows would have provided some gas ex-change to slow the buildup of carbon dioxide and given the crew even longer to notice the accumulating symptoms.

Even though it could only have increased the amount of warning time for the crew, I still wondered about the utility of the snorkel system . . . so, in line with the nature of an engineer, I decided to answer my questions with some math.

The US Navy's numerous experiments with hard-hat divers deter-mined that if you want to avoid a gradual buildup of CO_2, the correct ventilation rate for an enclosed gas space is about one hundred times the rate at which the people inside are consuming oxygen. Assuming the crewmen were cranking moderately, to meet this requirement the man at the bellows would need to pump gas through the *Hunley*'s 3-inch-wide snorkel pipes at a flow speed of 8.8 meters per second.

This flow speed is about twenty times the speed at which water comes out of the average kitchen faucet, and about a third of the speed at which water comes out of a standard modern fire hose. This speed is about half the wind speed required for a breeze to qualify as a tropical storm. To me, this task seemed like a challenge to achieve with a medium-sized, hand-pumped bellows. Closing my spreadsheet, I found myself agreeing with the accounts of history: At best, the snorkel system was probably pretty darn useless.

———

The last moments of the crew of the *Thetis* can be read between the morbid lines of their autopsies. The remains of the lost seamen had begun to decompose before their temporary tomb was finally raised from the ocean floor, but markers of carbon-dioxide asphyxiation were still evident inside the young men. Blood stained the normally translucent fluid inside the pleural cavities, the spaces outside the lungs that lubricate the internal motions of breathing. The same bloody contamination was found in the pericardium, the space around the heart that serves the similar purpose of allowing the heart to beat freely. This internal hemorrhaging is also a common sign of asphyxia in avalanche victims.

The carbon dioxide levels of Haldane's self-experimentations sometimes caused his entire body to seize with violent tetanic muscle contractions, and his urine to become so chemically basic that it frothed and bubbled like a child's science-fair volcano on the addition of a drop of acid.

With their eyes bulging and red, their pupils narrowed to pinpoints, some of the crew of the *Thetis* bit into their own tongues as the effects of lengthy carbon dioxide exposure set in.

Scientists do not like to throw around the word "proof." We couch our words carefully, always wary that we may be basing our conclusions on principles that one day could be proved wrong. We separate our opinions from our measurements, always vigilant against tainting our conclusions with our own bias. My cautious brethren and I are the reason gravity is considered a theory, not a fact.

Therefore, as a scientist, I will choose my words carefully: It is unlikely that the crew would sit in 0.07 atmospheres of carbon dioxide willingly for ten minutes. I personally would not endure those symptoms without action. But for me, I had surpassed the threshold of reasonable scientific evidence, and therefore, for me, the theories of suffocation and asphyxiation were eliminated.

The *Hunley* attacked on the surface. The crew of the *Housatonic* saw her coming, with her conning towers protruding above the ocean waves. She may have submerged after the attack, but still the crew would have felt in their chests the stifling burden of their own noxious exhalations long before the lack of oxygen rendered them unconscious. Most crews would not have sat peacefully and declined to open the hatches to the cool night air as they panted under an induced biological panic, slowly choking on their own toxic fumes. Nobody sinks their teeth into their own tongue in agony yet sits still, one hatch door away from freedom, without taking action.

So, on to the next common explanation: Had a "lucky shot" from the deck of the *Housatonic* sunk the *Hunley*? After all, they saw her coming.

CHAPTER 3

FISH BOATS

"You have to admit, at least, that your books have foreshadowed a number of great inventions and valuable experiments."

"No, a hundred times no," cried Verne. "The submarine boat had been invented some time before I published my book *Twenty Thousand Leagues Under the Sea.*"

—Interview with Jules Verne, 1902

Human beings have longed to explore the depths of the ocean since well before the Civil War and the construction of the *Hunley.* Aristotle wrote that his student Alexander the Great, curious about the ocean, decided to plunge in using a glass bathysphere in 332 BCE. Chinese sources from 200 BCE report the construction of a submarine that could fully immerse carrying one person, travel to the bottom of the ocean, and return to the surface. Some adventurers have focused purely on the scholarly, wanting only to discover and learn, but others have been fascinated with the military potential. Military minds have always understood that the water could provide unparalleled cover for subterfuge.

Cornelis Drebbel stood gripping the sharply curved wooden edge of a man-sized opening in the year 1620. This device was his largest and most magnificent yet, and he felt confident enough in its success that he had invited the king to watch.

Drebbel's machine was based on the drawings of inventor William Bourne, published a few decades earlier in 1578, but this was Drebbel's third-generation prototype of the design. The frame was wood, wrapped in leather to create a hull, then slathered with multiple thick layers of grease to keep water from oozing in through the dark walls. Men sat inside at the handles of oars that stuck through the hull and let them paddle through the water. Drebbel had installed two floating pipes as a snorkel system to supply fresh air to the hardworking crew, as well as to the multiple spectating passengers who had been invited to ride in the belly of the machine for the occasion.

Drebbel lowered himself down past the edge of the opening and pulled the watertight door closed behind him. King James I, his royal court, and thousands of the citizens of London watched as the machine disappeared beneath the choppy surface of the river Thames. They collectively held their breath . . . then released it as a roar when the submarine reappeared a few minutes later.

Drebbel's submarine has been recorded as able to stay submerged for three hours at a depth of 15 feet. The crew was either six or twelve men, depending on the account, working hard at the oars the entire time. No information is available on the size of the snorkel pipes, the volume of the boat, or the efficacy of the ventilation system. Some historians, given the ambitious estimate of three hours, have questioned whether Drebbel's boat truly submerged at all. Instead, some theorize that the boat's forward motion caused water to wash over the lowered bow of the vessel and provide the mere illusion of submersion to amaze the gullible crowds.

The *Hunley* had a heavy metal construction, but it still needed additional weights in order to submerge. Drebbel's, in contrast, was buoyant wood; therefore, it would need even more attached weights to sink. If Drebbel's submarine provided the same volume of gas per person as the *Hunley*, 952 liters, to each of six crew and two passengers, it would also be able to stay underwater for about thirty minutes before the people inside experienced problematic carbon dioxide levels. A submarine of this volume would require at least 7,600 kilograms of ballast to submerge fully in fresh water, equal to over four average-sized family sedans. If Drebbel's boat had a crew of twelve rowers with three passengers, providing each with six times as much gas so that they could stay underwater for the described three hours, it would need at least 86,000 kilograms of ballast. This mass is about equal to forty-eight sedans, or half of a locomotive train engine. It seems like a challenge to integrate this much weight into a hull made of wood.

Modern-day shipbuilder Mark Edwards constructed a successful small replica of Drebbel's supposed design, but the replica was propelled by only two oarsmen in a small space who dodged the problem of carbon dioxide by breathing from tanks of compressed gas. Historical accounts say that the alchemist Drebbel could completely refresh the air within his boat by dropping a few drops of an unknown magical mystery liquid on the floor. However, in the words of Simon Lake, a noted submarine pioneer who was well aware of the dangers of carbon dioxide, "Cornelius Debrell [*sic*] must have been either something of a joker or else he was much further advanced in the art of revitalizing the air than are any of our modern scientists." Nonetheless, Drebbel's constructions are considered the first submarine prototypes.

Over two centuries after Drebbel, German submarine inventor Wilhelm Bauer looked at his two panting countrymen slumped inside the hull of his creation. They had been trapped inside the submarine for hours, sitting and waiting for rescue.

The test day in 1851 had started normally. They had crawled, as usual, through the hatch in the angular conning tower above the bow and took their places: Bauer at the controls, and Witt and Thomsen each standing at one of the two massive hamster wheels that powered the boat's propeller. Bauer gave the command. Witt and Thomsen lifted their legs and began to step on the spokes of the wheels, spinning them slowly like a giant human-powered waterwheel. The submarine began to move forward through Kiel Harbor in Germany.

But when Bauer had expected a graceful and smooth disappearance beneath the surface of the water, like an elegant metal seal, instead the *Brandtaucher* ("Fire diver") had plummeted unexpectedly, caroming wildly in an awkward, unstoppable, and rapid descent down into a hole 16 meters deep. As she crashed into the seafloor and shuddered to a final stop the three men were hurtled unceremoniously into the bow of the boat. They pieced themselves together, shaken but uninjured. However, Bauer, Witt, and Thomsen slowly came to the realization that they couldn't get the boat out of the hole. They were stuck.

At first, they just waited. And waited. For at least five hours, according to them, they sat, wondering when rescue would come. Their dive had been witnessed by onlookers; they figured it was just a matter of time until the German Navy hauled them back up to safety and fresh air. Someone had in fact noticed, and eventually the clanking of chains and anchors on the hull indicated that boats and divers were poking around the wreck site. But Bauer was growing concerned about the air . . . and the anchors.

All the men were panting hard, pale, and sweating. "[Bauer] himself, he said, had a splitting headache and would like to be sick." Bauer knew the signs of carbon dioxide buildup. Their blood was becoming more acidic with every breath, and he knew that they did not have much gas supply left. He was also concerned about the anchors and chains that were striking the submarine so loudly, because he thought her thin hull might rupture from their repeated hits. He reached up a pallid, trembling hand, and he opened the seacock valve to flood the submarine.

Witt and Thomsen immediately pounced, one slamming Bauer down and sitting on his chest, the other scrambling to restrain his arms and close the valve. Wide-eyed, they yelled that he was trying to commit suicide and drown them too. But Bauer had opened the seacock because he was a man who wanted to live, and because he was also a man who understood physics.

The pressure inside the submarine was roughly 1 atmosphere because it got closed and sealed on the surface at 1 atmosphere. The pressure in the seawater outside, at a depth of 16 meters, was equal to about 2.6 atmospheres. Therefore, the pressure *difference* across the hatch of the submarine was about 1.6 atmospheres total. Converting the units, if Bauer wanted to force open the hatch to escape he would need to be able to move it against the 166 kilopascals of pressure pushing the hatch door closed.

The hatch door had a total surface area of roughly 1.5 square meters. One hundred sixty six kilopascals of pressure from the water times the 1.5 square meters of the door is equal to 249,000 Newtons of aquatic force shoving against the door.

Let's put that into relatable units; I choose to describe the force in units of Rachel. I personally am 160 pounds' worth of human-being mass, mostly comprised of cake, which in metric units is 72 kilograms. Therefore, according to Isaac Newton, to calculate the force exerted by me on the Earth, my 72-kilogram mass gets multiplied by the rate at which Earth's gravity wants to accelerate me downward, which is 9.8 meters per second squared. Seventy-two multiplied by 9.8 is a total downward force of 711 Newtons.

Therefore, I exert 711 Newtons of force on the ground just by standing there, doing nothing productive, converting oxygen to carbon dioxide. The force on the hatch from the water was 249,000 Newtons. If

Bauer wanted to leave the submarine, he would have needed to be strong enough to lift the 350 Rachel Lances standing on the hatch door.

Bauer opened the seacock because he knew that he needed to equalize the pressure differential. If he could flood the submarine and bring the pressure *inside* up to 2.6 atmospheres, the total pressure difference across the hatch door would drop to zero. The door would swing open with ease, and all three submariners could swim to safety. More likely the door would have blown open violently as the buoyant air tried to escape and shoot to the surface, but either way . . . exit pathway achieved.

Talked down by Bauer and his mastery of the laws of pressure, Witt and Thomsen released their captain and allowed him to flood the sub. The increase in the partial pressure of the carbon dioxide was temporarily difficult to tolerate, leading to gagging and choking, but the submarine flooded quickly and the pressure was equalized. The trio got blown out through the hatch and rocketed safely to the surface like they were the "corks of champagne bottles," as Bauer later put it.

Bauer, Witt, and Thomsen were the first three submariners ever to successfully escape a submarine. They did it in the year 1851, and they did it through a mastery of the scientific principles of the underwater world. A few decades later, the *Brandtaucher* was recovered from its mud hole in the ocean and conserved. It is presently on display in a museum in Dresden, Germany, and is the oldest submarine ever recovered.

By the time of the Civil War ten years later the military distaste for submarines was globally evident. They were dubbed "infernal machines," a common phrase used pejoratively to describe a variety of new inventions of war that could not be openly and fairly seen by their targets. The phrase was meant to conjure imagery of hell, and to suggest that these Satan-born stealthy devices were beneath the civilized warfare of respectable and dignified men. A respectable man looked you in the face and gave you a chance to shoot him back. In the South, the situation was a bit more dire, and therefore a bit less judgmental.

At the time of Lincoln's election in late 1860, the eleven states that would become the Confederacy had a potential fighting population of only 1.3 million white, male citizens in the age range of fifteen to fifty years old. The Northern states had a population of 5.6 million from the same demographic, over four times as many as the South, and in addition another 83,759 fifteen-to-fifty-year-old free black men, many of whom would prove eager to enlist. While women were not officially permitted in combat roles, modern research has found evidence of numerous female soldiers fighting undercover as men for both sides, and at least one black woman fighting undercover as a white man for the Union. However, not enough of these soldiers existed to sway the total numerical estimates. At the time the war started the Union Navy had a fleet of ninety fighting ships, and although not all were in superb condition, in contrast the navy of the Confederate States would later be described by historians as "nonexistent."

The citizens of the "Southern Slaveholding States" had watched the 1860 presidential election with intense apprehension. Lincoln, one of four candidates, was a member of the Republican Party, a party later protested in Georgia's declaration of secession as having the "cardinal principle" of "prohibition of slavery." Many plantation owners, firm in their belief that "none but the black race can bear exposure to the tropical sun," were concerned that a victory by the slavery-eschewing Republicans would lead to an end to their right to own slaves, and therefore an end to their estates and their livelihoods. After Lincoln's victory the cotton plantation owners led the charge. Starting with South Carolina, the collection of states one by one announced their determination to leave the Union.

The first official battle of the Civil War is widely considered to be the Confederate assault on Fort Sumter, an island fortress built just outside the harbor mouth of Charleston, South Carolina. The Union troops occupying the fort had been barricaded there for months, fighting off hunger and warily watching the escalating tensions between North and South following the declarations of secession. On April 12, 1861, the Confederate government decided it was time to take the fort, and on April 13 they succeeded. Sometime in the hours between, the bloodiest war in American history had begun.

Many in the South were confident there would be no war; they expected to leave the Union peacefully and without argument. As later stated by Confederate officer George Washington Rains, the war was "entered upon unexpectedly, as it was everywhere supposed in the South that the North would not seriously oppose the Secession of the States." A few months before the battle at Sumter, South Carolina senator James Chesnut Jr. had even been heard offering to drink all the blood shed as a result of secession because he was confident there would be none. So when the war did begin, the Southern states found themselves outmanned, outgunned, and short on supplies.

The obvious plan was to starve them out, and the Union immediately began a blockade of all the major Southern ports. They named the strategy the Anaconda Plan for the way they thought it would slowly choke the populace into submission.

Confederate president Jefferson Davis realized the strategic disadvantage of the relative lack of a Southern navy and promptly sent out a plea to the people for help. His wording did not hide how he felt about the fact that what he perceived as a simple secession had turned into a war, stating that he was "inviting all those who may desire, by service in private armed vessels on the high seas, to aid this government in resisting so wanton and wicked an aggression." In other words: Bring your private boats, we'll declare you and the boats to be part of the Confederate Navy, and together we'll show them they can't demand we stay.

The Confederacy offered monetary prizes to incentivize the destruction of Union ships, and the dollar amounts could be staggering. The prize value for each ship was determined case by case, but the pri-

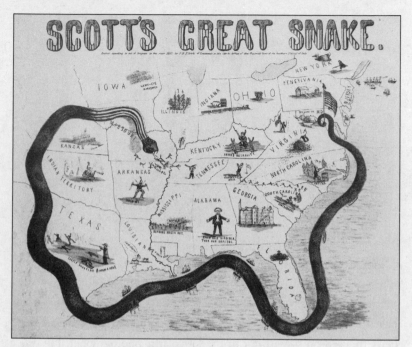

An 1861 illustration of the Anaconda Plan.

vateers kept almost all the reward. The reward included the value of the ship in addition to $20 per man aboard, so for a massive vessel like the USS *New Ironsides* the bounty for the lives of the crew alone would be about $9,000. This amount of money, equivalent to about $250,000 in 2018 even before adding on the cost of the ship herself, was sufficient to entice many young men who dreamed of making a fortune as well as those who dreamed of serving their home states. Three of these young men were Horace Hunley, Baxter Watson, and James McClintock.

Horace Hunley was born into an average farming family in Tennessee, but during his adulthood he became a wealthy man, and like many wealthy men he left behind prolific records of his life. The one confirmed portrait of him shows a young face with a sparse mustache and

Horace Lawson Hunley.

beard poised above a high, starched collar, and narrow-set eyes somberly focused on something to the left of the photographer. He was a
lawyer by trade with a degree from the university now known as Tulane,
but his real motivation, his real passion, seems to have been money.
After law school his adventures included holding a seat in the Louisiana
state legislature, dabbling in the export business, and working periodically in a highly valued and well-paid seat as a New Orleans customs
collector. Hunley's younger sister, Volumnia, was married to a substantially older, fabulously wealthy sugar-plantation owner named Robert
Ruffin Barrow, and Hunley unabashedly and repeatedly played that
connection to get loans from Barrow to fund his moneymaking exploits.
By 1860, the successful thirty-seven-year-old Hunley was able to purchase his own eighty-acre sugar plantation in Louisiana, including at
least the minimum of twenty slaves required to call it a plantation. The
outbreak of war presented blockade-running as a new industry, and the
entrepreneurial Hunley jumped at the opportunity.

The life stories of McClintock and Watson are far more mysterious.

They were true engineers: They were machinists and inventors before the title of "engineer" required an official university degree, back when it was a designation ascribed to a person who built and created. Portraits of James McClintock show a luscious swoop of hair, just beginning to recede at the temples, and heavy black eyebrows that frame deep, serious eyes. His broad mouth, set into a thin line, reminds me of the chagrin I often see in the faces of my modern-day fellow engineers when we are asked to waste time on frivolous tasks like sitting for a portrait.

James R. McClintock.

McClintock and Watson worked with their hands, and at the start of the war they invented a machine to mass-produce bullets for use by the Confederacy. McClintock, a former riverboat captain known for his engineering work on steamboats, made an effort on April 22, 1861, to organize his brethren handymen for the cause. He took out ads boldly declaring "ATTENTION, ENGINEERS!" in the local newspaper and held a meeting where he asked his fellow mechanics and inventors to join the newly formed "Louisiana Associated Engineers' Rifle Company" on behalf of the Confederate States.

At some point in 1861, while living in their mutual city of New Orleans, Hunley, McClintock, and Watson crossed paths. Their prototype boats would be largely financially supported by outside investors seeking to share in the bounty, but in general Hunley was the moneyman of the group, and McClintock and Watson were the designers. I have no evidence to support the theory, but I like to think that Hunley showed up to McClintock's advertised meeting that Monday night in the spring of 1861 looking for a wrench-turner who could help him beat the blockade. What is known is that by the following fall, the three men began to build their first design.

McClintock would later claim that he thought up the idea of a bomb-laden submarine on his own, without any outside inspiration. However, machinist John Roy wrote in his diary on April 22, 1861, that several days earlier he had carted an old copy of *Scientific American* with

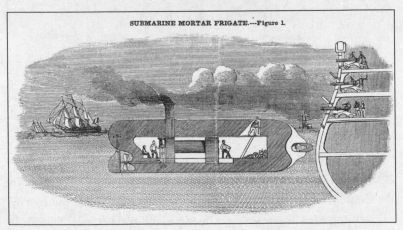

Early design concept of a torpedo-carrying submarine boat.

him to the foundry where both he and McClintock worked, and shown around an illustration of a torpedo boat that he thought could help menace the Union fleet. It seems plausible that this drawing may have been the reason that McClintock called the meeting: to search for more engineers to help him plan and build.

The submarine later dubbed the *HL Hunley* was not the first construction of Hunley, McClintock, and Watson's. Their first confirmed, known boat was the CSS *Pioneer*, the only ship of the three they built to receive an official Confederate commission and therefore to have a "CSS" designation. It carried only two men and was shaped from the repurposed panels of the boiler of a steamship, presumably pillaged by steamship engineer McClintock from some local graveyard of parts. Like the *Hunley*, she was powered by hand crank and had a generally cylindrical design. Unlike the *Hunley*, the bow and stern of the *Pioneer* sharpened to conical points, as if two waffle cones were stuck together by a short section of tube, instead of flattened vertical wedges.

Because of the pointed, conelike ends, the *Pioneer* turned out to be irredeemably unstable. According to McClintock himself, the design was extremely subject to small changes in weighting and position; shifting the ballast weights even a few inches forward or aft made her tip wildly and uncontrollably. This instability was not a great operational feature in a submarine. The designers therefore declared her unfit for service on the open ocean, but they still used her to patrol Lake Pontchartrain, the massive inland lake nestled in the crook of the crescent-shaped land mass that forms the city of New Orleans.

Additionally, when the tiny boat was fully submerged, the crew inside didn't have a visual frame of reference to see what was happening outside, or if they were even making forward progress through the water. McClintock provides one account of the crew, subject to an unstable plummet, driving the vessel headfirst into lake-bottom muck. Unaware that they were firmly stuck, they sat and continued to crank relentlessly, assuming they were moving the entire time. The crew in McClintock's retelling seems to have survived their unfortunate incident, but the *Pioneer* still carries a different fatal association.

Simon Lake is widely considered to be one of the two or three true "fathers" of modern-day submarines. In the year 1918 he wrote a book, and he took care to include a brief history of the devices that had predated his designs. Lake retells a story about the CSS *Pioneer* third-hand, courtesy of a photographer friend who heard it while in New Orleans from a supposed firsthand witness. The same friend supplied Lake with a photograph near Lake Pontchartrain for use in his book.

Slaves were forced to pilot the CSS *Pioneer* on a test run, according to the story. The prototype boat "was the conception of a wealthy planter who owned a number of slaves," and the planter wanted to show off the diving capabilities of the submarine on her trial run. Taking "two of his most intelligent slaves," he briefly showed them how to hold the tiller and turn the propeller before closing them into the vessel and launching it into the bayou in front of a crowd of invited spectators. The submarine never reappeared, and the planter vehemently and loudly swore his frustration at himself for trusting the two slaves who—in his opinion—had clearly just stolen his device to travel north to their freedom.

Years later, the submarine was found during a dredging operation, sunk in the mud close to where it had been launched. Lake quotes the alleged firsthand witness, who had earlier reported the values of the slaves at $1,000 per man when they went into the little boat: "And do you know, suh, when they opened the hatch them two blamed niggers was still in thar, but they warn't wuth a damned cent."

In 1864, US Navy fleet engineer William H. Shock was charged with inspecting the CSS *Pioneer*, which had been recovered from the lake bottom a few years earlier and was sitting on the shore of Lake Pontchartrain. Along with a technical drawing he commissioned of the *Pioneer*, he included a letter that reports a Confederate submarine test that is remarkably similar to Lake's tale, stating that "two contrabands [slaves] . . . were smothered to death" inside the vessel.

The number of slaves in both the stories of Shock and of Lake's photographer friend matches the number of men needed to pilot the CSS *Pioneer* and another submarine later found in the area. The tests in both stories occurred at the location that is known to have been used by Hunley, McClintock, and Watson to test their vessels. Hunley and McClintock were both, at that time, plantation owners with slaves, just as the inventor in the photographer's story was a plantation owner with slaves.

Machinist John Roy was living in New Orleans in the fall of 1861. His daily diary records his attempt to go watch the public demonstration of a "sub marine boat for blowing up ships" that took place on November 3, 1861, right around the time when Hunley, McClintock, and Watson would have begun testing. Roy frustratingly went to the wrong location and missed the demonstration, but other diary entries show that he and McClintock both frequented the same foundry, and that the men almost definitely knew each other well. If McClintock were arranging a public demonstration of his submarine prototype, Roy would probably have been invited.

The men lowered themselves into the foreign metal device, having only a cursory understanding of how the various levers and gears were supposed to work. They took hold of the crank and must have experienced the terrified certainty that the only way out of this situation was through it. They cranked furiously, stuck in the mud, with nothing to tell them that they were going nowhere, and eventually, feeling as if they were choking on their own breath, they became confident in the dawning realization that this experience would be their last.

Historian Mark Ragan, working "under the auspices of the Friends of the *Hunley*," did a massive amount of archival digging after Cussler announced his find in 1995. Ragan, who refers to himself as *"Hunley* project historian," was the first to wrest the Shock letter from the microfilm caches of the National Archives. He was so enthralled with its "historical significance" that he stated in one of his books about the research that this letter was "worth reprinting in its entirety." So, in the book, he included the entire text of the letter to make it more accessible to the world. With it reprinted and republished, nobody would ever need to look up the original microfilm and read it themselves. The Friends of the *Hunley* later used the drawing from Shock to build a full-sized model of the CSS *Pioneer*, and they now display the model in the lobby of their museum. By 2000, Ragan was serving on the board of directors of the Friends of the *Hunley*.

There is one major problem with Ragan's archival work, and his reporting: He changed a key word in the story. Where the original, handwritten Shock letter reads that two "contrabands" died, Ragan altered the word in his transcription to read "men" instead. He repeated the change in both of his books containing the quotation. He leads readers to believe that the letter must tell the story of two noble Confederate men, trying to sink a federal warship, editing the deaths of the enslaved men out of history.*

The *Pioneer* was reportedly scuttled. The fall of New Orleans in late April 1862 meant that the Union was in charge of the city, and Hunley, McClintock, and Watson were afraid their own technology would be used against them. On May 13, 1862, Union troops arrested

---

*The Friends of the *Hunley* keep an onsite compilation of all historical records at the Warren Lasch Conservation Center. As far as could be determined, every author who wrote a book about the *Hunley* between 1995 and the writing of this book collaborated with the Friends of the *Hunley*. To date, only one book or report could be found that links Shock's letter, which is often described as a work with questionable credibility, with his drawing, which is consistently given the highest credibility. Friends of the *Hunley*–affiliated author Brian Hicks is the only author who could be found who mentions the letter in his book with proper attribution to Shock and in connection to the technical drawing of the CSS *Pioneer*. However, he summarily dismisses the story about the contrabands as a "local rumor" without providing any supporting discussion that the story is only a rumor, and he even seems to chastise Shock for repeating it. Historian Tom Chaffin was the only author found who correctly quoted the Shock letter.

Charles Leeds, the owner of the foundry where the Confederacy had been manufacturing cannons and where the group had worked on their submarines. Shortly after this arrest, the three submariners decided it was time to move on. McClintock later stated that they had sunk their boat before heading for the nearest major Confederate port: Mobile, Alabama.

Newly housed in the Parks and Lyons machine shop in Mobile, Alabama, the trio got back to work. Their next design was dubbed the *American Diver*, but McClintock's original plans and drawings of the vessel were lost long ago, and only general descriptions remain. He made some attempts to build the boat with either electric or steam power, but he ultimately abandoned both new ideas and returned to the hand crank.

However, this vessel actually got a real trial run. The little *Diver* traveled successfully throughout Mobile Bay, but the man she was showing off for, Confederate admiral Franklin Buchanan, was unimpressed. The slow speed of the vessel coupled with the fact that she later sank and nearly killed her entire crew meant that he politely recorded the entire affair as "impracticable." In 1852 the US Navy had rejected the advances of poor submarine inventor Lodner Phillips with the simple line "The boats used by the Navy go *on* and not *under* the water," and in 1863 the Confederate Navy was still not interested.

After the loss of the *American Diver*, Hunley, McClintock, and Watson rallied the support of even more financial backers and set out to create what would become their most famous design: the submarine that history would eventually remember as the *HL Hunley*. They dubbed it *Fish Boat*.

True to McClintock's steamboat roots, the *Fish Boat* was hammered out of multiple wrought-iron plates, thought to have come from the boiler of a steamship. The new design reflected the lessons learned from the previous fish boats: It had glass deadlights to let light into the hull, and it had windows in the raised conning towers that a pilot could use for navigation. She was more stable too, with tall, wedge-shaped bow and stern pieces that ameliorated the "dirt dart" plummeting behavior of the CSS *Pioneer*.

McClintock would later declare that he had no knowledge of the submersible boats built in the centuries before him, but his work inarguably showed that he and the other inventors were all evolving toward the same basic physical principles for a working submarine. Like the submarine *Turtle*, built by David Bushnell in 1776, the *Fish Boat* used a simple but reliable hand crank connected to an external propeller. Like the cigar-shaped submarines built by Lodner Phillips in 1852, the *Fish Boat* had a long, sleek shape that was both stable and hydrodynamic. And even though historical documents indicate the *Fish Boat* was originally designed to tow a torpedo behind her on a lanyard, the constant fights between this lanyard and her spinning propeller meant that she would eventually be modified to transport her weapon on a spar attached to her bow, like Robert Fulton's submarine *Nautilus* in 1801.

On July 31, 1863, the newest submarine finally managed to impress cantankerous old Admiral Buchanan. She towed a black powder torpedo on a rope behind her, dove beneath a barge placed in a river specifically for her trial, and reappeared about 400 yards on the other side of the shattered sacrifice. Buchanan promptly wrote of the victory to his colleagues in Charleston, South Carolina, advertising the sensational *Fish Boat* as the perfect way for them to destroy the Union ironclads lurking in their harbor, blocking their access to supplies. So, at the beckoning of Confederate general P.G.T. Beauregard, the submarine was loaded on a train and shipped from Mobile to beleaguered and battered Charleston, the largest Southern city that still remained under Confederate control.

The *Fish Boat* never received her commission; she therefore never carried the label "CSS," even later, after she was renamed the *HL Hunley*. At the time she arrived in Charleston, she was still civilian-owned and operated by the partners who built her. The partners, familiar with the history of her design iterations and their multiple sinkings, approached her operations in Charleston with a level of caution and risk aversion that the military men found unacceptable. They wanted the blockade lifted, and they wanted it lifted quickly. The Confederate Army lost patience, seized the vessel, and staffed her with a crew from the Confederate Navy, dashing Horace Hunley's hopes of bounty and fortune. Unfortunately, despite the change in command, the luck of the *Fish Boat*'s predecessors had traveled with her from Alabama.

———————

Serving as crew on the *Fish Boat* came with perks, specifically higher pay and more notoriety about town. The public demonstrations with the little vessel had ensured the crew was well known, especially among the other soldiers and sailors.

On one average day, Lt. John Payne stood with his head and torso up out of the boat, ready to begin such a demonstration. His crew was waiting for him inside the boat, ready to crank but relaxing for the moment. They were under tow, hatches open and breathing fresh air, with the CSS *Etowah* (sometimes referred to as the CSS *Etiwan*) doing the work for them until they got to the site of the demonstration. Payne just needed to free the towline then lower himself down into the vessel, sealing the conning-tower hatch behind him. The plan was the same as the plan for all the previous dog and pony shows: Dive under some obstacle, resurface on the other side, accept applause from the adoring and hopeful populace who wanted the blockade broken so very badly.

Rocky waves were making the job difficult, however, and the towline was a disaster. Payne struggled, trying to free himself from the line, but he slipped. Jammed partly inside the conning tower but still partly outside the hatch, his legs scrabbling for purchase accidentally knocked the long lever that controlled the dive planes. The narrow fins on the port and starboard sides angled in response, and the *Fish Boat* dove. The submarine sank, unsealed, beneath the surface. Water began to pour in through the open conning-tower hatches.

Payne managed to get himself fully out via the fore conning tower, and crewman William Robinson squeezed out of the conning tower near the stern. In order to escape the flooding metal cylinder, the men in the middle would need to slither through a deadly obstacle course. The twisting, circuitous pipes of the crank formed a broad spiral down the starboard side of the 4-foot-wide tube, and the long pine crew bench shrank the available vertical space on the port side. Each man was wedged in place, head and shoulders slouched to fit in the narrow hull, with his legs crammed between the bench and the crank, his arms pressed between the shoulders of his neighbors. The tiny deadlights overhead let in some sun, but the small circles of imperfect old-fashioned glass could only dimly light the interior of the trap. To escape, each man would need to keep calm in the dark, keep his head above the rapidly rising water, thread between the crank and the bench, stay hunched over inside the narrow hull, avoid the ballast blocks placed throughout the bilge, and find his way to the small target of a conning tower. Even then, they could only exit one at a time, unable to begin the process before their neighbors gave them space to move. Meanwhile, the ocean kept gushing in as the boat continued to plummet.

Crewman Charles Hasker was seated second in the single-file row of people inside the boat, and he took immediate action. Fighting against the torrent of water flooding through the open forward conning tower, he clambered over the bars and levers that controlled the boat, only to get halfway out of the hatch before the door slammed shut on his back. He worked his way out while she continued to descend through the water, until only his left leg remained trapped. As the submarine finally settled with a thud against the rough ocean bottom, the hatch door was jostled open and Hasker escaped for the surface.

Five men couldn't make it. They died wedged in the jam-packed labyrinth between the bench and the crank. When the submarine was recovered, their corpses were "so swollen and so offensive" from their days in the warm summer seawater that they needed to be dismembered before they could be removed in pieces through the narrow ovals of the conning towers they had been trying to reach.

Some accounts differ in the details, stating that instead a wave swamped the open hatch door, but these accounts are generally suspected to be polite alterations of the truth to spare Payne's pride. Whatever the true cause of the flooding, Lieutenant Payne was required to arrange for the purchase of coffins for his drowned crew, and to write a letter to his superior officer justifying the expense of extra-large sizes to fit the bloated bodies.

The five men of this first lost crew were exhumed in 1999 because their bodies had been mistakenly paved over to build a new parking lot for the football stadium of the Citadel, the Charleston military college. It took months to find the grave of the fifth drowned crewman, Absolum Williams, because the free, black nineteen-year-old grandson of a slave was not buried in the same resting place as his white crewmates. Beneath the thick layer of pavement, the discovery of telltale custom-dimensioned coffins and dismembered bodies confirmed the long-standing story of Payne's unfortunate accident. The limbs of the men were placed next to their torsos and heads, and the extra-large coffins were hastily stacked one on top of another, two to a grave. The hands of several crewmen were inexplicably missing, and were never found.

A mere sixteen days after the accident, the *Fish Boat* had been recovered, cleaned, and assigned once more to Lt. John Payne. Five days after that, Horace Hunley audaciously suggested in a direct letter to Beauregard that he should personally be the one to lead the next crew. Beauregard agreed.

Hunley enlisted a group of eight volunteers, with Lt. George E. Dixon at the helm of his ship. The crew began to practice, again making repeated dives underneath ships, often towing a dummy torpedo behind them on a long line. One day, for an unknown reason, Hunley decided it was his turn. Seven men crawled into the boat to take the crank, and Hunley assumed the tiny wooden pilot's bench beneath the forward conning tower.

The submarine was seen approaching the CSS *Indian Chief,* a favorite practice target. As usual, it was seen to dive below the surface of the water. However, this time, the submarine never reappeared. Unfamiliar with the controls and unpracticed in the boat's operations, the proud Horace Hunley had plowed her nose-first into the ocean floor. Unable to raise the boat, he and the rest of the crew asphyxiated inside.

When the vessel was raised, the ghastly remains of the men were found huddled in anguish. They had tried to undo the bolts inside the keel that would have released the weights and sent the boat to the surface, but they did not finish in time. Hunley himself, doubtless panting and feeling the anxiety of the building carbon dioxide, was found curled tightly inside the forward conning tower, apparently trying to bash his way through the hatch door. With three Rachels of force pushing the small oval door closed, Hunley did not think to equalize the pressure like Wilhelm Bauer did. The hatch remained firmly sealed.

The stories of the sinkings have been muddled by time, the spread of rumors, and faulty human memory. As a result, historical documents report at least six separate stories about alleged sinkings in Charleston Harbor with up to fifty fatalities, but many seem to be exaggerations and variations on the same events. The general consensus among historians is that the *Fish Boat* sank twice in the summer and fall of 1863, killing a total of thirteen men. These fatalities earned her the nickname "the peripatetic coffin."

Despite her horrid track record of killing her crew, one of the most common statements made in the modern press about the *Hunley* is that she was "ahead of her time." I respectfully disagree. I think we underestimate "her time." By 1862, James Clerk Maxwell had published his ingenious set of mathematical equations to describe the complex relationships between electricity and magnetism. The first practical refrigeration units were a cool twenty-plus years old (sorry, I had to), grain elevators and steam-powered locomotives were in everyday use, and electricity was becoming common enough that the circuit breaker had already been invented. The Americans of the 1860s may not have had cars and plasma TVs, but they had already witnessed more advanced technological innovations than we tend to give them credit for.

Many people mistakenly believe that the only way for a design to be noteworthy is for it to be complex and "ahead of [its] time." For an engineer, a cleanly built machine that simply fulfills its purpose has a profound, inherent elegance and beauty. The hyperbaric chamber, a straightforward metal ball that holds gas, has this beauty. The *Hunley*, a tube with a basic hand crank and gears, has it too. Non-engineers tend to overlook these devices, ignoring them because they are not impressively elaborate, so it is easy to forget they exist. Even though it was unsafe, the *Hunley*, like almost every machine built by a good engineer, perfectly reflects the intersection of purpose, budget, timeline, and available materials. For that reason it has its own notability. McClintock made periodic deviations into new innovations like electric motors, but eventually he gravitated back to the robust, proven design parameters that he could get to function reliably on his urgent schedule: muscle power, a propeller, and one big-ass black powder bomb.

That is why she was ultimately the first submarine to be successful in combat. Her simplicity of design but complexity of story is why I was fascinated by her, despite the dark and devastating aspects of her history. That is why, after my study on suffocation was complete, I wanted to keep working on this problem. I needed to know why she failed, not in combat, but as a machine fails.

I stared down at the poor-quality black-and-white printout in my hand. It was my way of tempting Dale, of getting permission to work on this problem more. Dale was a scientist too, and the best way to intrigue him was by offering him mental candy in the form of a testable mystery. The printout was a screen shot of the *Hunley*'s conning tower, and it showed a fractured section that, according to the Friends of the *Hunley*, may have been broken by the bullets fired by the crew of the *Housatonic* in a last-ditch effort to defend their ship. The lucky-shot theory stated that the submarine then flooded through this broken chunk, drowning the crew.

It looked somehow wrong to me. The chunk missing was massive, and cleanly broken at the edges. Most of my knowledge of bullets was either as a navy civilian living in the gun culture of the deep South or as an injury biomechanist; therefore, most of my personal understanding of terminal ballistics at that time focused on how bullets ripped and tore through paper targets, mounds of red Southern dirt, or people. Both paper and people tear much differently than cast iron does, but still, my sneaking hunch was that the damage looked far too large for a Civil War round, with not enough tearing at the edges.

I was sitting in our lab's weekly meeting, holding this piece of paper and waiting for my turn to speak. Once a week, at the appointed time, we would hear Dale's boots *thunk* their way toward the shared departmental conference room at the end of the hallway. The noise signaled the beginning of our meeting, when the nine of us who carried the title of "graduate student" were expected to sit around the long wooden table and inform Dale of our progress.

I loved lab meeting. I thought it was thrilling. We would each take our turn talking while Dale clicked away at his laptop either taking notes or (for all we knew) doing something entirely unrelated. Each student reported their progress, their problems, their new victories, and their frustrations. The purpose of lab meeting was to help one another when we got stuck, and to share in the quiet, cathartic feeling of victory that comes with each new piece of data that signifies a tiny scientific step forward into undiscovered knowledge. We learned from one another, and even if we had nothing in common outside of science, my lab mates and I had the deep, common roots of curiosity and endless questions about the world. These were the shared traits that had brought us all into graduate school and into that meeting.

I passed my printout down the human chain of my lab mates to Dale at the far end of the table while explaining the lucky-shot theory. I had outlined in my head a careful plan to test the plausibility of the theory with minimal expense: Do the math to see how long the *Hunley* needed to drift before she sank in the location where she was found. Do the math to see how quickly she would sink with holes of different sizes. Create complex three-dimensional models of both the bullet and the conning tower, then run dozens if not hundreds of simulations to test various ways they could crash into each other, each time making small but critical changes to numerous variables like the material properties and the velocity of the bullet. The first two tasks I knew I could handle, but the last one was intimidating.

Dale began to slowly shake his head at me. Letting out a single bark of a laugh to interrupt the rapid flow of my words, he declared my new plan.

"Rachel," he said. "Buy some cast iron . . . and shoot it."

He passed my printout back. I loved lab meeting, but some were better than others.

CHAPTER 4

THE FURY BENEATH THE WAVES

One should not let one's self get out of the mindset that all manufacture of Black Powder is dangerous. Some methods may be less dangerous than others, but should never be considered as safe.

—Ian von Maltitz, black powder expert

Billowing clouds of rust-colored dust spewed out from the tires of the station wagon as it pulled into the small dirt parking lot. I watched from behind a giant mound of protective soil as the wagon parked next to my blue sedan, and decided I should probably go say hello. With the weather we expected for today, the only person who could be driving was the reenactor.

As Chris Kelley raised his average-sized frame out of the low-slung car, I saw why my straightlaced US Navy coworker Al had affectionately characterized him as "eccentric." Chris's pale red hair moved in unkempt, autonomous whorls in response to the gusts of wind from the threatening storm, and his round glasses contained easily the thickest light-warping lenses I have ever seen. Sticking out my hand, I introduced myself. Chris greeted me with a gigantic smile and a firm, callused shake right before he wiped his hands on his old yellow T-shirt and began to unload several mysterious wooden boxes from the trunk of his car. Civil War reenactors prize authenticity above all else, and Chris's passion for his hobby was already evident. The large wooden boxes were without modern trappings such as wheels or clever latches, and they boasted enough scars to pass for well-worn 1860s antiques.

After Dale's directive to "buy some cast iron and shoot it" I sent out feelers into every community I knew, trying to find someone with a period-accurate rifle. My navy friend had put me in touch with Chris, an old buddy of his from their active-duty days who just happened to live near Duke. Chris took his role as a Civil War reenactor with the 42nd North Carolina very seriously. He had proudly sent me a sepia-toned picture of himself in full reenactment regalia, standing in the woods with a swollen face, happily tolerating a massive pollen-induced allergic reaction because—as he stated—Benadryl had not yet been invented in the 1860s. The picture, combined with the fact that his email handle was a reference to *Mad* magazine, gave me the impression of someone passionate who had long ago stopped caring what anyone else thought of him and his hobbies. I was delighted to find I was correct, and that he was willing to volunteer his time and rifle to my little project.

"So this is finally happening, huh!" he gleefully declared.

"Ha! I know, right?" I replied sarcastically, rolling my eyes. Our attempts to set up the experiment had been plagued by weather: Our first test date had been canceled by a thunderstorm, and then the backup date brought us an actual hurricane. Today was cloudy and rain was expected but not until the afternoon, so I had optimistically declared that it was finally the day to head to the firing range.

In North Carolina, it is legal to discharge a firearm pretty much anywhere as long as you are at least 600 feet from someone else's building of residence, and people often do. In my neighborhood, some sit in their backyards in camping chairs on the weekends, drinking beer and firing .22 rifles at old pans and bottles. This is not unusual. The legitimate firing ranges in North Carolina, therefore, are designed with the assumption that people have bothered to make the trip to use only their really big guns.

The massive firing range that agreed to host our science had been carved out of the hilly, forested terrain with heavy machinery, and the displaced red Carolina clay had been piled high into towering berms that separated the numerous firing stalls. After Chris refused to let me carry any of the enticing-looking aged boxes, instead arranging them on his shoulders with an ease and grace clearly born of practice, I descended with him into the excavated pit. We walked around a crook in the path to disappear behind one of the massive clay walls, and I showed him to the stall I had claimed at the far end of the row.

My undergraduate student, Henry Warder, looked up from his squatting position as we trundled into the isolated strip of grass. Henry had been assigned to me by Dale a few weeks back, and it was part of my job as his graduate student (so I was told) to help mold Henry's young scientific mind. I had liked the tall, lanky Henry immediately because he was unique among undergrads in his willingness to ask questions. He understood that I was sleep-deprived and wanted efficient honesty, not polite reverence, and he told me right away when what I had just requested made no sense to him instead of hiding from me for two weeks before admitting he had been confused.

Henry was scrounging in the dirt and grass, making tiny piles of pebbles. The clouds had begun to release sparse droplets of rain, and he wanted to prop as many of the electrical junctions off the ground as possible. The cables stretched the length of the entire pit, connecting a remote trigger to the high-speed video camera positioned just next to our targets. This way, we could stand at a safe distance while controlling the recording. Henry and I had soldered together a custom electrical harness to connect the camera to two boat batteries as an improvised yet effective remote power source, and the entire setup was protected by thick plastic sheets propped up to guard against ricochets. We would stand and wait in the rain, because the expensive camera and its batteries had first rights to the lab's only portable rain shelter. As Henry unfolded from his squat to come say hello, Chris thunked the boxes down on the covered picnic table in the corner of the pit and began to open them.

The men on board the *Housatonic* reported firing at the oncoming *Hunley* in the moments before the attack. The lucky-shot theory stated that one of these bullets sank the sub by damaging the fore conning tower and allowing the boat to flood. Of the firearms the crew used, the most powerful would have been their standard-issue Springfield rifles; however, the vintage firearms from that period are no longer considered safe to fire because of material changes that occur to metal bodies over time. Chris Kelley "fought" for the South and therefore had a replica Enfield rifle instead, but like an authentic Springfield, it fired the same malleable, lead, hollow-ended Minié bullets of the time period. And more important, like a Springfield it had a muzzle velocity of about 300 meters per second.

A target does not know the political allegiance of the gun that fired at it, or its date of manufacture. All it knows is the kind of bullet and the velocity of the bullet at the moment of impact. For the purposes of this test, therefore, Chris's replica Confederate gun would convincingly pretend to be an authentic Union weapon.

As the sparse but fat rain droplets began to plunk down around us, Chris brought out his tins of black powder. He poured a small dose of the tiny black granules into the muzzle of the gun, added a bullet, and gently tamped it down before taking aim at the first cast-iron target. The sharp crack of the rifle reverberated between the walls of the deep pit, and an immediate white cloud of smoke consumed Chris as the sulfurous smell of fire and rotten eggs filled the air. As Chris shot at each of the numerous cast-iron targets, it became clear why he had chosen a grungy T-shirt to wear for the test day: With each firing, another thin coat of pungent smoky residue added to the layered accumulation of black powder crud that soon enveloped his entire body.

He licked his lips to clear them of some of their caked black coating, looking down at the ground and softly muttering profanity after a missed shot. Returning to the picnic table to reload, he licked his sooty fingers and used them to help wipe some of the obfuscating accretion from his thick glasses.

"Stuff gets everywhere," he said. The smoke from the powder had painted Chris like a cartoon caricature of a chimney sweep.

The lucky-shot testing took two days, nestled in the deep orange-red pit of the firing range. Drenched and chased away by the rain halfway through the first day, Henry and I returned to the lab to regroup and to find more cast-iron samples with a wider range of thicknesses. By the end of the second day we had not only accumulated a small crowd of curious North Carolinian gun enthusiasts, but the results of the testing were clear: The thinner samples had shattered, splintering apart in radial patterns that propagated all the way to their edges, fracturing them into a million razor shards. The thicker samples had been penetrated cleanly by the bullets, with plastic deformation and tearing around the edges of the small holes as the bullet pushed the iron wall backward before breaking through. These two patterns were how the material of cast iron failed in response to bullets. In the process of this discovery we had also shot to death one wooden stool and irreparably warped two metal ratchet straps.

Neither of the two patterns of failure matched the clean-edged, medium-sized chunk that was missing from one section of the unshattered conning tower. While it was possible that rifle fire had smashed the glass of the small, forward-looking navigational window or damaged one of the metal rings holding that glass window to the conning tower, the grapefruit-sized chunk neatly excised from the body of the otherwise intact tower more than likely hadn't been taken out by a bullet.

———————

Back in my narrow office and sheltered from the rainstorms, Henry and I spent weeks scribbling equations on the whiteboard and programming them into a computational script. Our goal was to determine how the physics that dictated the sinking behavior of the boat compared to the narrative of the lucky-shot theory. The failure patterns of the cast iron didn't fit the theory, but as scientists we still needed more data to declare it debunked.

The theory stated that the boat started sinking immediately after the attack on the *Housatonic*. In our system of equations, the downward force of gravity fought against the upward force of buoyancy to see which could tug the *Hunley* harder. The force of water pushing inward railed against the resistance of the gas pressure building up inside as the internal air was compressed. Our code calculated the rate at which water would fill the submarine through various-sized holes in the conning tower, from as small as the bullet holes in our samples to as large as the chunk actually missing from the recovered *Hunley*. For each size of hole, we calculated a length of time the boat would take to sink.

When the submarine was found, she was discovered with her bow pointing back toward the *Housatonic*, oriented exactly as if she simply drifted out to sea on the outgoing tidal current. The next obvious question, then, was how long it would take her to reach that position. Henry and I looked at the tides that would have slowly pushed the submarine seaward after her attack, and we badgered patient, helpful professors from the Duke ocean sciences department with our innumerable questions.

Charleston Harbor is one of the sites known as a "harmonic station," which means the harbor's tides follow a simple, repeatable pattern and can be calculated accurately for any date in history. The patterns of the tides in Charleston Harbor that night in 1864 almost exactly matched the tides from February 21, 2013, a modern date with recorded data taken from a buoy stationed near the *Housatonic* wreck site, data that told us the speeds of the tidal currents, in the area. Based on the changes to Charleston Harbor over the centuries, such as dredging open the entrance, all of which would have increased the outflow of water from the harbor mouth, the speeds of the currents that were recorded in 2013 were more than likely the upper limit of the speeds the doomed *Hunley* could have experienced.

At the end of the analysis, we had a whiteboard full of equations, a stack of printed ocean-science references about Charleston, and a few key numbers. For the *Hunley* to reach her final location 310 meters seaward of the wreck of the *Housatonic*, she would have had to drift outward on the 2013-speed tidal currents for roughly fourteen minutes. Therefore, if she was floating along in the slower currents of 1864, she had to drift for at least fourteen minutes or longer to reach her final resting place. From the analysis of the fill rates we calculated that if she were filling through a grapefruit-sized hole like the one in the conning tower, she would have hit the silty bottom in at most five minutes. This five-minute time period was not enough time for her to reach her final resting place. If the damage to the tower caused the boat to sink, and the damage had been done by a lucky shot, then the *Hunley* would have settled to the ocean floor much closer to the wreck site of the *Housatonic*.

The *Hunley*'s crew did not set their bilge pumps to pump out water from inside their vessel, and the crew would not have sat, relaxed, and curiously watched the slow trickle of intruding water as it drowned them. The submarine was found much farther from the *Housatonic* than she would have been if she had swamped immediately. Therefore, she must have stayed afloat to drift for some distance after she was shot at by the *Housatonic*'s crew.

The lucky-shot theory went the way of the theory of suffocation as Henry and I crossed it off our mental list of possibilities. Three months after the publication of the academic paper describing our scientific results, which was our second paper on the topic of the *Hunley*, the collaborative group including the Friends of the *Hunley* stated in an informal web article that they thought the submarine would have needed to drift for about thirteen minutes to reach her final resting site, further supporting our conclusions.

———————

Chris, Henry, and I had begrudgingly dealt with black powder to make our gunshots as period-accurate as possible, but in the 1860s the messy substance was the unavoidable lifeblood of both the Union and Confederate militaries. Without it, the most effective wheels of warfare would grind to an immediate halt: No guns could be shot, no cannons could be fired. Nothing would have been possible but bayonets and swords and fistfights in the mud. Black powder isn't a powder in the fluffy, soft sense of flour or snow; it's a coarse, pearlescent sand with large granules. The polished grains have an unmistakable smell, and everywhere they travel they leave behind a trail of telltale soot like so many minuscule black chemical snails.

Chris had repeatedly packed small doses of the powder into the muzzle of his rifle for shot after shot, and each time some of the grains had escaped and pinged off the picnic table, rolling away along the edges of the wood. I would press the tip of my index finger down on them, sticking the dots to my damp skin so that I could stare at their little spherical shapes. Individually, these granules were harmless. Light a match to one single grain of rifle powder and it will simply vanish, almost unnoticeable in its reaction. But assemble enough grains to fill the muzzle of a rifle, and their cumulative heat and gas can fire a bullet with lethal speeds. Compile an army of grains, enough to fill a beer keg, and you can destroy a ship. They're like ants: harmless alone, powerful in numbers.

The modern granules rolling down the table were the refined product of thousands of years of bloody evolution. Originally invented by alchemists in China around the year 220 BCE, black powder expanded to ubiquity once its utility as an explosive became apparent. Since then, each generation of warfighter has tried to improve upon the substance, sometimes succeeding in enhancing the power of the product, but more often blowing themselves to pieces. By the time of the Civil War, the dangerous process for making black powder had been refined to only three deceptively simple ingredients: sulfur, potassium nitrate, and charcoal.*

The sulfur, a soft, dusty, pale-yellow element with the chemical code name S, usually forms a mere 10 percent of the final powder by weight. However, even in such a small percentage the sulfur was the reason that the burnt powder caking Chris Kelley's face had the overwhelming smell of rotten eggs. When the sulfur burns it forms hydrogen sulfide, and the odor comparison is not a metaphor; the exact same chemical is produced as eggs begin to decompose. Hydrogen sulfide also spews from the mouths of volcanoes alongside the ash and lava, earning sulfur a place of honor in the Bible's description of hell under its other, much more famous, name: brimstone.

The simplest way to make black powder starts with mixing pulverized yellow sulfur together with the powder produced from ground charcoal. The black and the yellow swirl together in the mixing bowl beautifully, creating tiger stripes before blending to a homogenous, dark dust. The charcoal, only 15 percent of the final black powder by weight, is how the explosive product receives its signature color.

The magic ingredient contributed by charcoal is its carbon, a fundamental element denoted simply by the capital letter C. Carbon-to-carbon bonds are the I-beams that, when assembled neatly, construct a diamond, when laid flat into tidy sheets make graphite, and when jumbled into a degree of chaos become charcoal. Chemist Walter White

---

*Black powder is unstable during manufacturing and it should not be tried at home. I have included the steps required to describe only the chemistry rather than providing a full description of its manufacture, and this description is intentionally insufficient to generate an effective explosive.

said in the television show *Breaking Bad*, "Carbon is at the center of it all," meaning all of life and most of chemistry, and his words are absolutely true for the chemistry of black powder. Together the sulfur and the carbon are building blocks, eagerly waiting to be rearranged into lower-energy states, releasing their inherent energy as heat, light, and sound in the process.

The charcoal for black powder can and has been made out of pretty much any wood in the world. The type of wood will lead to some variation in powder performance, but what is truly crucial is the actual process of making that wood into charcoal. The wood must be carbonized, which means heating it to a specific, extremely hot temperature, then quickly depriving it of oxygen to stifle the burning reaction. All the water is burned off, the other miscellaneous components are burned off, and what is left is a pile of smoldering coals. These coals are scorching-hot little nuggets of desiccated tree. They have been reduced down to the carbon-carbon bonds that provide the wood's structural essence.

The dark, dusty concoction in the mixing bowl, still just a blend of yellow sulfur and black charcoal, is not yet an explosive because it is missing an oxidizer. The main difference between an explosion and an everyday, normal fire is the rate at which the material burns. In a normal fire the materials burn slowly, and in an explosion, the materials burn at warp speed. Explosive materials can burn so quickly because they include their own oxidizer.

Any fire or explosion requires the same three elements, each a leg of the so-called fire triangle: fuel, oxidizer, and heat to start the reaction. The carbon and sulfur are fuel alone, with no oxidizer or heat yet, so the mixture in the bowl is like a pile of wood stacked beside a pit: full of potential energy, but not yet ready to be a fire. The oxidizer delivers oxygen rapidly and forcefully into the chemical reaction that is breaking down the fuel. For a normal fire fit for roasting marshmallows, air with its 0.21 atmospheres of oxygen is sufficient. The air can waft in and out through the properly arranged logs of a well-constructed bonfire, combining with the heat of the flames and the fuel of the unspent wood to keep the reaction going. However, air alone is insufficient to enable an explosion. The most common oxidizer used to make black powder is a nondescript, innocent-looking white chemical called potassium nitrate, disturbingly purchasable as a fertilizer from any local grocery store for $5.95 per half pound.

The potassium nitrate, also known as saltpeter, commonly comprises about 75 percent of the final product by weight, a large fraction that emphasizes the extreme importance of oxidation when making an explosion. It is shocking how many seemingly inert everyday materials, like titanium or most rubbers, become eager to explode when force-fed enough oxygen.

After the addition of the oxidizer, the crude black powder in the mixing bowl is, at least in theory, complete. It is a mixture of fuel and oxygen in solid granulated form, missing only heat to create an inferno. In the words of a popular blast textbook, for all types of explosives, "all methods of initiation are basically thermal in nature," meaning whether the explosion is black powder, TNT, or C4, whether it is started with a match, a detonator, a sharp impact, or a tiny arc of unintended static electricity, it all starts with some kind of heat. For most modern high explosives, the heat must also be coupled with hydrodynamic effects, the additional forces caused by moving materials inside the charge, to achieve detonation. This requirement is why modern high explosives are far more stable than black powder. For example, the explosive C4 was designed stably so that a brick of it will not explode unintentionally even if it gets shot. But like a stack of dry leaves soaked in lighter fluid, ultrasensitive black powder "only takes one little spark to set it off."

This instability is why the next step in the process is so discomfiting: The powder gets ground aggressively. Crushed in a pit beneath massive, beastly rolling metal wheels, the impact-sensitive explosive sand gets milled for hours. Even when doused in water to make the process slightly less dangerous, the powder is still itching for the opportunity to convert itself into a lower-energy state, which would blow the mill wheels, the mill operators, and often the walls of the entire mill building to pieces. The grinding brings the fuel and the oxidizer into even closer, more intimate contact, as the eager molecules are further intermixed and smashed into tighter proximity by the friction of the spinning metal wheels.

The last remaining American manufacturer of black powder is GOEX, located deep in the heart of Louisiana. Large, deep, water-filled containers that look similar to bathtubs punctuate the GOEX campus. These tubs are protective refuges for the employees in case of a milling accident . . . if the employees can get to one in time.

The wet milled powder is then set out to dry, and it forms into chalky cakes. The cakes are broken into particles of the desired size, and the volatile, jagged little crystals of explosive are thrown into a tumbler, where they are bounced and spun until they take the final form of the tiny, rolling black spheres that I pressed from the surface of the picnic table into the skin of my finger.

These spheres are designed to burn. Every step in the process is designed to optimize the eagerness of these little spheres to burn as rapidly as possible to create the fastest explosion possible, and every step that occurs after the addition of the potassium nitrate carries a risk of an unintended blast.

During the Civil War, a common test for the quality of black powder was to create a small pile of grains in the palm of your hand, then light it on fire. If the pile disappeared in a flash, leaving your hand unharmed, then the powder burned quickly enough to be considered good quality. If it lingered, scorching your flesh, then the burn was too slow to be useful.

The explosion of black powder, although engineered to be as rapid as possible, is still not fast enough to be called a detonation; instead, the explosion of black powder is called a deflagration. The term "detonation" is reserved for explosive materials that have achieved an important accomplishment in the world of fire: The flaming front of the chemical reaction burns through them faster than the speed of sound. A deflagration is slower than the speed of sound, a plodding, deliberate movement of the burn as it jumps from granule to granule. Both are proper explosions, both can be lethal, but the physics in each case is different. Unlike a detonation, the blast pressure produced by a deflagration also varies based on the type and strength of the casing that contains the explosive material.

In a black powder explosion, first something causes an ignition, whether it is a mercury fulminate cap like in the *Hunley*'s torpedo, an arc of static electricity, a sharp impact, or one of a hundred possible alternatives. Regardless of what it is, *something* transfers sufficient heat to the first granule at the ignition site for it to catch fire. This tiny black ball then spews heated gas and particles outward as it burns, and the gas and particles smash into the neighboring granules. The neighbors catch, their polished spherical surfaces burning first before the reaction moves internally, and they too spit out gases and particles and more heat to even more neighbors. The burn front moves forward in this way, consuming sphere after sphere as it rages outward from the initial point of ignition. The gas pressure builds and the heat grows with each grain consumed.

Eventually, as the internal pressure grows, the casing containing the powder reaches its failure point. If the powder is spread out on the ground it simply burns, with little damage and no explosion. Because there are no walls to confine the gases, they release into the air, and the reaction occurs relatively uneventfully. If the powder is lightly confined by a weak container, the walls rupture easily at a low pressure, and the gases of the explosion are therefore released at that low pressure. Hollywood takes advantage of this feature by filming explosions made by black powder that is confined by weak paper tubes. The tubes rupture easily and therefore release lower, less-dangerous levels of pressure than an explosive like C4 would, but still create visually impressive smoky blasts.

If the powder is strongly confined instead, for example in a sturdy casing of steel or copper like the torpedo on the little submarine's spar, the gases build until they reach pressures strong enough to destroy the thick casing material. As the powder burns the pressures rise, growing until the casing, unable to control the fury, begins to melt and shred from the inside. The pressure is released as a pop, a sudden, massive, cathartic bursting, an overinflated balloon finally yielding but on an awesome and fatal scale. The casing becomes shrapnel flying outward, and the gases and by-products of the burn become the characteristic plume of smoke and destruction that is the signature image of an explosion.

Common, everyday pressure cookers are designed to cook food quickly by strongly containing unusually high levels of pressure. For this reason, pressure cookers filled with deflagrating explosives have become a popular bomb design with terrorist groups such as al-Qaeda. This bomb design was used in the Boston Marathon bombing on April 15, 2013.

———

By the time we had finished testing at the firing range, I was on a full-tilt mission scavenging for historical blast-test data using black powder, and I had dragged Nick into the quicksand with me. He had not been chased off by the visit to the *Hunley* museum in Charleston and the time with my parents, and he now sat in a desk chair across from me. We were both scooted up to opposite sides of a long table in the austere National Archives reading room in Washington, DC, and archivists clad in light-blue collared jackets roamed silently among the fervent researchers. The high ceilings sent every noise pinging back and forth across the room in a million echoes between the towering shelves of books, so the other hopeful patrons and I were all doing our best to search quietly through the yellowed pages of the priceless historical documents we held on our desks. I was leafing slowly, delicately, through fragile handwritten papers with their detailed descriptions of Civil War gunfire tests. I glanced up at Nick, and he quickly redirected his gaze to pretend that he hadn't been staring at the top of my head, psychically trying to persuade me to declare we were finished for the day.

Nick was a firefighter and had multiday breaks as a normal part of his work schedule. He had donated one of these breaks to travel to DC with me and add his eyes to my search. The National Archives contain a bottomless supply of history that is limited only by the number of hours of life a researcher can dedicate to staring at old-fashioned handwriting. We had been rooted to these seats for days, trying to find information on Confederate black powder and, while we had found many other invaluable *Hunley*-related historical nuggets, as far as useful data about black powder testing, we had mostly come up empty.

The performance of black powder can be erratic and inconsistent even with tightly controlled modern manufacturing methods. Its behavior often varies substantially between seemingly identical lots whose only difference was that they were manufactured on separate days. I wanted at minimum to get an idea of the manufacturing processes that would have been used to fill the *Hunley*'s torpedo so that I could estimate how much the performance of the Confederate powder might differ from that of modern powder. I didn't have any extra years or limbs to sacrifice to copying their process and making my own replica powder, so instead I had decided to turn to the archives for data.

The faint siren of a distant fire truck disrupted the silence of the reading room, and its cry grew to a wail as it passed beneath the windows of the National Archives Building. Nick's spine stiffened in response to the call of his profession. He jumped from his chair and bolted to the window to smash his hands and face against the glass like a deranged car-window Garfield toy, his whole demeanor screaming that he wanted to be part of the emergency instead of reading more documents. My bellows of exhaustion-exaggerated laughter rang out through the long room, and tears streamed down my face from the much-needed release. After finally recovering my breath I was forced to admit to myself that we were both at our limit of cognitive usefulness, that the Confederacy's black powder secrets had been preserved elsewhere, and that it was time to go home.

I was hopeful I had arrived "elsewhere" as I pulled in to the Hagley Museum. The drive from North Carolina to Delaware had been long, and the sun had already gone down on the closed museum property. Mine was the only car in the small parking lot at the remote back entrance, and a thick downpour gushed over my windshield. Crouching under my little red umbrella, I ran toward the hewn stone edifice of the darkened building I guessed was the former blacksmith shop, where I was supposed to stay for the week. After punching the key code on the locked door of the unoccupied shop, I was relieved when it creaked open to allow me in out of the deluge.

The Hagley Museum is not a normal museum. It is a former black powder mill, built by French immigrant Éleuthère Irénée du Pont in 1802. The famously wealthy du Pont name is now firmly associated with a diverse portfolio of chemistry and innovation, but E. I. du Pont first established the base of the family fortune by grinding black powder at this mill. As all the other American powder manufacturers shut down, one factory at a time, each sent their black powder documents for preservation to the du Pont–funded library and archives at Hagley. The working steel rollers of the museum's mills still turn inside their massive stone hutches, powered by the endlessly churning waters of the Brandywine River, but now they grind away at nothing and serve only to delight visitors.

"They have everything ever written about black powder," the woman in charge of research at GOEX had told me when I had called her begging for data. "Everything." And after a $400 travel grant provided by the good folks at Hagley, I had finally arrived to bury myself in their historical treasure.

The archives at Hagley are stashed in a building called the Soda House. Tucked away on the back of the mill property, the gorgeous stone Soda House and its arched high ceilings used to guard staggering white mountains of sodium nitrate. Also called nitrate of soda, hence the building's name, sodium nitrate is an oxidizer that replaces potassium nitrate in the specialized black powder destined to blast open mines. These days the statuesque building serves as a wedding venue, and the high arches are home to black powder documents instead of ingredients. They contain shelf upon shelf filled with the same gray filing boxes found in every archive in the world, all tended by an ingenious man named Lucas Clawson.

Lucas knows the archives of Hagley; he knows them as if he had been born in the aisles between the stacks. I sat at one of the long tables in the massive, vaulted, white-walled reading room with my camera, tabletop tripod, and document stand ready for action. I was instinctively quiet even though I was the only one there. Lucas would silently appear carrying filing box after filing box, placing them on the table for me to photograph before he once again disappeared without a word back out the door to the stacks. Between his meticulously groomed handlebar mustache and his deliberately antique fashion style, I felt as if I were being handed the secrets of the *Hunley*'s torpedo by my own personal Civil War ghost librarian.

It was through Lucas Clawson that I first met George Washington Rains, military chemist and Confederate black powder demigod.

George Washington Rains was a man of intensity. Given the unlimited options provided by a long weekend, he once declared that the best possible use of the time was for his friends to join him on a

90-plus-mile hike from Fort Monroe, Virginia, to Richmond. He then insistently set for them a furious and unyielding pace of 30 miles a day at 17 minutes per mile. The determined young chemistry professor, carrying a sack full of food and wearing his military cap with a pair of torn, ill-fitting trousers, mustered the group at four o'clock in the morning and never once paused in his relentless tempo. After three long days, drenched to the bone from a torrential downpour, Rains led the march into town, sodden, victoriously on schedule, and in search of more whiskey to refill yet again the flasks the men had already emptied many times on the road in toasts to fallen soldiers.

Born in 1817 in New Bern, North Carolina, Rains came from a family of genetic intensity. After excelling his way through school, he graduated and left to join his older brother Gabriel in "Indian Territory," described as "a primitive wilderness inhabited only by savages." Successful brother Gabriel received promotion after promotion in the US Army, one of which was a reward for the invention of one of warfare's most notorious innovations: the land mine. He would construct sensitive black powder charges and hide them, leaving them for a Native American warrior to step in the wrong spot and trigger the explosion.

Whatever George Rains saw during his time shadowing Gabriel clearly convinced him of two things: First, he needed to join the army, and second, his job also needed to involve explosions. After the year with his older brother, the younger Rains returned to enroll in West Point with the goal of studying chemistry.

George Rains's career with the US Army then became a relentless search for ever-greater excitement. He was originally appointed to the Engineer Corps, but a politely phrased obituary would later state that "the quiet and monotony of the Engineer Corps became irksome to him," and he promptly requested a demotion to allow him to access the fireworks that he assumed would come with a job discharging heavy artillery. His request was granted, and he was knocked down the pay scale. At first, the 4th Artillery seemed to have everything he had wanted, but again it was soon revealed to provide insufficient adrenaline. Rains became known for writing letters and pamphlets arguing that even in peace the artillerists should be given more shells to use for far more frequent practice. By 1844, a year of relative peace for America, the bored and disenchanted twenty-seven-year-old Rains was willing to accept a placid appointment back at West Point as a professor of chemistry, geology, and mineralogy. However, at the outbreak of the Mexican War in 1846, he immediately clamored to be sent into combat.

There was only one person to whom George Washington Rains wanted to write to express his excitement over his love of battle: his older brother, Gabriel. In one particular letter full of lengthy and delighted exclamations about battles and troop movements, the only hint that the two men shared anything besides warfare is shoved in as a final sentence, jammed awkwardly beneath the printed lines on the stationery as a token and seemingly obligatory admission that something exists besides battle: "Give my love to Mary & Stella & Lauren, Affectionately, Your Brother, George Rains."

With the unexpected outbreak of war in 1861, both militaries found themselves short on powder. The Confederacy had stockpiled at most a few months' supply, and the secessionist states did not contain a single modern industrial mill capable of supplying the military with more. Almost 1.2 million kegs of black powder were made in America in the year 1860, but less than 0.9 percent of those were manufactured in what would become the Confederate States. Of the 747 total American employees trained in the art of black powder manufacture, 13 lived in the South. By the time of the war, not one former powder-making employee was available. But despite the "appalling" situation, Confederate president Jefferson Davis knew immediately where to turn: George and Gabriel Rains.

By the time of the request, the North Carolinian Rains brothers had already left the US Army to voice allegiance to their home state as true "Sons of the South." They had the chemical, strategic, and creative acumen to supply the entire Confederate nation with black powder and munitions. And they did it so abundantly that by the war's end they would earn a menacing nickname: "the Bomb Brothers."

George Washington Rains had never made black powder before, and he had never even seen it being made. But the relentlessly high-octane man was armed with a pamphlet, a degree in chemistry, and a "carte blanche" from Jefferson Davis to do absolutely whatever he needed to do to supply the Confederacy. Bolting to begin his mission even before he received his official commission in the Confederate military, Rains spent the next several months endlessly traveling the Southern states, sleeping in railway cars to save time while on his quest. He needed to find the perfect site to build a black powder mill, and then he needed to gather the personnel and equipment required to do so.

His treasured pamphlet, the only resource he had for knowledge on how to build the mill, was an old publication by the Waltham Abbey Gunpowder Works in England. It described in forty-two short pages—with zero photographs, drawings, or diagrams—how black powder was made. Eventually Rains tracked down a former employee of Waltham Abbey named Frederick Wright, and the two claimed a strategic, militarily defensible spot near the railway lines and waterpower of a canal running through Augusta, Georgia. Together, they began to build. Within seven months they had erected a factory capable of supplying the entire Confederacy with all the powder it could ever need.

Rains designed his factory to explode, using a plan very similar to the mill buildings where I clambered over shattered stones at Hagley. The task of grinding the powder was subdivided between multiple separate buildings in an attempt to minimize the batch size, and therefore reduce the size of each accidental explosion. Each mill building with its massive 5-ton roller wheels had three sturdy walls, each at least 4 feet thick. The fourth wall and the ceiling were deliberately made of flimsy material, "so that but slight resistance would be offered, upwards and outwards, to the explosive force." The hope was that, when the mills did inevitably explode, the flimsy fourth wall and ceiling would allow the force of the blast to be directed outward and away from the rest of the complex.

The mills at Hagley saw 288 explosions during their 119 years of production. Rains proudly boasted that his mills only ever saw 3. One of these incidents was thought to have occurred because a careless worker dropped a match on a floor dusted with scattered black powder, but the cause cannot be stated conclusively because no witnesses survived. The chain reaction ignited an estimated 3 tons of powder, which "vibrated the air for a mile around." Eight were killed inside the mill building, with only small pieces of their bodies found, but a sentinel outside fell where he stood, externally intact. Rains said that "the sentinel was killed by the shock, but his body was not otherwise disturbed."

After long months of deciphering Rains's tightly curled handwriting with its looped *h* tops, I was finally able to conclude that the black powder used by the Confederacy would more than likely not have suffered in its performance because of Rains's need to create the powder works from scratch. Rains had optimized the milling process, utilizing his full engineering and chemistry backgrounds to employ the same ideal procedures that have still not been further improved by today's black powder manufacturers.

The chemical components of the powder, however, can also have an effect on performance, in addition to the influence of the manufacturing procedures. To evaluate the performance of the powder, I would also need to assess the quality of the ingredients Rains had used. But as I learned, he had optimized his ingredients too.

The charcoal made by Rains was manufactured from cottonwood and willow trees, using the well-established procedures prescribed by

Waltham Abbey. All published texts on black powder manufacture speak highly of willow charcoal, and experimental data confirm that this charcoal type optimizes performance and burn. Rains said confidently that his own experiments showed that cottonwood worked just as well as willow, and the modern data support his statements. Again, in his selection of charcoal and in his means of making it, Rains had maximized the performance of his powder.

Finding supplies of sulfur was a nonissue, as it could be obtained easily and in a pure form through natural sources. However, potassium nitrate was a constant concern. The incredibly valuable saltpeter formed three-quarters of the final product and was therefore in high demand by the militaries on both sides. Even with an efficient new mill, lack of saltpeter would mean lack of powder, and lack of powder meant losing the war.

Rains's first move was to rally the support of the populace. Potassium nitrate, also the critical ingredient in fertilizer, is a normal byproduct of decomposition. It oozes into the soil as organic materials such as leaves and fecal matter decay, but it can be washed back out by rain. However, the soil in covered places like caves, stables, and cellars are not only subjected to a constant onslaught of animal feces released by creatures taking shelter, but they are also protected from the cleansing effects of raindrops. The soil inside these shelters can be mined and processed to yield pure, snow-white potassium nitrate, suitable for both vegetable gardens and bombs.

Rains, the former professor of chemistry-combo-geology, issued detailed pamphlets on how to process this sheltered soil, valiantly declaring to the citizens of the South that "the individual who makes a pound of saltpeter each day contributes in fact more to the ultimate success of his country than if he shouldered his musket and marched with all his sons to the tented field." Hundreds grabbed shovels and marched into local caves, digging up dirt to supply their military with the much-needed oxidizer.

In addition to the saltpeter supplied by the people, Rains also heavily utilized blockade-runners bringing potassium nitrate from Europe. As the Union Army closed in, taking control of one cave-containing territory after another, the blockade-runners who managed to sneak past vessels like the USS *Housatonic* became an increasingly critical source of the precious saltpeter.

Even though Rains managed to create an admirable supply using digging and blockade-runners, the long-term plan for potassium nitrate relied on neither the people nor the passage of ships. Instead, the agriculturally minded South would farm its own. George Rains established potassium-nitrate farms, which were extensive systems of 2-foot-deep trenches. The nitrate farmers filled the trenches with decaying matter such as leaves, feces, and the rotting carcasses of stray dogs. They also periodically wet them down with more organic liquids . . . most likely urine. Eventually, the decay of the biological materials would yield an embarrassment of soil so profoundly rich in potassium nitrate that it could have supplied the Confederacy with all of the saltpeter it would ever need. However, the trenches would have taken at least eighteen months to fully "ripen," and the war ended before their fruits were truly ready.

Rains left abundant records of his refinement process, which clearly took advantage of his extensive chemical knowledge to create the purest, most powerful potassium nitrate possible. His powder benefited from advanced manufacturing techniques, the optimum choice of wood for charcoal, and exhaustive attention to detail in the refinement of each ingredient. The performance should have been unparalleled in its time, and equal to any modern powder I might use in my testing.

———

A farmer somewhere in the South dug up several cubic feet of soil from inside a cave on his land. He processed it according to the pamphlet he had read, boiling and mixing it until a fine white powder condensed out. He packaged up the final product, selling it to the military for 35 cents per pound and shipping it off to Augusta, Georgia. It was added to a pile of identical white powder freshly brought by blockade-runners, who had risked their lives dodging the artillery of Union ships to deliver their packages. The saltpeter was ground and refined again, reaching a near-perfect level of chemical purity.

Somewhere else in the Confederate States, a cottonwood tree was chopped down and hacked into nuggets. The nuggets were brought to Augusta, where they were heated to the ideal temperature before being deprived of oxygen and cooled into condensed pods of carbon. The pods of carbon were ground into a messy black dust, which was then mixed with yellow sulfur.

The black mixture was gently stirred together with the white saltpeter, then poured into the metal bin of the massive mill contraption inside one of a long series of identical stone buildings. The mill operator ran to take shelter outside the building before starting the rollers, exhaling a sigh of relief as the wheels uneventfully began to churn and grind the mixture into a uniform, even blend. The black-colored powder, now an explosive, was dried, caked, granulated, and polished until it formed beautiful, even, nearly identical tiny spheres.

George Washington Rains ordered the spheres shipped to Charleston, South Carolina. The recent battle of the ironclads off those shores had consumed almost 22,000 pounds of powder, depleting the stores of the entire city and ensuring that the massive machines built by Rains would need to provide General Beauregard and his warfighters with an entirely fresh supply.

George's brother, Gabriel, waiting for the shipment in Charleston, used much of the powder to assemble torpedoes. Gabriel had been sent to Charleston to riddle its harbor and waterways with hidden deadly torpedoes, underwater versions of his land-mine invention, and to create a lethal maze to deter the Union ships from encroaching any closer. Gabriel used his brother's powder to fill even more of these torpedoes, sinking them in the waters of Charleston until they were "as abundant as blueberries."

A massive quantity of the powder was reserved for a special torpedo. This torpedo was built with thick, robust metal walls to maximize its confinement, and therefore its destructive power. The deadly black sand was poured into the copper casing, and the cap with its fuse was sealed tightly in place. Then, the torpedo was bolted onto the spar on the bow of a submarine.

CHAPTER 5

ANATOMY OF AN EXPLOSION

> Every day we walked into the city and dug into basements and shelters to get the corpses out, as a sanitary measure. When we went into them, a typical shelter, an ordinary basement usually, looked like a streetcar full of people who'd simultaneously had heart failure. Just people sitting there in their chairs, all dead.
>
> —Kurt Vonnegut, on removing corpses from bomb shelters in Dresden during World War II

Nine people died during the most massive explosion of George Washington Rains's powder works. Eight of them, seven men and one boy, were inside the building containing the powder when it blew. According to Rains, the tragic explosion likely occurred because one of the men, after lighting a cigarette, callously flicked his extinguished but still-hot match onto the powder-dusted ground. Smoking in the literal powder keg was forbidden, but the usual supervisor was off work that day. The stray granules littering the floor ignited, one at a time, passing the flame like water flowing over the ground, and the deflagration radiated outward to reach the large volumes of powder in storage. The smoke plume from the resulting explosion could be seen for miles. The eight people inside the building were, not surprisingly, "reduced mainly to small fragments and dispersed."

However, Rains's brief description of the sentinel, the lone man standing guard outside the building, presents the key to understanding blast trauma: The sentinel was found dead but intact. "His body was not otherwise disturbed," according to Rains; he had not been hit by shrapnel, and more important he seems to have been found dropped to the ground where he had stood.

Author Kurt Vonnegut more famously described the same phenomenon. He spoke in an interview about his time in Germany during World War II, right after the firebombings that decimated Dresden. His job had been to excavate the bomb shelters and basements to remove the rotting corpses before the entire city started to stink of human putrefaction. The people he found had usually died without moving, without any signs of struggle, and were often still seated peacefully in their chairs. They were not outwardly wounded; they were not blown wildly across the room.

There are multiple ways for victims to die in a firebombing, and Vonnegut's cases cannot be retroactively declared to have all occurred solely because of one single cause. However, they share the same key descriptors as the sentinel in Rains's factory blast: undisturbed, no external injuries, simply dead where he stood. To a blast researcher, this scenario sets off all the mental alarms. It starts our heads screaming that we should at least suspect what is called by our field a "primary blast injury."

Medically speaking, the injuries from an explosion are neatly categorized into one of four tidy bins. A blast victim can receive only one type, or they can receive a sloppily assorted grab bag of trauma containing any delightfully painful mixture of the four. Helpfully, the injury types are numbered for easy reference: primary, secondary, tertiary, and quaternary.

Quaternary trauma is a sort of "other" category. It covers the grotesque and myriad injuries that *can* occur as the result of a blast, but do not necessarily occur consistently or predictably from every type of blast. The umbrella of quaternary trauma covers adventures like burns, radiation sickness, and infectious biological goodies that may have been intentionally dispersed by the explosion.

Tertiary trauma is the injury type that most people expect. It is the classic scene from the action movie: Our sweaty, grease-covered hero flips on the wrong light switch and a massive red-and-yellow fireball propels him wildly flailing across the theater screen. When he stands up, he grimaces. He is unswayed in his determination to save the helpless yet busty heartthrob with the long flowing hair, but first he needs to stretch his lower back so the audience can appreciate how much pain he is shaking off in order to continue this mission. His lower-back pain is a tertiary injury: an injury incurred from "whole body translation," which is engineer-speak to describe someone getting physically thrown by the blast.

Secondary injuries are unfortunately an overwhelmingly common injury type, especially with the rise to prominence of improvised explosive devices (IEDs) in the combat zones in Iraq and Afghanistan. This injury type is the result of objects getting thrown and hitting a person because of the blast. The objects are often shrapnel from the charge casing, or sometimes nails and ball bearings included solely for the purpose of inflicting more harm. Secondary injuries frequently take the forms of trauma to the limbs, cuts deep enough to reach the skeleton, and amputations.

These three injury types—secondary, tertiary, and quaternary—are logical, meaning that they make obvious sense and even people with zero blast experience can predict that they are expected possibilities. In contrast, primary blast injuries—the kind likely incurred by Rains's sentinel, and possibly incurred by the victims in the Dresden bomb shelters—are an impressive, strange, and horrifying fluke produced by the bizarre physics of explosions mixed together with human frailty. Primary injuries result from the pressures produced by an explosion, usually—but not always—because of a shock wave.

To understand how a shock wave maims, first it is crucial to understand how a shock wave is born. Normally, sound moves like billiard balls on a massive, smooth felt table. First, a noisy event occurs, like an impact or a vocal cord vibrating into movement. A gas molecule in close proximity to the action gets pushed away: This is the cue hitting the cue ball. The cue ball travels outward until it hits the 4-ball, another gas molecule. *Clunk.* They impact, and the cue ball transfers some of its energy to the 4. Both balls now move, slightly slower and in an outward direction, until they impact other balls, hitting their next closest neighbors. The overall wave front of the motion moves forward, but each individual ball travels only slightly across the table. The motion gets passed outward, expanding and slowing just a bit with each collision as the leading edge of movement travels across the table.

Sound travels outward, each molecule of material transferring energy to the next, growing in reach but decaying in strength as it moves. Eventually it hits an ear and gets heard, or a wall and echoes back toward the source. It moves the same way in water as it does in gas, except faster, because the molecules start out closer together in the denser liquid.

A shock wave occurs when the pool cue is placed in the hands of the most furious, most irate patron in the hall. He is a high explosive. Apoplectic and red-faced, the explosive burns quickly. In fact, the burn front moves through the entirety of the explosive much faster than normal sound. Therefore, the entire reaction happens too fast for the gaseous products created by the burn to expand outward in a normal way. The material is burned and gone before the balls can travel outward on their own, too quickly for them to *thwack* their neighbors at their natural speed. The whole charge has reacted, is consumed, becomes a tiny, compressed, superheated ball of hyperpressurized gas before the 4-ball ever gets the message. The resulting gases expand all at once, together, suddenly, violently, and the pool cue is shoved, hurtled, *rammed* down the length of the table, picking up ball after ball and adding them to the front of the wall of molecules moving forward, picking them up faster than they can move on their own.

This is how a shock wave develops. The molecules accumulated at the wave front are densely packed, shoved together tightly by the gas urgently expanding behind them. They are so densely packed that each molecule can reach its neighbor more quickly than it could in a normal situation, and so this unique wave moves faster than the speed of normal sound.

The molecules downstream get hit without warning. In its purest form, the shock wave goes straight from zero to its maximum pressure in an instant; on a graph it is a vertical line followed by a sloping decay back down. If it were a car it would go from 0 to 60 in *exactly* zero seconds.

When they reach high enough pressures, these waves can disintegrate everything in their paths. The substantive fabric of objects gets jerked into motion fast, too fast, by the instantaneous rise of the shock, and they break apart into chaos like a fragile porcelain teacup getting hit by a rapidly moving concrete floor.

Most of the human body handles mild to moderate levels of shock surprisingly well. Severe pressures will cause tissue disruption, which is a polite phrase that describes a horrifying concept. However, the lower-pressure shock waves can travel through most of our anatomy without harm. These waves can move straight through water without much chaos and disruption, and human bodies are, after all, mostly water. It's the gas pockets inside certain organs that cause the real drama.

In the chest wall, which is mostly water, sound moves at roughly 1,540 meters per second. In a gas pocket, which is basically air, it moves at roughly 343 meters per second. Therefore, waves moving through the body that hit a gas pocket are forced to slow down at the interface by about 80 percent. And as they are forced to slow, that energy must get transferred somewhere.

To make a bad situation even worse, the human lungs are basically two lumps of bubbly fluid. The bubbles are the alveoli containing the gas that gets moved in and out by the lungs during breathing, and the blood vessels and tissues surrounding the alveoli are curvy lines of fast water surrounding a network of pockets of slow air. Together, the structures make a maze for the pressure waves. As the pressure waves navigate the circuitous pathways of the labyrinth, moving quickly through water lines but changing direction and bouncing off walls of air, they are forced to slow down even more. Way down, much slower than they would if they could travel straight through a simple pocket of normal, uncomplicated air. They slow down to a measly 30 meters per second. The phenomenon of this extreme slowdown in the water-air maze is called "the hot chocolate effect" after the delightful frothy bubbles of the delicious beverage.

If the shock wave is like a runaway semi-truck traveling through the watery tissue of the chest wall, racing headlong at over 1,540 meters per second down a mountain, then the lungs are the gravel pit of a runaway truck ramp. The truck is slowed to 30 meters per second, less than 2 percent of its prior speed—it has no choice—but its energy must go somewhere. The gravel flies outward, everywhere, a rampant hailstorm of dispersed energy and momentum. So too respond the delicate tissues that form the walls of the lungs. They rupture and shred, and blood sprays into the alveoli, filling the precious gas pockets needed for breathing. This process is called spalling.

Gas pockets in the intestines can cause a similar problem, leading to bruising and tearing of the intestinal tract, but the intestines have a higher threshold for injury and are less commonly damaged than the lungs. The same is true of some of the smaller bones in the skull, particularly the ones that form the fragile archways around the sinus cavities. These bones will on occasion show spider webs of fracture from primary blast, but they are sufficiently difficult to injure that these patterns are typically only seen in autopsy reports.

The delicate tissues of the brain can also experience forces from the blast, which can cause traumatic brain injuries without ever disrupting a perfectly undamaged skull. These injuries occur via a different and far more complex mechanism that is still the subject of active research. Critically, the brain remains intact after a primary blast injury, and the only potential sign of trauma is a faint inkblot of blood that may be spread across its surface.

Fatalities from primary blast occur at lower pressures than the pressure levels required to translate a human body. To rephrase that in plain English: A person will die, choked with blood, from a shock wave that was far too weak to move them.

During World War II, the bombings of German cities led to civilians dying in exactly this way. It was common for blast victims to be found dead, looking externally peaceful, with no other signs of trauma except the occasional trace of bloody foam around their noses and mouths. These victims often had no damage to their muscles or bones.

A shock wave will have a 100 percent fatality rate if it reaches a peak overpressure level of 350 kilopascals and lasts for 7 milliseconds ($\frac{7}{1000}$ of a second) before it drops back down to zero. When a blast hits a typical adult, it will be impacting approximately 1 square meter of surface area. The 350 kilopascals of pressure multiplied by 1 square meter of area gives a resulting total force of 350,000 Newtons. This force is equal to 492 Rachels, the narcissistic unit of force I made based on my weight while standing still, and the pressure is equal to the water pressure at a depth of 25 meters below the surface of the ocean. However, it lasts for a mere fraction of a moment.

Using a quick back-of-the-envelope calculation, engineer-style, this shock wave could move a 72 kg person a maximum of 0.2 meters—less than the length of an average adult's foot. That is assuming no friction, and no resistance to motion of any kind. Therefore this wave, even though it would be universally lethal, provides barely enough impetus to knock someone over.

Recreational scuba divers plunge to depths below 25 meters every day without harm; the pressure level alone is not the problem. But in a blast the traveling shock wave rises quickly from zero to maximum pressure, and it also impacts one side of the body rather than simultaneously immersing it from all sides. The shock wave jerks the blood and tissues into motion, even though it is a small amount of motion, before they can adapt.

The sentinel falls where he stood. The citizens, huddled in their bunker, die seated in their chairs. Autopsies frequently show no skeletal damage from the primary trauma, no broken bones or fractured skulls, just blood in their lungs, and possibly in their intestines or on the surfaces of their brains. They are unmoved. They are un-translated. Our action hero, thrown across the room by the winds of an explosion, is not standing up and dashing off after a mild back injury; he is dead from blast lung, 100 percent of the time.*

———————

Each major war comes with advances in military technology, and fresh young soldiers almost always become the first victims. During the Civil War, the Rains brothers brought mayhem with their inventions of land mines and underwater torpedoes. By World War I, machine guns and high explosives were deployed to the trenches, rendering cavalry charges obsolete and introducing the first widespread patterns of blast

———————

*This section describes the physics and injuries from conventional blasts. Nuclear explosions, in contrast, are so powerful that they behave differently and can sometimes violate these general rules. For example, the blast durations from nuclear bombs are in fact so atypically long that they may theoretically translate a human being without requiring the high overpressure levels that would kill them from primary blast trauma. However, even during the forceful blast winds of Operation Plumbbob, one of the largest nuclear test series in global history, freestanding mannequins exposed to pressures just below lethal were displaced a maximum of only 11 feet. Although these mannequins may have theoretically escaped primary blast trauma, they nonetheless received whole-body patterns of severe burns despite being wrapped in heat-resistant foil, indicating that surviving these exposures was still highly unlikely.

trauma. World War II brought submarine wolf packs roaming the seas and atomic bombs, and along with them came innumerable medically novel in-water and nuclear-blast victims. In Iraq and Afghanistan, the rise in popularity of IEDs caused so many blast-induced traumatic brain injuries that these injuries became known as the "signature wound" of the conflicts.

During peace, militaries seek to prepare for the next war by developing innovative, more effective ways to kill. Then, when the war starts, soldiers are shipped home with different injury types than in the previous wars. Medical scientists and researchers, who take a long time to produce answers because of the tedious, exacting nature of scientific research, struggle to keep up with the technological advances in weaponry.

Blast casualties are uncommon in the civilian world, especially when compared to other traumatic events like car crashes, so the way the field moves forward is usually because a war starts. Soldiers come home wounded or dead. The country wants to know why, and decides it is finally willing to fund the science. To explain it, and to please oh please hopefully stop it, people like me head to the lab to once again take up our Sisyphean race against the development of new weapons. When the conflicts are over and the dead seem to rest in peace, we are the ones who can be found sifting through the wreckage, still trying to figure out what really happened.

During the violence in the 1970s in Northern Ireland, soldiers and civilians alike were routinely hit by blasts. Two British military scientists studying the casualty reports began to notice a disturbing pattern.

As British military physicians they treated only the British soldiers, so they saw one combat narrative repeat itself over and over again. A gelignite charge was placed. This soft, moldable charge carried the chemical heritage of black powder, as it used both potassium nitrate and wood pulp in its reaction. The explosive charge, originally manufactured for the innocent purpose of blasting open a commercial mine, was instead detonated in a public place. Its shock wave propagated outward into the lungs and brains of nearby human beings, along with jagged flying missiles.

The physicians, Graham Cooper and Susana Mellor, began to track the patterns of the cases. By 1984, after fourteen years of slowly accumulating macabre forensic reports, they had reached a surprising conclusion: Those wearing the rubber foam–based body armor of the British military may have been less likely to die from the secondary trauma of shrapnel and blast debris, but they unexpectedly seemed *more* likely to die from the primary trauma of blast lung. One hundred and forty of the soldiers in their case reports died without a single sign of any injury beside blood in their lungs.

The trend seemed counterintuitive because the life-saving vests provided an additional barrier between the soldiers and the shock waves, a line of extra material that should have guarded the lungs from the blast. Logically, it seemed that any additional barrier around the soldiers should *reduce* the risk of blast lung. It took another several years, but eventually Cooper was able to set up an experiment to explain the anomaly.

The burst of an overinflated Mylar party balloon releases a small but legitimate shock wave. The air inside the balloon is pressurized slightly compared to the outside, squeezed together by the balloon's strong walls, and when the gas is released suddenly it travels outward in the same manner as the gases created by high explosives. The mini shock wave gets heard as a *pop*.

Volcanic eruptions also suddenly release pressurized gas, and thereby create shock waves. The explosive eruption of the volcano Krakatoa in 1883 produced a shock so powerful that it was heard almost 3,000 miles away and circumnavigated the globe seven times.

High explosives are not the only way to make a shock wave. They work by creating a ball of high-pressure gas, but their rapidly burning chemical fury is not the only way to create a ball of high-pressure gas.

Scientists take advantage of this convenient fact by using devices called shock tubes. These strong metal tubes have one closed, sealed end that gets pressurized, called the driver. The driver is separated from the rest of the tube by a replaceable plastic membrane. This membrane, usually Mylar, just like a fancy party balloon, pops when the driver is sufficiently pressurized. The pressure releases and propagates down the rest of the length of the tube, forming into a beautiful, smooth, and predictable shock wave without most of the mess and danger of high explosives.

Cooper mounted his hefty shock tube to the ceiling. He let the long metal tube hang from the rafters, aiming its lethal maw downward into a gigantic tub of water. He secured one disk of material on the surface of the water at a time, either foam rubber, Kevlar, or thin sheets of copper, and he repeatedly triggered the shock tube. With each building-shaking *pop* he measured the pressure waveform that propagated into the water.

The water represented the chest wall, and Cooper's elegant experiment showed that the foam rubber used in the British body armor of the time was actually amplifying the shock waves being transmitted into the bodies of the soldiers. When he blasted the water through a disk of foam rubber, the peak pressure levels in the water were about 25 percent higher than when he blasted the water alone with no rubber on top. The material of the body armor increased the overall amount of energy transmitted into the simulated "chest wall" by 230 percent. Normally a large portion of the shock wave would reflect directly off a soldier's chest, but a fluke of the bubble-filled rubber softened that reflection and allowed more to carry forward into their bodies instead. Cooper's experiment proved that the suspicious pattern of trauma was real, that the soldiers wearing body armor were at higher risk of primary blast injuries. He and Mellor had been right.

Cooper not only proved that the effects of blast could propagate straight through solid materials, but he showed that the wrong choice of material, the wrong configuration between a soldier and his environment, could in fact amplify the fatal potential of an explosion.

Modern-day body armor is designed with this effect in mind, and the Kevlar used in most bulletproof vests also massively reduces the amount of blast pressure that can get transmitted into the lungs of the wearer. It is actually because of this protection that traumatic brain injuries have become so common in Iraq and Afghanistan; the Kevlar protects the lungs of the wearer, so they survive a blast that should have killed them from primary lung trauma. However, their brains are still vulnerable. In a cosmic twist of fate, Kevlar, now being used to protect people from explosions, was invented by chemist Stephanie Kwolek while she was working at DuPont, a company founded by explosions.

———

A shock wave, by definition, skyrockets in an instant from zero pressure to its maximum pressure. The rate of increase is literally infinity. Once you can measure the rate of increase because it occurs over some known length of time, then the wave is no longer technically a shock. Instead, it is simply a pressure wave.

Pressure waves are less likely to cause damage because they allow their targets that little grace period of a few extra milliseconds' time to adapt to the coming impact. The material might be able to flex and respond without failing, like Silly Putty, which can stretch when pulled slowly instead of tearing when jerked rapidly. Structures are more likely to survive, but human beings, unable to adapt to these rapid time scales, can still be injured and killed by sharp-rising pressure waves.

When the US Navy performs underwater explosives testing against ships using high explosives, nobody is allowed to loiter on the deck of the ship being tested; it floats alone and unoccupied for safety reasons. The shock has too much potential to tear and destroy the vessel, and the equipment inside. It is too risky. However, when the testing is performed with air guns, which create fast-rising pressure waves that aren't quite shocks, curious engineers and scientists are sometimes allowed to stand on the deck to feel the *ping* of the high-pressure wave bouncing off the hull.

The data suggest that 2 milliseconds is the cutoff when predicting risk to humans. In other words, any pressure wave that reaches its maximum in less than 2 milliseconds can be considered to maim and kill like a shock wave. Scientists established this limit using an influx of blast-research cash that came with the escalating tensions of the Cold War.

Our lungs are fragile. We bleed easily. A "not quite a shock" wave is still enough to destroy us.

———————

At the tail end of the Gulf War, a military blast researcher triggered a controlled detonation in his laboratory. The charge he detonated was a small lump of C4. It sat on the floor in the center of an enclosed room, a room designed to mimic the inside of a US Army tank. Armor-penetrating missiles had been causing blast-like trauma to American soldiers inside tanks during the Gulf War, and the goal of this experiment was to understand how. Coincidentally, the room was also roughly the size of the inside of the *Hunley*, albeit a different shape.

The researchers wanted to see how the shock waves behaved when they were trapped. They already knew that the pressures would bounce wildly off the walls, ceiling, and floor, like a sound echoing in an empty room, and that each time the echoes intersected with one another they would combine and amplify. They knew that, like a whisper reverberating loudly through an empty cave, the blast waves, when trapped, would rebel against the walls and build on their own reflections to grow in magnitude. But what they needed to know was this: After all that echoing, would they still kill?

Sheep were positioned at various locations around the room, suspended from webbed harnesses. They were alive but anesthetized by veterinarians into a pain-free unconsciousness. After the detonation of the charge, a military blast researcher named Johnson and his colleagues examined the externally uninjured sheep for signs of lung trauma. They discovered that the patterns of trauma were much worse than what would have occurred if the same charge had been detonated in an open field, because the reflections had massively increased the lethal potential of the blast.

The shapes of the waveforms that were measured inside the room were crucial: The waveforms were no longer polite and tidy shock waves with an infinite rise followed by a smooth, sloping decay. Instead they were jagged monstrosities, with one or two large peaks somewhere inside the long time span before the pressures finally dissipated. The rise times of the big peaks were under the 2-millisecond cutoff. The unfortunate injuries of the unconscious sheep showed that the jagged pressure waveforms were still inarguably lethal, that they were still essentially comparable to shock waves for the purposes of causing and predicting human injuries.

Only a few years before the 1995 discovery of the *Hunley*, Johnson and his colleagues reached a determination that would prove crucial to understanding the fate of her crew. They determined that the risk of blast injury was dependent not just on the first wave passing into an enclosed space, but on the maximum pressure level that was achieved at any time while the blast wave ping-ponged around within the echoing volume.

These conclusions were again consistent with the case reports from World War II. In one particular incident, a shell detonated just outside a train station bunker. Many people took shelter in the tunnel that led down to the station, hoping its walls would shield them from the effects of the bombs. These unfortunates were found dead exactly where they had last been in their final moments, still standing up and clutching one another for comfort. They had been protected by the tunnel walls from any shrapnel, from any secondary injuries to their limbs or bones, but nonetheless the shock wave had reverberated down the narrow passageway. For many of them, the only trace of injury was a slight dust-covered froth at the mouth.

Johnson's conclusions would again be reaffirmed in the most unfortunate possible way only a few years later, in a separate conflict, when the same pattern was revealed in the victims of terrorist bombings in Israel. Bombs set off inside buses resulted in over six times the fatality rate when compared to similar bombings that used nearly identical charges, but instead occurred outside in open, unconfined spaces. Furthermore, every single one of the bus victims died because of pulmonary failure. Even though the bus victims had experienced far less secondary wounding than the open-air victims from shrapnel and projectiles, the reflections inside the enclosed space had nevertheless sealed their fates.

———————

Iraq and Afghanistan too brought new blast scenarios. American vehicles were frequently subjected to roadside bombs. Naturally, this scenario also warranted scientific testing, led by a scientist named Howard Champion.

Seventeen kilograms of C4 is a little cube of nondescript gray putty, roughly 25 centimeters per side, and unless you understand its power it is unexciting to look at. The particular pile that was sitting on the ground for an experiment a few years before 2009 had a target: an armored vehicle. As the clock ticked down to the moment of detonation, the rugged armored military vehicle sat quietly a mere 3 meters from the pile.

Vehicles and inanimate structures do not have lungs; they cannot experience spalling of blood. They are destroyed differently than human beings. Structures are far more resistant to shock than the fragile tissues of the human body, and it takes roughly a thousand times higher pressures to "kill" them.

The pressure gauges positioned immediately outside the armored vehicle measured a long-lasting blast with a maximum pressure of a blistering 760 kilopascals, more than double the limit where every person exposed would have died of fatal lung trauma. However, unsurprisingly, the armored vehicle, in contrast to a frail human body, was fine.

Even though the vehicle itself was fine, the squiggly lines produced by the gauges *inside* the armored vehicle were stunning. These lines showed a sharp-rising pressure waveform, a waveform that was not quite a shock wave but was still fast-rising enough to kill, with a long and jagged tail. The peak pressure inside was only 48 kilopascals, giving theoretical occupants a mere 4 percent chance of serious blast lung injury. Low odds, but the squiggly line still proved that some transmission was in fact occurring.

The armor of the vehicle protected its occupants against shrapnel, and against almost all of the blast. But like Cooper's body armor, some pressure still got through, and then, like the blasts inside Johnson's enclosed room, the penetrating waves reflected around the inside of the vehicle to increase the chances of trauma.

The day after my adviser, Dale, wandered into my office to declare, "What about the *Hunley*?" he and I looked at the drawings of the massive beer keg of black powder, the photos of the spar with its cartoonishly peeled-back copper shards, and the stationary skeletons seated at their battle stations. We knew about the hallmarks of blast trauma, about the body armor of Cooper, the case reports of World War II, the small rooms blasted by Johnson, the armored-vehicle transmission data published by Champion. We suspected that—for the first time in our field—the decades of experiments by our scientific ancestors had all intersected to explain a case of fatal trauma that had occurred inside a protective metal structure.

The original plan had been to build a computational model using the US Navy's proprietary software called DYSMAS, the program I had already been using to gauge the blast exposure levels of World War II soldiers swimming in the ocean. However, the black powder was proving difficult and fickle. The scientific literature about black powder was all over the place, describing performances that varied wildly based on the powder's composition, its confinement and exact setup, and a million other variables. Unlike standardized high explosives like TNT and C4, which had well-known and polite equations to describe their behavior in every situation, the physics to describe black powder seemed to make most blast scientists simply give up in frustration.

We finally decided the computer model was a no-go. The black powder introduced too many variables. With its slow burn rate, the results produced by any computer model could change dramatically based on the construction of the theoretical charge casing. And after the powder exploded, the casing burst, and the bomb released its pressure into the water, black powder's unusually slow rise time to peak pressure might have strange and unpredictable effects on the wall of the submarine that could be difficult to model accurately.

The DYSMAS code wasn't designed to model the pressures propagating into closed, air-filled volumes like the *Hunley*. It was designed to examine the walls of a structure, see what they would be exposed to, and determine whether they would fail. Modeling the trampoline-like way they could flex and push a secondary *whoosh* of air into the inside of the submarine was something that had never been done with that model, and had never been tested to work.

To test our theory, we would need to do live experiments. Or, in the words of Dale . . .

"Build a model of the submarine, Rachel, and blast it."

———

During the Civil War, engineers conducted their own explosive experiments with black powder in order to gradually evolve the technology. For my own tests I would be able to lean upon decades of work by other researchers, but in the 1860s the largely undeveloped state of the field meant that novice blast experts in all areas were eager to develop the first reliable underwater mines, and many of them lost their lives and body parts in the process.

One ambitious such inventor was engineer Francis Kemp. He thought his experimental "water rocket" might come in handy against the Union forces prowling Lake Pontchartrain, menacing his Confederate home city of New Orleans. The recent secession had created a need for defenses to guard the port city, and like the citizens building fish boats, he too wanted to weaponize the water. The torpedo was his rudimentary experiment in blast science, his attempt to optimize an explosive technology he thought could help. The shore he had selected for the test was near Bayou St. John, the site of the tests of the submarines.

As Kemp prepared the charge, the sensitive black powder somehow accidentally received the minor jolt it needed to start the chemical reaction. Bent over to work on the device, Kemp's face and head absorbed the full force of the blast, including shrapnel from the casing. He was expected to die, with "part of his head shattered to pieces," but after a long month he mostly recovered . . . minus the loss of one eye.

———

Demure Chicago lady Mrs. E. H. Baker was hoping to observe a more successful one of these underwater blast tests. She picked up her skirts and gingerly stepped down from the carriage. She paused to wait for her friend to join her, then together the two women sauntered with their picnic basket toward the festive crowd gathered along the shore of the James River, south of Richmond, Virginia. Mrs. Baker's dear childhood friend happened to be married to a high-ranking Confederate officer named Atwater, and he had invited the ladies to join him for the day.

As they approached the jovial crowd of Confederate officers and their accompanying women, Mrs. Baker noticed a dilapidated old scow bobbing silently in the middle of the river: the target of the day's test. She waited with apprehension while an innocent-looking green float bobbed nonchalantly toward the unsuspecting target. The float paused, then gradually reversed its direction and retreated. The crowd waited in anticipation.

A massive gush of water hurtled the scow into the air. The scow burst upward while its hull exploded like fireworks. Mrs. Baker felt the ground tremble and heard the muffled rumble of the underwater blast. The crowd roared in delight as tiny airborne fragments of boat plunked slowly down into the river, and Atwater could not contain his elated surprise at the destructive power of the new weapon.

Mrs. Baker, in contrast, was doing her best to hide her sorrow. The green float was attached to a small model of a submarine that was being prepared for use in waters farther south. The personnel within the submarine had destroyed the boat by attaching a torpedo, retreating to a safe distance, and triggering the charge. The test was a display to show the officers on the shore how the full-sized vessel would strike terror into the Union sailors and help break the blockades. Baker understood the devastation such a submarine could wreak on Union men.

She gleaned as much information as she could from Atwater, wrote it down, stayed with him and her friend a few more days to be polite, and then returned to Chicago. There, she promptly delivered her notes to her boss: famed spymaster Allan Pinkerton. Visiting her childhood friend had been a ruse. Pinkerton, an ardent abolitionist and supporter of the Union cause, sent the information about the submarine directly to Union general George McClellan.

The North knew that the South was building submarines, and they soon began guarding their warships against such attacks. It seems plausible that at least some of the warnings they received were from Allan Pinkerton and his network of spies. The major problem with Mrs. Baker's story, its fatal flaw, is that there is no other evidence that Mrs. Baker existed. Dozens of modern books retell her story, but they all trace back to the single source of Allan Pinkerton's book *Spy of the Rebellion*. Baker and her husband do not appear in any US Census records for the state of Illinois. She is not in any of Allan Pinkerton's corporate records, except for references to the story in *Spy*. She does not appear in his private listings of the spies he employed during the Civil War, and she does not appear in any of the extensive personal notebooks he kept cataloging all his known spies, employees, criminal contacts, and informants. None of his known female spies used the alias Baker.

Pinkerton writes affectionately about Atwater. The text of *Spy* contains several paragraphs about how Atwater never really wanted to be part of the secession, how he despised slavery, and how he secretly hoped the North would win the war. From Pinkerton, a vocal and vehement abolitionist, the words are unexpected and exaggeratedly heavy praise that read like an attempt to exonerate a Confederate officer . . . possibly because the officer had been sending him information about submarine tests in secret.

Pinkerton was famously unwilling to release the names of his operatives and informants. At one point the US government insisted that he would only be paid once he submitted the spies' complete names, but Pinkerton still refused.

"The names of any employees (or operatives, as I usually style them) should only be known to myself," he wrote. He explained further, "Already some of my Force have suffered death at the hands of the Rebels."

Pinkerton's detailed billing documents, which list spies by the initials of their real names, show no trace of Baker. Unfortunately, the detailed billing documents that Pinkerton submitted to the US government for his Civil War espionage have only been preserved starting with the spring after the Baker story was said to have taken place. However, they show no trace of a trip to Richmond. The spy who incurred each charge is listed by their initials, and Baker's initials are not listed for any other missions.

Only two Atwaters seem to have reached the rank of captain in the Confederate Army, and only one of them would have been an officer of sufficient rank and near Richmond at the time of the test, which was the fall of 1861. His full name was James W. Atwater, and he seems to be the Captain Atwater of Pinkerton's story.

Atwater was married, but his wife died just before Pinkerton claims that Mrs. E. H. Baker traveled to visit her. Capt. James W. Atwater was also "a man of strong convictions" who "hated all manner of shams," so much so that the phrases made it into his obituary. Given that the submarines were considered "infernal," it is possible Atwater considered them a "sham" as well.

Pinkerton believed in protecting his sources above all else. Some of Pinkerton's information about the submarine is accurate. It is possible Pinkerton fabricated the entire story, using bits and pieces from the newspaper articles about the 1864 *Hunley* attack to fill in the details to publish his book in 1883, but none of these early publications contain details about the loop of wire or the number of men in the prototype vessels.

It wasn't long before the experimental boats and spar torpedoes were taken into action. After a failed early attempt, a Confederate officer, Lt. William Glassell, found himself glowering at a Union marshal with an angry smirk on his face. He had been fished out of the water and arrested. Now he sat in prison, silent, wearing head-to-toe gray to show his resilient Confederate pride, and refusing to answer any further questions.

He had been the leader of a tiny crew of four, wedged inside a long cigar-shaped boat of a class that was starting to be referred to as "Davids." The small boats, stealthy, sneaky, infernal, were designed to devastate the Goliath Union warships prowling outside the Rebel harbors.

His boat was made of wood, just under 2 meters in diameter, a rough cylinder with pointy tapered ends. This boat, also named *David*, couldn't submerge—a fraction of the wooden hull always stuck up above the waterline, the rest below, with a massive smokestack jutting upward to provide air to fuel the hungry engines inside.

Glassell and his crew had maneuvered their David close to the USS *New Ironsides* that night late in 1863, close enough to stab it with the 70-pound black powder torpedo on their spar. The big ship somehow survived, even though it would need to limp back to safe harbor for repairs. The *David*, however, was not so lucky; the frothy plume of seawater from her own blast had swamped her smokestack, partially flooded her interior, and extinguished the fires of the engines needed to propel the little boat home. She was stuck adrift, a sitting duck waiting to be hit by the small-arms fire of the crew of the *New Ironsides*.

Glassell and two of his crew had abandoned ship, preferring to take their chances in the open water rather than risk drowning in the partially flooded, narrow wooden tube. The fourth man, unable to swim, stayed put. Glassell and one other crewman were plucked out of the water by the sailors of the *New Ironsides*, put into shackles, and taken north for interrogation. The other two *David* crew escaped, got the engines restarted, and made it safely back to shore.

Glassell told his story to the US Navy interrogators in full, then staunchly refused to answer more questions. He sat in prison, spurning any clothing that wasn't Confederate gray, waiting to hear the Union government's decision regarding what would be his "final disposition."

The almost-victorious *David* proved to the Confederate officers in Charleston that a combat victory by a little cigar-shaped boat was possible. More stealth was needed, they concluded, from a boat that could fully submerge. A boat like the *Hunley*.

The *Hunley* herself had been tested in the rivers outside Mobile, Alabama, as Gen. Franklin Buchanan watched, and as other experimenters were testing their torpedoes and boats in Virginia, Louisiana, and other locations. The *Hunley* had been using a torpedo towed on a line at the time, but these tests quickly revealed that not only could the little submarines sink large ships with their torpedoes but also that the placement and configuration of the torpedo was key. Placing the torpedo beneath, rather than beside, the target increased the amount of damage it would do to the enemy vessel. Torpedoes that exploded above the waterline could cause some destruction, but much of the force would vent harmlessly out into the open air. When the torpedoes were triggered underwater and beneath the ships, the bombs would bite more massive chunks out of the hulls. The *David* had a spar that could be angled downward slightly but would have been more difficult to fit completely beneath an enemy hull, so the blast was less destructive than it could have been.

The science of the 1800s could not explain this phenomenon, but modern physics has mathematically solved the problem. The explosion of a bomb underwater causes a bubble of gas to form and burst outward, made up of the gaseous products released by the chemical reaction. As the bubble collapses, a rapid jet of water follows it and smashes against the hull of the target ship. The combined forces of both the pressure wave and the water jet wreak havoc on the enemy structure. The bubble then travels upward toward the surface of the water, repeatedly collapsing and expanding as it moves. Submarines in World War II would later learn the destructive power of these pulsating gas bubbles, as boats unfortunate enough to pass directly over mines were easily shredded by their motion.

Positioning a torpedo beneath a ship combined the destruction of the pressure waveform with the destruction of the gas bubble. The experimenters of the Confederacy learned the technique through trial and error.

The high density of the water also means that the blast pressures can propagate away from the bomb and toward other objects in the water, like a waiting submarine, more efficiently and with less loss. If a target is 5 meters away, a blast that occurs underwater transmits pressure levels that are more than twenty times higher to that target than if the same blast had occurred in air.

Objects near the surface are less vulnerable, shielded from the full potential of the blast by their proximity to the air. Deeper objects, positioned farther down in the water and therefore farther away from the protective effect of the surface, will receive the full, unmitigated wrath of the blast.

Hunley, McClintock, and Watson tested their boat by setting off a torpedo that was a full 400 yards away in one of the rivers of Mobile. Kemp's face felt the wrath of his much smaller bomb, but in the air where the pressure waves were less destructive. "Mrs. Baker's" submarine also used a long line to pull the trigger, waiting to set off the charge until the submarine was much farther away. Glassell and his David crew used a smaller bomb than the rest of the boats, a bomb that could not submerge as fully. The men of the *David* were also positioned inside a vessel made of wood with a thick hull that sat farther out of the water, and was therefore protected by proximity to the surface.

The torpedo of the *Hunley* carried a much larger charge than the almost-successful *David*. Her spar sank farther down into the water, with a bend at the end to allow the black powder torpedo to be positioned completely beneath the hull of the *Housatonic*. The *Hunley*'s thin hull was metal, a material more eager to transmit pressure waves than wood. She was sunk farther down into the water, nestling her into a cocoon of the ocean, a cocoon that surrounded her in a saltwater medium that could more efficiently transmit the full force of any blast.

I explained all of these design features out loud as I sat in a conference room, patiently clicking through one slide at a time during my preliminary exam. With each slide, the members of my advising committee riddled me with a gauntlet of scientific questions about blasts, injuries, and physics. The five men—four professors from Duke, including my adviser, and one US Navy PhD underwater scientist from my base in Florida—were the panel of judges who would one day determine whether I would be deemed worthy of graduating with my PhD. To get my degree I would have to be proclaimed "done" by this committee. The preliminary exam was a rite of passage to determine whether or not I was worthy to continue my work and use it to aim for graduation. Fail the exam twice, and you are asked to leave Duke.

So much of science comes down to measuring the correct squiggly line on a computer screen. Without the benediction of this committee, I would not get the chance to move forward with this project and experimentally measure the squiggly line of pressure inside the boat. And without that measurement, my theory would have to stay an opinion.

CHAPTER 6

PREPARATIONS

I know damn well that if there had been a way to get to success without traveling through disaster someone would have already done it and thus rendered the experiments unnecessary, but there's still no journal where I can tell the story of how my science is done with both the heart and the hands.

—Hope Jahren, *Lab Girl*

After the three-and-a-half-hour interrogation of the preliminary exam, my advising committee deemed me worthy to continue in my quest for science. I smiled weakly through the fog of blissful exhaustion that had descended upon my brain, and each committee member shook my pale, perspiring hand in congratulations on his way out of the conference room. I now had permission to set up the *Hunley* tests, and a budget of $4,000 metaphorically clenched in my tight, sweaty fist.

Early the next morning I slowed my car to a crunchy halt in the grass-overgrown gravel outside our lab's test building, a place we lovingly called the Farm, with a capital *F*. Duke had given my adviser this white concrete structure, buried deep in the woods down a winding dirt road beyond an unmarked barbed-wire fence, largely because nobody else had wanted it. The students of our lab spent years gradually reclaiming the building from the forest, uprooting small trees from the gutters and evicting the intrepid rodents that had rampaged freely through the facility. We slowly made it our own: a working lab space, with no climate control, but with enough solitude that our massive shock tubes could tremble the walls without risking complaints from neighbors. The impressive main blast room hid inside the ramshackle building like a Corvette engine inside a rusted-out old Hyundai.

Dale had given me permission to open and claim two large, previously unoccupied cinder-block rooms. The rooms were currently used as storage, and were filled with pieces of old experimental setups hurled into haphazard heaps. One room was ringed by brown, dented metal benches, and the concrete floors featured a Tetris pattern of dingy, broken linoleum squares. The two rooms were connected to each other by a closet-sized steel passageway with a heavy metal door on either end, a creepy feature that had originally been installed for some past, forgotten generation of researchers to wash large pieces of equipment. Industrial-sized drains were dug into the floor outside both doors of this wash closet, perfect for either a serial killer or an underwater blast researcher who was about to make a mess.

The test space needed a water tank. The Farm was fully outfitted for blast tests in air, but we had no facilities for blasting in water. I needed something that was cheap, easy to modify, and common enough that I could easily replace it if I accidentally smashed it to smithereens with a shock wave.

I found a beauty in a For Sale post on the internet, a post whose text showed that the water tank's current owner did not fully appreciate the scientific potential of his neglected treasure. She cost $60, a steal for such a gorgeous hunk of heavy-duty plastic reinforced with metal bars. She had originally been used for shipping liquids and grains, and now she slumped lonely and unloved in a heap of similar tanks on a farm outside Durham. Our lab tech, Jason, and I soon found ourselves in his truck, on a mission to collect my prize.

Setting up a blast trial can be an exercise in learning how to improvise a believable story. Like with home repairs, no first day of testing ever goes exactly according to the original plan, and trips to the hardware store to concoct a Plan B are virtually guaranteed. Helpful and inquisitive store employees become human-sized obstacles that I have to dodge like traffic cones, because in their kind dedication to their jobs they feel the overwhelming need to confirm that I am in fact buying the correct products for my mission. I can't tell them the honest truth: "It's part of my experimental test setup to blow stuff up," because I don't feel like cashing out my bank account for bail money.

During one trip I bought a massively atypical amount of pipe insulation, long, black foam tubes designed to wrap around copper water pipes and help them transmit hot or cold water more efficiently. I needed the foam to wrap around my gauge wires, both to make them float and to shield them from the water. I had cleaned out all the boxes of stock for pipes with diameters between 0.5 inches and 1.5 inches, and I stood in the aisle staring at the empty cardboard containers, thinking about asking if there were more in the back storerooms. I awkwardly clutched the assorted soft, dark noodles in an untamed bundle in my arms.

Like clockwork, Greg the employee appeared by my side, a traffic cone materializing out of nowhere. His tidy salt-and-pepper hair and his meticulously knotted, clean apron gave him the appearance of a man with careful attention to detail. A man who was probably very experienced at completing precisely planned home repairs . . . and therefore a man who would ask me a lot of questions. I could feel his eyes running over my arm-spider of foam tubes, noting their varying dimensions.

"Can I ask what you're working on?" he asked. "Looks like you've picked out a couple different sizes." He continued to look at me, the kind curiosity in his eyes slowly converting to sadness as I stood with my mouth open, waiting for an answer to materialize in my brain. "Are you sure you know what size pipes you have at home?"

"I'm fine, I'm fine, I don't need help," I tried to reassure him, clutching at my noodles. "Do you have any more? I don't care what diameter."

Wrong answer. I had confirmed Greg's worst fears: I had no idea what I was doing. I didn't even know what diameter pipes I had at home! Several of the foam tubes tumbled out of my arms as Greg looked at me with the profound pity of someone unable to save a train rushing headlong toward a cliff, someone who was sure I was wasting my money and would be back at the store soon. He somberly helped me gather the tubes, one at a time placing them back on top of the pile still in my grasp. Greg reluctantly allowed me to proceed to the cash register.

By the time I drove with Jason to obtain the tank, I was tired, and I neglected to concoct a just-in-case tale during the drive. As Jason passed me the end of a ratchet strap and I tightened the precious water tank securely into the bed of his truck, the farmer asked the fatal question.

"So, what're you gonna use it for anyway?" he drawled.

I froze. My brain decided to disappear on me. I told the truth.

"I'm going to take it back to the lab and blow shit up in it."

The farmer looked up at me, a youngish city dweller in a grimy T-shirt standing in the bed of a borrowed truck, and not even a flicker of concern or judgment crossed his face after my openly suspicious response.

"Well, if you break it, I've got plenty more." Then, the man invited me into his home to use the restroom before we headed back to Durham.

After Jason and I body-slammed the hefty vessel into place above the floor drains at the Farm, Henry the trusty undergrad got to work sawing off its roof while I heaved a garden hose around the side of the building to fill the plastic-and-metal beast with water. Henry and I carefully lowered in the new partial shock tube we had constructed, a stubby monstrosity made of over 40 pounds of steel. We took cover behind the heavy metal door of the wash closet, and then I selfishly insisted that I wanted to be the one to press the big red button.

A gush of high-pressure helium filled the space in the shock tube behind the sturdy Mylar membranes. *POP. SPLASH.* A dozen failed trials later, we had evolved our equipment into a working setup. We would use the shock tube to test each pressure gauge to exhaustion, until we knew their quirks like they were tiny members of our family. These pressure gauges were responsible for measuring our squiggly lines once we got to black powder test day; if they chose not to work properly, we would have no data, and therefore no proof.

The water tank was far too small to perform the actual tests, even though I planned to use a scale model. Blast problems can be scaled down in size, to a certain degree. While there is a lower limit, in general if the variables are altered correctly, scaling can be used to conduct experiments that are cheaper, easier, and just as informative as full-sized explosions.

Mathematician G. I. Taylor performed one of the most famous examples of blast scaling when he used photographs of the detonation of a nuclear bomb that were published in an article in *LIFE* magazine in 1947. Armed with only the photographs, a ruler, and a thorough knowledge of scaling, he calculated that the bombs had an explosive yield of 22 kilotons (22,000 tons) of TNT. The actual yield, which was highly classified information at the time, was an impressively close 20 kilotons.

I wanted to scale the *Hunley* problem down to one-sixth the size of the actual 40-foot-long submarine, which meant our model boat would be 6 feet and 8 inches long—this was the biggest size scale I could carry myself and fit in my sedan without having to rent a flatbed truck for each test day. I needed a water volume at least as large as a pond. Duke was not an option; Dale and I knew without even asking that the safety office would never allow live explosives on campus.

Imagine how quickly you hang up on a telemarketer. Now imagine that the unknown telemarketer is asking you, not for money, but instead for permission to come to your home and set off live explosives on your property. Finding a test site had become an exercise in humiliation. Call after call, my pleas were sometimes met with polite rejection, but more often they were met with immediate, outright laughter. The army, calling me back from Fort Bragg in North Carolina, had semi-mockingly suggested that I "go find where those MythBusters guys set off their charges instead." If only I had my own TV show.

By this point in the testing, Nick and I had moved into a small apartment together. He got home from his twenty-four-hour shifts at about nine a.m., and on those days I would go into lab late so that he could tell me about his night over hot tea and scrambled eggs. Our narrow wooden porch overlooked the featureless pavement of the apartment complex parking lot, but we had outfitted it with cheap, comfortable, blue plastic patio chairs, and the routine of curling up in one and listening to him talk always sent me to work in a good mood.

"They talked about farm equipment most of the day," he sleepily muttered while watching the tea swirl in his mug, "so I mostly just hung out quietly in between calls." Many of Nick's fellow firefighters were also farmers on their off days, so farms and farm equipment were frequent topics of conversation at the station. That day, though, Nick's comment snagged on one of the problems churning away in my brain. My forkful of eggs froze on its way to my mouth.

"These farmers, Nick," I began. He looked up at me questioningly. "Do any of them have *water* on their property?" Nick slowly set his mug down. He nodded. He already knew what I wanted.

"I'll ask around."

———

The *Hunley* herself was also something of an outcast. The fatal sinking in October 1863, the one that killed Horace Hunley, drew additional negative attention to the boat. The remains of Hunley and his crew had been "ghastly," and "the blackened faces of all presented the expression of their despair and agony." Feeling the painful effects of carbon dioxide in their last moments, the doomed crew had "contorted into all kinds of horrible attitudes." Confederate general Beauregard wrote that he didn't want the boat used again. Basically, he wanted her buried away as a failed experiment. The *Hunley* and her torpedo were as unwelcome as my scale model and me.

By then the bombardment of Charleston had also begun, with Union troops nightly lobbing shell after shell into the city and all surrounding forts. The area was no longer safe.

Diarist Edmund Ruffin had previously made it a point to visit the little torpedo boat regularly in Charleston. He was especially curious about her as a tool for breaking the blockade. But after the October sinking, the *Hunley* disappears from his entries until months later, after he hears of her victory. She had been moved somewhere else, tucked away from sight.

Bert Pitt thought I had built a full-sized submarine, and yet even with that misconception, he had still invited me out to talk about the project.

"How will you get any pieces of the sub back out of the pond?" he asked. "Because we like to fish in there." His family and favored neighbors considered the pond a prime fishing hole.

Nick had valiantly lobbied at the fire stations on my behalf, and he had struck experimental-setup gold. Firefighter Michael Phillips was Bert Pitt's son-in-law, and they all worked the family farm together: an isolated, expansive tobacco, cotton, and sweet potato farm that included a man-made pond. Bert, the family patriarch, asked me to drive out to talk before he agreed to the project. Understandably, he had some questions.

I arrived at the Pitt family home at a time I thought of as early but was apparently several hours into their average morning. The statuesque main house stood proudly at the end of a long lane bordered by the smaller homes of the other relatives who worked the family farm, including Phillips and his wife and young children. Climbing the front steps of the traditional, two-story wooden farmhouse, I knocked loudly on the edge of the screen door then stepped back onto the broad wraparound porch.

A woman with shoulder-length brown hair swung open the solid inner door and stood looking at me through the screen. I assumed she was Bert Pitt's wife, but based on her facial expression and bathrobe I suspected that her husband had given her no warning whatsoever that someone was coming to visit.

"Hi! My name is Rachel Lance, I'm here to see Bert Pitt." Her eyebrows flicked briefly but perceptibly downward. I was coming across as a solicitor! "He's expecting me," I gushed out, smiling as widely as I could in the hopes it would convey good intentions. "He asked me to come by to talk about a science project he might let me do in your pond." Mrs. Gwen Pitt's face opened into a warm, welcoming smile. She reached out a hand to push open the screen door, and graciously invited me inside with the immediate hospitality characteristic of the South . . . if you are not an uninvited salesperson at eight a.m.

"This is for you," I said, shoving my arms forward to present her with a paper plate piled high with a heavy burden. It was my Grandma Lance's recipe for Southern red velvet cake, carefully wrapped in foil to guard it during the hour-and-a-half car ride away from the urban island of Durham. I was hopeful that baked goods would help me create a positive first impression, especially since I had nothing else to offer in exchange for the massive favor I needed. With the cake and its piles of traditional boiled frosting chilling in the fridge, Gwen called Bert in from the fields.

He was an average height but atypically tan and lean, his appearance a marked contrast to the soft, pale shapes that most of us have assumed after years of working in offices. I knew he had grandchildren, but his age was impossible to determine visually; decades of nonstop physical activity on the farm meant he still moved smoothly and quickly, without the creaking caution that often sets into knees and backs with the inconvenience of age. Wearing a baseball cap that covered what seemed to be a full head of mostly sandy-brown hair, Bert sat next to me on a barstool at the white kitchen counter. We looked together at pictures of the *Hunley* on the smudged screen of my laptop as I explained the project. His many questions came out rapidly, and with the same molasses North Carolina accent I had grown up hearing from my father's parents.

After he asked about the danger to the fish I happily clicked to the next slide and explained that I was using a scale model, not a full-sized 40-foot sub. I didn't plan to sink her, but if something unexpected happened the carcass of the boat would be easy to retrieve with basic scuba equipment. And fish are surprisingly robust, because fish don't have bubble-filled lungs to smash the traveling blast wave to a halt. Some fish have gas-filled swim bladders, but experiments driven by blast fear during the Cold War showed that these non-bubbly gas spaces are much more difficult to damage than human lungs. As long as the fish weren't within a half meter of my charges, they might be annoyed, but they shouldn't be harmed. Bert nodded briefly on hearing this, then gestured through the kitchen's sliding door toward the silver pickup truck sitting outside the back of the house.

"Well," he said, "let's drive out there and see if the pond has got what you need."

The moment Bert walked out of the kitchen, a thick-coated golden retriever adhered herself to his heels. The dog, whose name I learned was Dixie, clambered into the bed of the truck while her master walked to the driver's-side door, in a routine they clearly performed many times a day. I hopped in the passenger's seat, and Bert drove me down one of the red dirt roads crisscrossing between his fields, past the personal cemetery that housed generations of his family, including a few head-stones for ancestors who had fought for the Confederacy.

The pond was beautiful, both traditionally and from a scientific perspective. Dug by people, it was free of detritus and major obstacles—no sunken trash for me to cut myself on, no huge rock formations to crash my model sub into, no weird bottom features to cause unusual reflections of the blast waveform. It was at least a quarter mile from the nearest electrical outlet, but I was an engineer, so I shrugged that prob-lem off. I would figure out a power supply later.

"It's all yours if you think it'll work for what you need," Bert said, watching me sidelong as I stood on the wooden pier, looking out over the water. I suppressed my joy into the gruff, emotionless male mode of communication in which I was most comfortable because of my lifetime as a tomboy. I offered my right hand for a firm shake.

"It's perfect. Thank you."

A few weeks later, Bert Pitt and Mike Phillips watched from metal folding chairs on their pier as I squirmed into a wetsuit and plunged into the murky water for the first time. I had badgered three friends from another lab to come help me in exchange for home-cooked fried chicken, and together they waded through the muck of the shoreline while I spent hours swimming back and forth along premeasured lines of string to gauge depths and characterize the bottom topography. As I had hoped, the smooth, shallow bottom of the pond matched the ocean floor at the scene of the *Hunley*'s original explosion. The pond was perfect.

———

Sometime before early 1864, a few short months before her final mission, the *Hunley* had also been tucked away in her suitable new location. She was safely lodged on Sullivan's Island, a long, narrow stretch of land whose southernmost tip was the northern edge of the mouth of Charleston Harbor. The island contained mostly sand and military fortifications, and it was distant enough from downtown that it escaped the nightly bombardments. Because of the narrow, sandy nature of the island, it was relatively free of civilian buildings, and therefore had few prying civilian eyes.

About halfway down the length of the island was a narrow channel called Breach Inlet. The inlet funneled not just the tidal waters from behind the island but also the currents contributed by three rivers. This strong outgoing flow of water would vigorously push along any fish boat, helping spare the crew from some of the cranking. Even today, the inlet is known for its strong, outgoing flow of water during the ebb tide. "Breach is notorious for drownings and other crises spurred by its powerful currents," wrote one Charleston newspaper recently. The inlet was also protected by Battery Marshall, an armed fortification positioned just next to the opening.

The *Hunley* wasn't the only fish boat hoping to launch from Breach. By then, the Confederacy was hard at work building additional small vessels in the template of the *David* torpedo boat, which were also kept in the area. Diarist Edmund Ruffin frequently traveled specifically to see them, taking careful measurements and making illustrations in his notebook. The plan was for four or five of these vessels to attack one or several blockade ships in perfect synchrony, in one of the first submarine wolf packs.

From their new location, the *Hunley*'s crew also finalized their perfect target. The Union knew to expect a submarine attack. The attack of the *David* and the information gleaned from spies meant that they were aware of the new technology, and some of the Union ships had taken preventative measures. They dropped nets and spars in the water to block torpedo-carrying boats from reaching their hulls, and set up more nets to trap them. The nets don't seem to have actively foiled any at-

U.S.S. HOUSATONIC. CIVIL WAR SLOOP BLOWN UP BY MINE NEAR CHARLESTON.

Contemporary drawing of the USS *Housatonic*.

tacks, but they were definitely a deterrent for the Confederate troops when trying to select a target. The *Hunley* would fare best against an unguarded ship, it was decided, and so the little submarine set her sights on the unguarded vessel closest to her departure point: the USS *Housatonic*.

When Gabriel Rains churned out torpedoes for the defense of Charleston Harbor, he had at least one distinct advantage over me. Since torpedoes were new, there were basically no laws restricting their use. I, on the other hand, had a test site but would still apparently need a permit.

"Is this Rachel Lance?" the woman on the phone asked, a stressed note in her tone.

"Yes, this is she."

She spoke assertively and rapidly. "You can't set off black powder without a permit. You *really* need a permit." I had left her a voicemail, and she had called me back almost before I had even put my phone down. "I'll send you the forms."

There had been some confusion about the amount of paperwork required to set off black powder, since it was a low explosive and therefore less fearsome than something like C4. I had been less than confident that there was a difference in the eyes of the law, and wanted to ask the Bureau of Alcohol, Tobacco, Firearms, and Explosives (the ATF) just in case. As it turns out, that was a good life choice. Dale was correct that we could buy all the black powder we wanted fairly easily, but only for use in rifles.

We sent in our application packet, listing Pitt Farm as our test site, and then we waited. According to the ATF, we should expect the permit process to take at least six months . . . six months before I could even buy the powder for the tests . . . six months of doldrums waiting to make experimental progress.

One day shortly afterward, Dale materialized in the frame of my office door. "JENNIFER LOPEZ IS ON THE PHONE!" He belted the words at me before pivoting on the squeaking rubber toe of his boot and darting rapidly back down the hall without further explanation. I swept up my keys, lab notebook, and a pen, and slammed the door shut in my rush to run after him.

J Lo was indeed on the phone, but this one worked for the ATF. She was calling about our permit application, and much sooner than anticipated. Dale and I swung ourselves hurriedly into chairs in his office as her voice began to pipe through his speaker phone.

"We were all very interested in your project," she said, ambiguously. "Normally we process applications for big, ongoing projects like blasting open mines. Something this small is unusual.

"One of our agents is actually a history buff, and he's offered to volunteer his help. He already has every permit imaginable, and he would come to all of your test days to help with the charges. That way you wouldn't have to apply for a permit of your own. It would save you months of waiting and a lot of trouble."

YES!

And that was how I first heard about Brad Wojtylak, the amazing explosives expert with the utterly unpronounceable last name.

A few weeks later, Brad himself walked into my office and sat in the old blue wheelie chair where Dale usually roosted. His job hunting drug dealers with the ATF took him all over the state of North Carolina, and he had paused on a trip zigzagging past Durham in his behemoth black work-issued pickup truck with a locking bed full of body armor. He was a former Marine who now sported a slight slouch from his time lurking undercover in the world of heroin, and he described himself as "a rare breed of ginger who can tan." His cargo pants and T-shirt gave the impression of someone who valued function over frills. I liked him immediately.

The lab's new medical student, Luke Stalcup, walked in and took the only remaining chair, the one shoved in the corner collecting dust. Luke was a former army explosive ordnance disposal operator, a specialty dedicated to safely defusing terrorist explosive devices and often referred to colloquially as "the bomb squad." After his time in the military he came to Duke to learn how to continue saving lives with a scalpel instead. His ever-present rust-speckled facial scruff seemed like a minor rebellion against his former military life.

Duke's medical school sends its students out into science labs for their third year of education, telling them they should somehow learn the extraordinarily complex field of experimental science in one measly year. Luke had chosen our lab because of his history working with explosives, and he had agreed to help me with my research if I agreed to help him with his. The start of the academic year meant undergrad Henry Warder's time was nearly fully absorbed by his classwork, and I needed other assistance to conduct my experiments. I also lacked live explosives experience of my own, yet wanted to keep all of my fingers and toes, so I eagerly agreed to Luke's deal.

The three of us sat in the narrow confines of my office. I had printed out oversized copies of the technical diagrams of the *Hunley*'s torpedo from the National Archives and spread them out on the desks. Luke picked up a dry-erase marker, spun toward the wall with the white-board, and began to sketch potential charge designs.

All three of us were avid scuba divers, with interests in underwater technology and physiology. All three of us were blast specialists, with different angles of expertise. We were ATF, EOD, and Duke. We were former Marine Corps, former Army, and Navy Civil Service. The three of us were the *Hunley* test team.

We had a test site. We had a permit. We had a place to test our gauges. We had the expertise. But we still needed a boat. I needed to find someone who could make me a flawless steel cylinder.

The first thing I noticed about the metalworking artist Tripp Jarvis was his hands. Manicures and engineering work make awkward partners, so around women and some more fashionable men I often feel the need to hide my functional hands, with their calluses and hastily lopped, un-polished fingernails. But when I met Tripp, his sturdy fingers were as black as gangrene.

He held one soot-caked hand down over the high ledge of the loading dock, and when I grabbed it, he helped me heave myself up from the parking lot of the Liberty Arts Foundry. He wore square-rimmed glasses and had wispy, sandy-blond hair, both also made darker by the same black welding scuzz. At a later date, over Thai noodles, Tripp would laughingly tell me he had once been described as having "a heart of gold, but the physical essence of the dwarf Gimli, from *Lord of the Rings*."

The Liberty Arts Foundry was a collection of local artists in Durham, with each artist claiming a workspace inside one shared massive, high-ceilinged warehouse. Beautiful, miscellaneous pieces of art lay visibly scattered just beyond the doors, but because the casting furnace and metalworking equipment had heated the inside to a scorching temperature, Tripp invited me to take a seat outside. We each scooted a chair up to a round metal table that was positioned beneath a monolithic piece of art made of stacked steel geometric shapes. When I admired the sculpture's smooth, uniform welds, Tripp told me it was his. The physical work of welding and hammering to create clean geometries was a kind of mental therapy for him, a therapy he had begun sharing by organizing art programs for veterans. I glanced back at him with new confidence. If he made this sculpture, then making me a simple tapered tube should be no problem.

I had used my computer rendering of the *Hunley* to create technical engineering drawings on extra-large paper, complete with dimensions and tolerances. I edged my chair closer to Tripp, spread the papers on the table, and began to explain the project.

The submarine would be round in the center so it could be rolled out of one solid piece of mild steel $\frac{1}{16}$ of an inch thick. The *Hunley* was not perfectly cylindrical but was close, so the shape was a reasonable approximation that would greatly simplify the construction. The original submarine was made out of wrought iron, but wrought iron is extremely hard to come by in the twenty-first century. I had selected mild steel instead because this type of comparatively malleable steel is similar to wrought iron in the material properties that govern how they physically respond to blast waves, such as impedance and modulus of elasticity.

The boat needed working ballast tanks. The water sloshing about in the ballast tanks, especially the one in the front, could potentially affect the way that the pressure entered into the vessel. However, I had concluded after some careful calculations that I could eliminate the ribs that were inside the crew compartment, instead making the boat one solid piece. In the pressure ranges of the *Hunley*'s blast, the ribs should not have any effect.

A series of exhaustively detailed publications by the brilliant blast physicist Michelle Hoo Fatt describes how cylinders respond to the pressures of explosions, and how their physical responses change when they have internal support structures made of ribs with different spacings. Using her work I had concluded that the *Hunley* would be below the exposure pressures where its ribs would affect the way the walls moved and changed in response to the blast. The ribs began to matter if the pressures were more extreme and caused permanent damage and deformations to the cylinder. However, the blast pressures from the black powder should be below that level, and the real *Hunley* confirmed the hypothesis because its walls showed no permanent deformation from its full-sized torpedo. Therefore, no ribs would be included in the model.

As I explained the design, Tripp listened, waiting patiently for me to stop talking with his eyes wide beneath his smudged lenses. His face was making the concerned expression I have learned means that people are trying to follow me, but that I have jumped too rapidly into an unfamiliar topic. He jabbed his right index finger onto one of the dimensions on the clean white paper, leaving a dark black smudge, then worriedly tried to brush the smudge away with the same hand, making the mark worse by dragging it across the page.

"So, this is the length of the boat?" he asked. "And you want it round in the middle? Is it more important that the welds look good, or that they be watertight?" He was always the artist.

"Watertight. It has to be absolutely watertight. I don't care what they look like." I pushed the drawings toward him. "These are for you to keep. They have all the dimensions you should need."

"Yeah I can do that," he said, looking at the figures, now understanding. He confidently picked up the sheets of paper that, because they were now his, he could more comfortably smudge with impunity. "Might take me a couple of months, I have some other work going on now too." While he was working, I would spend my time testing my gauges.

———

By the middle of January, out at the Farm, I could barely feel the steel of the shock-tube driver in my frozen hands, but I knew it was slipping. My knuckles were engorged with fluid; I could only partially bend my fingers to grip the 40 pounds of metal. Repeatedly dunking my arms in the cold water of the test tank had caused my hands to swell in a cartoonish way. The Farm had no heat, and after a recent temperature drop in the weather, the test rooms and therefore the water of the tank had both settled to a constant 40 degrees Fahrenheit. All sensation in my hands had been reduced to a vague numbness and tingling, with occasional vicious spikes of pain. Luke and I had built ourselves an improvised "warming hutch" by duct-taping scavenged panels of pink wall insulation to the sides of the steel washroom next to our test tank, and with two space heaters running full throttle we could coax the tiny box up to 55 degrees.

After each shock-tube blast, one of us had to reach into the tank, plunging both arms fully into the chilled liquid, and pull the tube driver out. Luke and I took turns. Whoever retrieved the driver got to huddle momentarily in front of a space heater to warm their bare, dripping arms. The other person lugged the steel across the building to the pneumatically powered impact wrench, opened the driver, and exchanged the spent Mylar membranes for fresh ones.

For each test, the driver sat facing upward in the center of the tank.

Every test used four gauges, one between the driver and each corner of the tank, the same distance apart in a four-pointed star. Because the test setup was symmetrical, each gauge should measure the same signal . . . if they measured signals at all.

I was ready to smash our gauges with a sledgehammer. We had started with hydrophones, little baby carrot–shaped devices coated in black rubber that were designed to measure sound underwater. They had, in this test, measured absolute gibberish, recording only signals that vibrated wildly, and boldly declaring pressures higher than what could be physically possible.

We had moved on to using fiber-optic gauges, thin blue plastic wires that measured pressure with light and could be surgically threaded inside the human body to measure the pressures inside veins and arteries. The fiber optics measured the first few milliseconds of the shock wave, then completely gave up, recording only a dead flatline for the rest of the signal.

Neither the hydrophones nor the fiber-optic gauges could hack it because neither could take data fast enough to come anywhere close to the sampling rate we needed, and as a result they were outputting garbage. The gauges our lab normally used in air would not work underwater because they were not waterproof. Luke and I next tried a specialty gauge, designed specially for measuring underwater explosions, and it too captured only a few accurate milliseconds before producing a chaotic zigzag that looked more like a mountain range than a shock wave.

One magic fiber-optic gauge worked—gauge number 8—and if it were connected to port number 4 and *only* port number 4, then it would produce a beautiful, clear graph of the shock wave. But one gauge was not enough; these tests were too important to rely on one magic gauge that worked for mysterious reasons. We were nearly out of ideas to try to get the gauges to work. Luke and I had been trapped at the Farm, testing them systematically, for weeks. Change out the membranes, dunk the driver, take shelter, push the button, grimace at the results, change the gauge setup, pull up the driver, towel the water off, repeat.

My swollen digits couldn't hold the weight of the slick driver anymore, and it slipped out of my control. I clutched feebly at the steel bolts as it fell, and it hit the floor with a resounding *clang* that prompted Luke, still curled tightly in front of the heater in the other room, to yell to ask if I was OK. The driver had smashed into the ground within inches of my grasping hands, and as I positioned it back in the bitingly cold water for what felt like the millionth time, all I could think about was how a few broken bones might have been worth the pleasant warmth of a pile of hospital blankets and a tray full of Jell-O.

My struggles were nothing compared to the struggles of the *Hunley*'s crew. The crew was dependent on their own muscle power to crank the sub out to the Union blockade, and to help ensure success they practiced every day. In the middle of winter, they sat hunched in the cold, dark recesses of the submarine for at least two hours a day.

Ultimately, my gauge salvation came from the most likely, predictable source.

When I first began puttering around with DYSMAS, the navy's hydrocode computer program I used to model the blast exposures of unprotected World War II sailors suffering in the water, a navy engineer named Greg Harris patiently answered every one of my questions about the code. Every time I lay awake at night obsessing over some arcane facet of underwater blast physics and I wanted to talk it through with someone, I would type up a lengthy nocturnal email to Greg Harris, and he would invariably send me a thoughtful and equally nerdily excited reply by the next afternoon. When I was searching for obscure, un-digitized reports on historical underwater experiments, he invited me up to the Naval Surface Warfare Center where he worked in Indian Head, Maryland, and kindly supplied me with sandwiches so I didn't have to take breaks while I pillaged his towering stash of old blast documents. So, when I couldn't get my gauges working, when I ran out of ideas completely, when I began daydreaming about how pleasant an injury might be if only to give me a break from the problem, I turned yet again to Greg Harris.

Greg has an imposing presence, both because of his actual size and because his resonant baritone voice somehow seems to take up physical space in a room. He is tall, with a full head of thick hair shot through with more than enough silver to provide him with the immediate credibility that gets assumed for all scientists nearing retirement. Greg is free with his professional opinions and he will tell you the facts of physics immediately and clearly, and often accompanied by a cell-phone photo of the mosh pit at the most recent rock concert he attended. Greg Harris is an underwater blast expert, working for the same patriotic team that is the US Navy, but with a focus on undersea weapons design and damage to inanimate targets instead of damage or injuries to people.

"Sit tight," Greg replied promptly to my emails of gauge distress. "I'm going to connect you with Kent Rye. He's the navy's gauge guru."

Kent and Greg not only had a long-standing collaboration based on a mutual love of the explosion business, but Kent soon proved to be equally as magnanimous, endlessly ping-ponging ideas and theories back and forth with me as we reworked every aspect of my tank setup.

Greg invited me to see their pressure gauges working in action in a live-charge test. I basically drooled on my keyboard at the opportunity; I wanted so badly to learn more about the way other naval researchers were setting up their underwater experiments, to make sure I was getting every detail correct the first time rather than waste days, weeks, or months refining my processes. Greg knew I was interested in the *Hunley*, so he invited me up for the black powder tests he was about to conduct. His goal was to examine the in-water pressures output by a full *Hunley*-sized black powder charge. He was conducting the tests as part of a group that was intrigued by the same mystery I was, but they were investigating a completely different theory to explain her sinking. My manager in Panama City gave the visit the thumbs-up, the proper authorities rubber-stamped the official approvals to visit Greg's test site at Aberdeen in Maryland, and I packed my car for the road trip up to underwater blast mecca.

The day of testing went mildly awry, as testing often does, but with profoundly inconvenient timing. The harness to hold the gauges broke on the first day and could not be fixed immediately, so I did not get to watch a single explosion. But I did get the opportunity to talk all day about the US Navy's custom-made blast gauges and how they were used.

They were tested by tapping with a pen because the touch of a human finger can induce electrical signals that will create a false temporary pressure readout. The tiny, polished ball of tourmaline crystal inside will flex and compress in response to the pressures of the blast, creating electrical signals through the it's-not-witchcraft-it's-science of piezoelectricity.

Finally, while standing huddled on the shore of the Aberdeen site and looking out over the cold winter water, we collectively concluded that the fundamental problem was not my test setup. My test setup was correct. The problem was that I was working with gauges that simply weren't capable of doing what I needed them to do.

Everything looked so easy at Aberdeen. When something needed attention in the middle of the pond, they took a small boat out; they didn't have to swim. They had a full lab, complete with a roof to protect them from the weather, right next to the water. They had electricity. I was deeply jealous. My pond site was much lower-cost—it was free—but it was not nearly so luxurious.

After I returned home, Kent Rye mailed me pressure gauges. Two tiny, clear tubes with round silver balls suspended inside by wires, squeezed lovingly between sheets of soft, black foam packaged inside a stiff cardboard box that could have held an expensive bracelet. The gauges were handmade by Kent and the blast specialists at the Carderock, Maryland, navy base (officially called NSWC Carderock Division), and Kent considered them mutual US Navy property. He was willing to send them to me as a courtesy, since I was another naval employee working in a similar research area.

I slid the gauges down the dark-green high-strength fishing line I had installed in my water tank to mark the four carefully measured symmetrical locations around the shock tube. Magic fiber-optic gauge number 8 took a third spot. I bundled the red wires of the new navy gauges together carefully and routed them through the crack in the door of the washroom, where the sensitive recording electronics inside were protected from the spray from the tank. Luke pressed the big red button. *POP. SPLASH.* We jerked our heads toward the computer screen and psychically willed it to show us the curves. I held my breath as the signals processed.

All three gauges recorded the shock wave. Identical, beautiful waveforms. Sharp, infinite rises, straight up to the maximum pressure. Almost the exact same value for the peak pressure. (Some variation is inevitable.) Smooth, continuous slope back down. Magnificent.

———————

It was time to build live charges. The in-water gauges were measuring the pressure waves properly and consistently. The gauges that would go inside the sub were air gauges that had been used successfully by students in our lab for years. I had installed them inside a small metal tub and blasted the tub in the tank to check, and they were perfect as usual. Tripp was done with the boat, and I had proved it was watertight by floating it in the chilly community swimming pool of my apartment complex even though the pool was still technically closed for the winter, with the staff watching apprehensively from the main office windows.

The charges were the only puzzle piece left before we could trek out to Pitt Farm and blast. Luke and I drained the test tank and turned our attention to making casings.

The design of our charges would parallel the design of the *Hunley*'s torpedo as closely as possible, but with a little help from modern technology. The 1864 *Hunley* team had used a plunger rod that sprang backward to hit a little nugget of highly impact-sensitive mercury fulminate. The design was effective, but dangerous. A small jostle could prematurely set off the charge. We would replace the unstable contraption with a squib—a small capsule that provides a tiny "match strike" starter explosion when you apply the right voltage.

The most common torpedo design used by the Confederacy during the Civil War was Singer's torpedo. Not surprisingly then, the writing on the drawings from the National Archives states that the torpedo used in the attack was a Singer's. However, the trigger used in the Singer's design was actually a spring-loaded plunger device that was positioned completely externally to the body of the torpedo. The technical diagram in the National Archives drawing shows an internal plunger mechanism.

Torpedo legend Gabriel Rains was in Charleston during or just after the sinking that killed Horace Hunley, as in his records he wrote that "the boat was brought to the wharf & left for a long time where we were preparing torpedoes, but on account of the mishaps, I would have nothing to do with her."

Rains also wrote that his compatriot Capt. M. Martin Gray was in charge of "making & managing" the torpedo used for the attack on the *Housatonic*. Rains's records contain a technical drawing of the pressure trigger designed by Gray, and this trigger is mechanistically consistent with the trigger in the National Archives drawing. The trigger has a plunger that protrudes slightly externally, but otherwise is mostly internal, and the plunger is held in place by a retaining wire with a spring to launch it backward into a mercury-fulminate cap.

It therefore seems likely that the design in the National Archives drawing is generally accurate in its description of the charge configuration, but that it may have been incorrectly labeled as a Singer's torpedo.

Luke and I hammered and shaped glossy sheets of copper into cylindrical tubes. We sealed the seams.* We stood looking proudly at our small army of shiny orange tubes, each standing on its end in a geometric battalion covering the battered metal lab benches. They needed only black powder.

———————

I was trying to meet Brad Wojtylak to obtain free black powder, donated to the project courtesy of one of his ATF coworkers. My parents drove down from Michigan allegedly to visit Nick and me, but really because they wanted to watch some explosions, and I made the mistake of mentioning to them that I was meeting Brad vaguely near a doughnut shop. My father then became rather insistent about the doughnuts.

Brad's text messages to me had contained normal English phrases the day before, but as they crossed into the morning, the communications had become more and more abbreviated. He was following a suspected drug dealer, tracking some kind of remote signal, and the nocturnal gentleman was unknowingly dragging Brad on an all-night, cross-state road trip. The doughnut shop was just off the highway he was traversing. As my parents and Nick ate their frosted sugar bombs, I

---

*Again, I am intentionally leaving out or altering some of the details of how the charges are made, both in this section and in future sections.

heard the aggressively throaty rumble of Brad's high-powered work truck pull into the parking lot, and I grabbed a cruller in a napkin before heading out to meet him.

"What is that, some kind of cop joke?" he protested as he stepped out of the cab and saw me holding the doughnut.

"No, I've just seen how you eat," I quipped back at him. He chuckled and walked around the back of his truck to unlock the bed, then he reached inside to open the separate lock on a sturdy, ruggedized box. With his head buried under the lifted bed cover, he began to rummage with his right hand, and he handed me the first bag of black powder with his left.

I stood awkwardly, cruller in one hand, big pink static-free bag in the other. The sloppy grease-pencil handwriting on the bag loudly and proudly declared that it contained black powder, and since the bag was transparent it was clearly an unreasonably large quantity. As Brad nonchalantly handed me a second pink bag, I shifted my feet and awkwardly looked around to see if anyone was watching us.

"Uh, Brad?"

"Yeah," he responded.

"What do I do if I get pulled over with this stuff?"

"It'll be fine. Just have them call me." He glanced up at me with bleary, pink-rimmed eyes, his fatigue thinly veiling his confusion over my concern. Having a badge must make it easier to explain things to people, I thought. "Maybe put it in the trunk," he conceded as he handed me a third bag full of explosive material.

———————

Brad, Luke, and I stood in front of the row of copper tubes lined up on the metal lab benches that ringed our room at the Farm. We were tethered to the bench by springlike yellow bracelets to prevent static electricity; the thin wires running through them kept us constantly at the same electrical potential as the metal table. Luke had also powered off the two dehumidifiers that normally ran nonstop. Without a centralized heating system, the palpable atmospheric sweat that defines the moist climate of the Deep South had rapidly oozed in through every pore in the walls to bring the indoor humidity up to a clammy 80 percent. We were not risking any miniature static-electricity lightning bolts jumping between us and the table to ignite the stray powder dust and granules.

Luke looked at me and rolled his eyes with a mocking smile. Brad was bent over the table, intently focused on the digital readout of the scale as he slowly, meticulously filled his copper cylinder, dropping in one single, tiny grain of powder at a time.

"Hey, Brad, it doesn't have to be that exact," I said, interrupting his laser focus. "Plus or minus a gram is fine. These little bombs aren't that precise."

"Hm, sorry," he said, straightening back up and removing his tube from the scale so Luke could get started on his. "I'm too used to heroin. A gram is like $200. Those guys are really precise in their measurements. Oh, and Rachel?"

"Yeah?" I was already watching Luke zero the scale to fill his charge.

"Stop calling them bombs. These are pretty weak, so we want to avoid calling them bombs if we can. That word carries some specific meanings it would be better to avoid."

I looked back at him. "OK. So what do we call them instead?"

Luke, already hunched over the scale, spoke up without shifting his eyes. "Science tubes," he responded. Our first round of science tubes was completed by the end of the day.

———————

I spent the night before the testing lying wide-awake, staring nervously at the ceiling. I was still wide-awake early the next morning when my alarm clock sounded. We formed a caravan out to the Pitt Farm test site, with each car responsible for transporting one key element of the setup. Brad and Luke carried the squibs and the science tubes, kept carefully separate from each other. I carried the submarine and the data-acquisition equipment. Altogether, it was over 250 kilograms of gear.

Everyone had been assigned jobs in advance. We had practiced carefully for this day. Brad and Luke began assembling charges while I secured the gauges inside the boat. My dad trudged to the opposite side of the pond to sink into a lawn chair in the mud, ready to help pull the submarine out to the center of the water. My mother, unsure she wanted the responsibility of helping with the science, was in charge of photography and snacks.

By the time we got everything set up it was midmorning. The atmosphere among the people on land, in the thick green grass and the pleasant sunshine, was like a carnival. The pond had a broad shore, a wide circumference of closely trimmed field that eventually transitioned to expansive stretches of crops on three sides and dense North Carolina oak forest on the fourth. All our cars were parked at random angles on the grass, and we had scattered mismatched camping chairs between them. An exposed wooden pier stretched toward the center of the pond, with a bench at the end for weary fishermen, and the entire extended Pitt family had congregated by it to watch our blasts. While I tightened nuts and bolts, Nick tossed an orange foam football with the two young Phillips boys, Bert Pitt's grandsons, Mason and Austin.

Finally, we were ready. Crouched on the sun-bleached wood planks, I flicked the navy gauges with a pen, as I had been taught. They were working perfectly. Luke thwacked the bow of the submarine with a rubber mallet, and I watched as the gauges inside flickered to report the subtle resultant pressure wave. Brad handed Luke the first powder-filled copper tube. Luke and I attached the charge to the spar on the bow of the model sub, running the wires for the squib back to Brad's detonator equipment on the shore.

I sat at the end of the pier, huddled with my hat covering the screen of the laptop so I could read it in the sun. I flicked obsessively between the various screens for the gauges, trying to quiet the booming, insistent voice in my head that was terrified I had missed something critical. The equipment was set to auto-trigger, meaning that as soon as the in-water gauges read a pressure above a few kilopascals, the computer would automatically record the signal, back-dating it a fraction of a second to ensure it processed the entire waveform.

I held up a hand to show Brad I was ready. He counted down, letting the small children push the two buttons on the detonator box. Mason held down one button during the countdown as Brad guided Austin's hand to press the second button at the correct time. The charge went off.

When an underwater charge explodes, you see the explosion first and you feel it second, all well before you hear it. Light travels fastest, followed by sound in water, so the image of the plume and the sensation of the blast, having traveled through the water, into the ground, then up into your feet, both reach your brain before the *kaboom* can plod to you through the air.

This *kaboom* was small. It was too small, and the plume of water matched the sound in its unimpressive size. The gentle hum of the recording equipment told me that as it sat next to me, not processing data, instead still patiently waiting for the trigger. It had never received the signal to stop recording, and it was still waiting to feel some kind of pressure wave move through the gauges. Brad and Luke joined me at the end of the pier, and we sat staring at the heavy yellow box that was generating squiggly lines on the laptop screen. They were just noise, no blast waveforms.

We pulled the submarine back to shore and rechecked the gauges; they were all still working. Luke attached a new charge to the spar, and my dad pulled the submarine back out into the pond. Again, countdown. Two buttons. *Kaboom*. Again, too small. Again, the yellow box sat whirring, unperturbed, not having witnessed any pressure wave.

We tried a third time, but this time I switched the settings on the acquisition box and triggered the recording by hand. I zoomed in on the screen, staring intently at the recorded waveform, and finally saw a blip. A minuscule waveform at the time we had hit the button, but with a peak too diminutive even to reach the small pressure level required to trigger the box on automatic mode. A peak far too small for an explosive this size. Our baseball-sized charges were barely creating pressure waves.

Something had gone terribly wrong. A part of the experimental setup had failed. Or possibly many parts? There were about four hundred possible causes for this indeterminate catastrophe. I would have to pick through them one at a time.

CHAPTER 7

APPLE PIE WITHOUT APPLES

The great obstacle everywhere is scarcity of supplies. That is the controlling element to which everything has to yield.

—Robert E. Lee

Archaeologist Maria Jacobsen crouched awkwardly. She was shielded from the ubiquitous mud by what seemed to be the standard *Hunley* conservation team uniform: a hair net and a set of navy-blue coveralls with the words "Friends of the *Hunley*" embroidered on the right shoulder, a Clemson logo on the left. Panels of the submarine had been removed to allow the researchers access to the crew compartment, and Jacobsen's gloved left hand was coated in the thick ocean muck that still largely filled the inside.

"I've got it," she said.

"Say the words," someone urged her.

"I have the gold coin," she declared with more confidence. She removed her glove to squirt the mud in her left hand with a rinse bottle until the unmistakable hue of a large, golden disk shone in her palm.

The solid-gold coin was the stuff of legend, the Confederate version of digging up King Arthur's sword, Excalibur. It belonged to Lt. George Erasmus Dixon, the man who, based on the historical records, was thought to have piloted the submarine on her final mission.

And Jacobsen had just fished it out of the *Hunley*, near the skeletal remains that sat slumped on the pilot's bench.

The floridly looped letters engraved on the warped twenty-dollar piece were still clearly legible, the chemically inert gold having resisted the ravages of decades of salt water:

Shiloh
April 6ᵗʰ 1862
My life Preserver
G. E. D.

The engraved words and the subtle curl of the bent coin were physical evidence to support the legend: The man whose skeleton slouched at the pilot station of the *Hunley* was almost certainly George Dixon, and at the Battle of Shiloh the now-warped lucky coin in his pants pocket had taken the force of a Union bullet, saving his leg and probably his life.

As the archaeologists painstakingly extracted each human bone or artifact from the silt, the sundry relics began to tell the individual stories of each crew member. Tobacco pipes were found mixed in with several piles of the remains, and the rounded shapes of their stems matched chiseled, rounded gaps in the teeth of the crewmen who carried them; repeatedly clenching the pipe stem in the same spot eventually wore out a perfect notch. Two of the skulls had much smaller notches in their teeth, notches the size and shape of a sewing needle. A handful of metal Union buttons, the kind that would have adorned a standard-issue pea coat, showed that one of the Confederate men at the crank had been cold enough that February to wrap himself in Union-blue wool. Handkerchiefs, hats, and boots had been eaten away by time and the ocean, but the tattered remains nonetheless gave hints at how the men chose to dress before looking at the sky for the last time and wriggling through the narrow hatch of the conning tower.

Archaeologists carefully mapped the position of each bone before it was removed from the boat. Scientists separated the bones based on the crewman to whom they had belonged, and then laid them out on long tables so they could begin the exhaustive process of inspecting for evidence. The lungs, heart, and flesh had rotted and had been eaten by time, but the bones could still tell stories.

———

The strongest bone in the human body is the femur, a singular massive column of osseous tissue that acts as the infrastructure of the thigh. When the femur grows, it can increase in diameter all around the outside of the bone, but it can only extend in length through the creation of new tissue at the growth plates.

A growth plate is located at each end of the femur, one near the hip and another near the knee. During puberty these plates churn out cartilage, which then gets slowly replaced by other cells and minerals like calcium as it is built into solid bone, gradually extruding the entire femur by lengthening the central portion. As the new tissue extends from the growth plate, the bone organizes itself into lines, forming thin fibrous structures reminiscent of the threads of a steel cable. These fibers are called osteons, and the central portion of the long bone looks like a tightly bound bundle of their lines, a bamboo stalk with a hollow, marrow-filled core.

By the end of puberty, the general linear structure of these osteons has more or less been set for life. The growth plates stop making cartilage and then they solidify, and the length of the growth that they managed to create determines a person's height. The femur may undergo small alterations in diameter or composition because of changes in activity level or the onset of conditions such as osteoporosis, but the longitudinal structure of the lines of fibers will stay essentially the same.

The exception is injury. A fracture to a long bone like the femur

disrupts the even, smooth tendrils of the fibrous bundle, splitting osteons apart from one another and cleaving them into pieces. Like wood,
the tissue wants to split along the direction of the fibers, and as a result
the fracture usually propagates away from the original site of the
blow. The bone gets disrupted into jagged shards.

If the fractured pieces stay physically close together, the bone can
heal on its own. Blood leaks from the broken vessels and clots in the
area, carrying with it biomarkers, biological chemicals that act as bea-
cons to muster the body's defenses and stimulate new growth. Fast-
growing cartilage rushes in first to form a callus, providing a temporary
structure to stabilize the wound. Then slow-moving osteoblasts, the
cells responsible for building new bone, can take their time surrounding
and slowly infiltrating the bulge of cartilage enveloping the fracture.

After about four months, the callus of cartilage has been replaced
by a scattered, disorganized mesh network of bone, called woven bone.
It will take another several years for smooth lines of osteons to replace
this disorganized mesh with permanent bone, and even then usually the
scar of the original fracture still visibly disrupts the otherwise neat organization of lines within the column.

The middle bone of my right pinky finger is broken as I write this.
It has been reset and will heal, but long after my death a trained eye will
be able to look at the bone and see the old break. The bone will always
bear a line of chaotic osteons, wrapped around its middle in a thin spiral, indicating that it had once twisted apart.

If the victim is not lucky, the pieces of bone break apart from the
trauma, and they float isolated within the soft tissue of the surrounding
muscles. Too far apart, and they cannot sew themselves back together.
In the twenty-first century, surgeons can manually reassemble the
pieces, using cadaver bone and metal parts to fill in the gaps in the
structure and to provide support to join the broken elements together.
But they do so while wearing masks and sterile gloves to thwart the
legions of marauding bacteria that would happily grab a foothold and

grow in the exposed flesh. Despite antibiotics and sterile techniques, infection is still a constant concern.

In the time of the *Hunley,* bacteria ran amok. Louis Pasteur, one of the main advocates who convinced the scientific community that bacteria existed, did not present the results of his first experiments until the same month as Dixon's wound at the Battle of Shiloh; the doctors in America therefore simply could not have known. Bacteria, though anonymous, were a bigger threat than bullets.

Well over 620,000 soldiers died during the Civil War, but two-thirds of the fatalities were from infectious diseases. Bacteria could spread like wildfire in the close quarters of the unsanitary troop encampments, leading to ailments such as typhoid and dysentery rampaging unchecked.

Without knowledge of bacteria, there was also no knowledge of how to clean open wounds, and as a result gangrene too was epidemic. The soft lead bullets of the time stayed lodged in the body, expanding as they traveled through flesh, carrying in with them pieces of cloth and a smorgasbord of other contaminants. Surgeons learned that amputations performed within twenty-four hours of the wound led to higher survival rates compared to waiting for the nearly inevitable infection to set in. After a major battle it was not uncommon for them to operate nonstop for several days without washing their hands between patients, and boasting times as low as two minutes per amputation. The bone saw used to amputate infected limbs became the symbol of the battlefield doctor.

The femur of the skeleton seated at the pilot station showed signs of trauma. The lines of osteons running the length of the bone were disrupted, a scar that revealed that at some point the upper part of the femur had experienced a comparatively minor trauma that had healed on its own. Tiny flecks of lead stayed embedded in the bone. It was damage consistent with a gunshot wound. The man had been lucky—shards of his femur had not split apart inside his upper thigh because

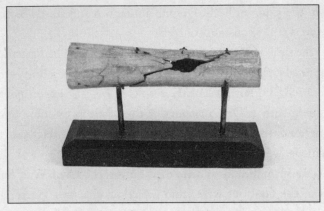

An unprotected femur fractured by a bullet during the Civil War. This wound was either quickly fatal or resulted in immediate amputation.

something else had absorbed the bulk of the impact of the bullet. He had not needed to risk the horrors of 1860s surgical techniques because something else had dispersed enough of the force to let the bone stay largely intact. More than likely, that something else was the warped gold coin inscribed "G.E.D." in his pocket.*

———————

Bones are dynamic, living things. Too often they get shortchanged and depicted as sedentary I-beams that hold up the soft tissues, but in reality, their cells are just as vivacious as those in any other organ in

———————

*The legend of the gold coin has previously stated that the twenty-dollar gold piece was given to Dixon by his sweetheart, Queenie Bennett. However, historians have begun to question that part of the story. The reasons include the fact that Queenie was only fourteen years old at the start of the Civil War, when Dixon would have needed to leave with the coin in the pocket, and that her family was of modest means. Twenty dollars at that time was equivalent to hundreds of dollars in modern currency. In addition, no written documentation has ever been found confirming that Dixon knew Queenie or the Bennetts.

the body. In a healthy person, the body continually remodels its bones, breaking down aging or unused tissue and replacing it with fresh material where strength is most needed. Osteoblasts construct the new mineral structures but trap themselves inside, where they convert to a new cell type as they become the permanent prisoners of a jail they built.

The building materials come from the most predictable source: our food. Like all known living things, our nonaqueous parts are predominantly carbon, the simple, stable molecule that also comprises diamonds and the charcoal that gets ground up for making black powder. Our carbon comes from the food we eat, which, even though it may have gone through a few intermediate phases as meat, eventually all traces back to plants.

The plants get it by pulling the carbon dioxide from the air, taking it out of gaseous form and turning it into energy and structural bits through the act of photosynthesis. But different plants perform this act differently, optimizing the chemical processes for the region where they live and the temperatures they experience. Maize, for example—usually called corn in America—is best suited for warmer climates, and uses the heat-optimized C4 type of photosynthesis, which unfortunately has no relationship to the famous explosive. Wheat, rye, and barley, hardy crops that enjoy cooler weather, take advantage of the C3 type.

Though it might seem unrelated, photosynthesis, as it turns out, is surprisingly relevant to decaying bones buried inside a historic submarine. The C3 and C4 types of photosynthesis process carbon differently, and therefore the people who eat the plants that use them end up with different proportions of the type thirteen-C carbon isotope inside their bodies. They are, literally, made of what they ate. The surviving bones, even after hundreds or thousands of years, will still contain a legible atomic signature that can tell modern scientists whether they are the product of cooler climates with a lot of wheat, or warmer climates with a lot of corn . . . cooler climates like Europe, or warmer climates like the American South.

The results of the carbon analysis showed that the man at the pilot station and the men at the third, sixth, and last handles along the seven-man crank were from America. The men at the first, second, fourth, and fifth crank handles had all come from Europe. Only two of the eight-man Confederate crew, those at the third and sixth handles, were born natives of secessionist states.

Like the scarred femur at the pilot station, the skulls too proved they could talk. The skull buried in the mud by the fourth crank handle, deep inside the belly of the sub, belonged to one of two crewmen with tiny notches in their front teeth. The small hole in his naked grin was the size and shape of a sewing needle, the result of the teeth being slowly whittled away by the force of clamping down around the tool. Called a tailor's notch, the distinctive missing chunk was unsurprisingly associated with those who sewed: tailors, cobblers, and occasionally sailors who had spent decades stitching sails.

Carbon testing revealed that the man had grown up in Europe, eating plenty of C3 plants. A combination of his estimated age at the time of death, historical documents listing the *Hunley*'s crew, and the process of elimination identified him as J. F. Carlsen. No known first name, no firm explanation of how he ended up in that narrow metal tube. At least, not at that time.

J. F. Carlsen's name popped up uninvited on my computer screen one day, in the most unlikely of places: a message notification from the professional networking site LinkedIn. Normally I delete these emails without thinking, but this one seemed far too tailored to my rather specific interests to be the typical marketing spam. The message was from a man named Adam Jon Kronegh. He was an archivist and a like-minded *Hunley* enthusiast who had tracked me down online, just as I had tracked down Michael Crisafulli of the Vernian Era website when looking for dimensions.

"Hi, I work as an archivist at the National Archives of Denmark and was able to identify the *HL Hunley* crewmember, J. F. Carlsen and his origins," he wrote. With that tantalizing lead in a private message, my unofficial network of fellow rogue, unsanctioned *Hunley* researchers grew a new branch across the Atlantic, all the way to Denmark.

Kronegh, as it turned out, had a bloodhound's nose for tracking old documents. He had spent eight years patiently sifting through page after crumbling, handwritten page, searching for the name of his lost countryman in the tight cursive of the faded texts. His efforts had paid off. He had found listed in the documents one Johan Frederick Carlsen, born April 9, 1841, in the Danish city of Ærøskøbing, located in the crook of the small, L-shaped island of Ærø in the cold waters just north of Germany. Carlsen was listed as a seaman in the 1860 census but disappeared from the official Danish paperwork shortly thereafter. . . . And he was the son of a cobbler.

With that, the skull at the fourth crank was given a first name, and a story. Pleased to meet you, Johan.

Seaman Carlsen had served aboard the *Grethe*, a coal-carrying brig, as one of a crew of eight, and in February 1861, he had stepped off the deck of the brig and walked into the soon-to-be-war-torn city of Charleston, South Carolina. For whatever reason, he decided to stay. The official records of the *Grethe* state that Carlsen "deserted" in Charleston, meaning he chose to leave prior to serving his full expected time on board; however, the word used did not have the deeply negative connotation that today is carried by its English translation. The war started three days after Johan's twentieth birthday.

Carlsen promptly signed up for a new shipboard opportunity, putting to work his skills as an island-born sailor. He took a spot on the privateer *Jefferson Davis*, a black-hulled ship that until recently had persisted in carrying human beings for the illegal slave trade. After her sale she had been rededicated to capturing the crews and cargos of merchant ships. It's possible that the new market for privateers, with its tantalizing offer of lucrative bounties, paid more or offered a better lifestyle than the hard labor of carrying coal with the *Grethe*.

On June 28, with Carlsen aboard, the *Jefferson Davis* eked past the US Navy ships outside Charleston that were beginning to form a nascent blockade, and within seven weeks she had captured or destroyed nine vessels along the Atlantic coast. She inadvertently ended her own orgy of profitable destruction by running aground after a storm in Florida that August. Without a ship to use, sailor Carlsen followed his captain back to Charleston.

It was from the records of the foundered *Jefferson Davis* that genealogists confirmed that Carlsen's name was spelled with an *e*, not an *o*, allowing archaeologist Maria Jacobsen to identify him as a fellow Dane. From there, Kronegh had picked up the trail.

While Carlsen was on board the *Jefferson Davis*, in late July 1861, the Union and Confederates met for the first major conflict since the attack on Fort Sumter. Before this battle, the First Battle of Bull Run, both sides thought the war would be over quickly. Many high-ranking officers and officials even packed lunches and brought their families so they could picnic on a hillside and watch the excitement of the battle unfold. Afterward, the relatively quick Confederate victory had reassured the South. Most thought this initial success in a major battle indicated that the North would give up the entire war fairly readily. It was not yet clear how dramatic the body counts would become for both sides, but with their smaller overall population numbers, the Confederate States nonetheless continued recruiting new soldiers, asking for a voluntary one-year commitment.

After the gory Battle of Shiloh the following April, both sides were struck with the horrific realization that thousands would die. Almost immediately the Confederacy passed the Conscription Act, the first compulsory draft in American history. Soldiers who had previously volunteered would not be released at the end of their single year after all, and other men aged eighteen to thirty-five had to enlist and serve the entire duration of the war . . . with a few key exceptions.

Immigrants were exempt. Men in trade positions crucial to the production of crops and the items used for warfare were exempt, if there was no one to take their place at work. Men who claimed ownership of more than twenty slaves were also automatically exempt from the draft starting that fall. The Confederacy believed that Lincoln's Emancipation Proclamation was part of a deliberate attempt to foment a slave rebellion, so the plantation owners were provided the exemption to stay home and "secure the proper police of the country" against "horrible insurrection" by the slaves.

When the Union instituted a draft, they allowed men to pay a cash fee in lieu of service. However, in both the North and the South, the wealthy with no trade skills could buy their way out of combat by providing a human substitute to take their place. These substitutes were paid by the original draftee, and they were usually immigrants. The practice was so prevalent in the South, with estimates of 50,000 to 150,000 substitutes serving, that it led many to speculate that the government had exempted immigrants from the draft specifically to create a pool of eligible substitutes. The practice of substitution was also allowed beginning October 1861, just after Carlsen's return to Charleston, to provide an escape for the one-year volunteers who no longer wished to serve.

German immigrant Frederick Scheuber signed up as a substitute for wealthy planter Robert Carter, in exchange for $20.83 per month and another $2,500 at the war's end, all to be sent to Scheuber's family. Scheuber, like most immigrants, was exempt from the conscription laws, but he nonetheless became one of many Germans who accepted sums of up to $5,000 in exchange for service. Scheuber died in combat, having lived for less than a year after making the deal. While records indicate that Carter dutifully paid the monthly sums for the duration of

Scheuber's survival, it's unclear if his family ever received the final $2,500.

Johan Carlsen also signed up as a substitute, taking the place of an unknown Southern gentleman. The draftee would have had to accompany Carlsen to the reporting station and wait with him until his substitute was declared suitable. Carlsen would have received a health screening, including careful inspection by a physician, before the military accepted the swap. As a German-speaker, Carlsen was then grouped by language into Wagener's Company, German Artillery Company A, where he eventually reached the rank of corporal. After several years of war, Wagener's men, Carlsen included, found themselves stationed at Fort Moultrie on Sullivan's Island, the final departure point of the *HL Hunley.*

Shortly before the *Hunley*'s final mission, two of the regular submarine crew were unable to continue, possibly because they were called away on other orders. Lieutenant Dixon (or his representative) ventured into the nearby encampments on Sullivan's Island and recruited both Carlsen and a second replacement, who was likely also from the local German-speaking troops. Carlsen was assigned the seat at the fourth crank handle.

The remains of three other European men with German-language last names were recovered from inside the *Hunley*: Becker, Lumpkin, and Miller. Arnold Becker could not be the second recruit because he was a known volunteer from the crew of the CSS *Indian Chief.* Lumpkin, first name known only as "C," is listed alongside three other confirmed *Hunley* crewmen in the pay logbooks titled "'Special Expedition' and Naval Detachment on Special Duty at Charleston, South Carolina." Lumpkin's duty as a special operative started October 1, 1863, or earlier, so he too can be eliminated as the second last-minute addition. The most likely candidate was Miller, at the fifth station along the crank.

Unfortunately, the common nature of Miller's last name makes him difficult to trace. Skilled forensics specialists created a reconstruction of his face, artistically adding skin, a heavy mustache, and dark side-swept hair to the bone structure of the skull excavated from the mud of the *Hunley*. The glassy but somber eyes of the artistic model of his severed head sit in a display case in the Friends of the *Hunley* Museum, staring relentlessly forward under a slightly lined brow.

Miller's skeleton showed that he had lived a lifetime of "harsh physical activity." Despite being only in his early forties, he showed signs of painful arthritis, of bone having grated directly against other bone in spots where the cartilage wore thin. He was found with a pipe and was thought to be a heavy tobacco user. Miller also sported the telltale scars of multiple healed fractures riddling his ribs, legs, and skull. Through his remains his life story is somewhat known, but even with the intimate details that his bones tell of his painful medical history, Miller stays largely anonymous.

The fourth and fifth positions required only cranking, no training or skills. Carlsen and Miller were at positions deep inside the darkness of the sub, far from either conning tower. They would have been some of the last out, if escape became necessary. There may have been a language barrier, but Carlsen and Miller were more than capable of providing the muscle to turn the crank.

Lieutenant Dixon recruited the rest of the crew—Becker, Lumpkin, Collins, Wicks, and Ridgaway—off the decks of the CSS *Indian Chief*. They were already actively serving the Confederate States, and they proved eager to volunteer for the "Special Expedition" duty. Money may have been one motivator for their volunteerism; all except Becker are listed in the official pay records, and they received a lofty $22 to $29 per month, a substantial increase over the $16 to $18 recorded as salary for most of the enlisted crewmen on board the CSS *Chicora*.

The best paid of the men at the crank was Boatswain's Mate James A. Wicks, at \$29 a month. Wicks, a born native of North Carolina, had enrolled in the US Navy as a young man long before the war broke out, then found himself fighting opposite his former neighbors when the Old North State decided to secede. After his Union ship sank off the coast of Virginia, the body-desperate Confederacy offered him the chance to switch sides, and he accepted. However, with him he brought his warm, wool US Navy pea coat, complete with its shiny, decay-resistant, USN insignia–embossed buttons.

The winter leading up to the year 1864 was an exceptionally cold one, even for the soldiers stationed down south in Charleston. Diarists in Charleston made repeated mentions of the relentless ice and sleet. Union soldier Adna Bates, serving on the USS *Canandaigua* as part of the offshore blockade, wrote home to his family numerous letters in the summer of 1864 that were riddled with complaints about the cold the previous winter. He repeatedly requested that they send him his heavy winter coat before the next fall. This cold also extended to the sea, sending the water temperatures below the chilly Charleston average of 50 degrees Fahrenheit for the month of February, cold enough to cause death from hypothermia in less than two hours.

The thin, wrought-iron hull of the *Hunley* would have sucked the heat out of the crew compartment and transferred it all to the endlessly hungry thermal sink of the wintery Atlantic Ocean. Chilly air can more effectively drain away warmth when it is humid because humid air is more conductive than dry air, but wrought iron is over 2,000 times more conductive still. And there is—of course—a scientific way to calculate how quickly that heat would be lost.

If each of the seven men at the crank were working at a strenuous rate, they could be expected to produce about 460 watts per person. The men are generating the energy in the form of heat, whereas a lightbulb consumes energy in the form of electricity—both are measured in watts, a measurement of energy per second.

Each person had 2.5 feet of shoulder space along the length of the crank. This width provides about 0.9 square meters of hull surface area for each cranking man, just along the length of the roughly 15-foot crank, omitting all the surface area of the rest of the 40-foot boat. This 0.9 square meters per laborer is therefore less than the actual amount of wrought iron that is working to transfer out as much heat as possible and sacrifice it forever to the thermal deities of the ocean.

The rate at which *Hunley* drew the heat out of the crew compartment was also a function of the amount of mixing of the air inside as the men cranked furiously along. More mixing means more airflow along the cold hull wall, which means a colder temperature inside, sort of like a lower temperature caused by wind chill. This value is officially known as the "convective heat transfer coefficient" but for the sake of efficiency and everyone's sanity usually gets written simply as h. Inside a refrigerator with the door closed, h is about equal to 10. In applications intentionally designed to maximize the transfer of heat, h can skyrocket up to the range of 100,000. Inside the *Hunley*, which was basically a cylindrical pipe filled with air with a large degree of mixing, I set h equal to a reasonable but moderate estimate of 50.

With these assumptions, and the men working hard without any breaks, the temperature inside the submarine would have settled at about 69 degrees Fahrenheit. A more practical estimate using twice the values for surface area and h calculates a final temperature of under 55 degrees Fahrenheit; this temperature still assumes that the men are cranking nonstop at a strenuous speed.* The air would have been humid

---

* The heat transfer calculations were performed assuming a lumped coefficient for the air and metal hull. The details (for my fellow nerds) were: K=0.027 W/m*K for moist air, K=59 W/m*K for wrought iron. Use of h=50 was mathematically determined by the relationship between Nu and Re. For turbulent flows, Nu can be expected to be ~1,000, which leads to a calculation of h=45 for λ=0.027 and L=0.6 m. However, it could be argued that the men in the hull are more comparable to turbulent flow inside a pipe, which would justify a much higher h-value and therefore calculate colder temperatures.

and therefore felt even colder, filled with not only the evaporated water from the bilge and ballast tanks but also the moisture produced by the lungs of the men as they exhaled. Every time the men leaned against the hull in the cramped quarters of the chilly, humid boat to take a short rest, they would have been pressed against the water-temperature, frigid metal.

When James Wicks climbed into the metal tube for the last time—leaving behind a wife and four children—to take his place at the sixth crank handle next to Miller, he wrapped himself in his old Union Navy pea coat.

The conditions inside the submarine may have been unpleasant, but the conditions in Charleston itself were calamitous. Charleston was the site of the first shots of the war, it was where the Southern leadership first voted to secede, and it was one of the last major Southern cities still standing by 1863. The city of Charleston and its harbor therefore were favored targets upon which the Union commanders focused their resentment, ire, and weaponry. Gen. Quincy Adams Gillmore, in particular, was determined to bring the city, including its civilians, to its knees.

Deciding that its geography made it resistant to an assault by land, the Union instead focused on attacking Charleston by sea, using a ring of blockade ships to hammer the city nightly with whatever weaponry they could find. The offshore Fort Sumter, already the recipient of thousands of shells, was "battered and crumbled almost to shapelessness" by the onslaught. Gillmore, once he became weary of chiseling away at Sumter, decided to increase his shelling range farther into downtown by building a platform for weaponry in the middle of the swamp near the harbor entrance. His engineers finished the construction while dodging long-range fire from Confederate weapons, and Gillmore placed massive guns at this battery, dubbed with the dark but affectionate moniker "Swamp Angel."

It was rumored that Gillmore had prepared not just regular shells but also shells filled with Greek fire, a chemical mixture designed to explode over a target and spread a destructive burn that would amplify the mayhem of the shelling. And in the fall of 1863, he sent an ominous message: Evacuate Fort Sumter, or we fire. But he never physically signed the message, so the letter was sent back without being delivered to the Confederate commanding officers. Gillmore's terms were therefore never met, and the citizens were never warned of what was about to come.

The city was in rough condition even before the bombings began. About a third of the downtown had been destroyed by a fire at the start of the war, crumbling many of the massive buildings to the ground at a time when there were no resources to repair them. The fire damage was then augmented by the war itself, when an estimated 13,000 shells rained down on the town and surrounding area.

After the first rounds of shelling in late 1863, some Union troops claimed they could hear the bells and sirens of Charleston's fire department hard at work, struggling to control the unruly flames.

Those who could evacuate did. "They like the rest of us are refugees," wrote young Artha Wescoat of his extended family members, all of whom had scattered from Charleston. Even after evacuation, the interminable salvos were audible from the relative safety of areas miles away, and the former Charlestonians listened daily to their homes being hewn to the ground.

"Early this morning the whole village was awakened by the thunder of distant artillery, and we knew by the quick reports that there was hot fighting going on around Charleston."

"We can hear the roar of the artillery all day."

"The enemies gun [*sic*] are within the last half hour again roaring."

One resident wrote from inside the city with an undertone of fatigue and resignation, "The rapidity of the cannonade while I write has decreased, but the discharges are deafening at times."

Lt. George Dixon himself stated that by February he had not been out of the range of Union shells, not even for a moment, for more than six weeks. And for those who decided to stay, the effects of the blockade too were wreaking havoc. Food supplies were dwindling, and letters out contained complaints that even the supplies of paper for letters were running low. A Charlestonian described that "Sundays are as plenty as there are days in the week now; all of our stores are fast closing, their proprietors following the patriotic example of our Bank, and 'skedaddling' with their property to some imaginary place of security."

The more resourceful citizens of the South tried to support the war effort by optimistically taking advantage of whatever they still had, rebuilding favorite recipes so that they used minimal ingredients and avoiding the perishables that would be in scarce supply. Recipes emerged for custard without eggs or milk, and apple pie that needed no apples.

The people of Charleston built new forts and defenses, often tasking slaves by the thousand with the hard labor of helping to erect the defenses to protect the slave owners who held them captive.

———

For some Charlestonians, innovations in naval warfare were their last hope to end the shelling. With each new boat, the citizens became hopeful: "The two gun boats now building here, when completed will be able to raise the blockade," one resident wrote. But so far, all of the innovations had failed.

Lieutenant Dixon heard the complaints of the citizens. Like the rest of the soldiers and sailors on both sides, he saw how his "splendid crew of men" was being forced to endure difficult conditions in the

Charleston, South Carolina, after the war.

pursuit of victory. The gold fillings in his teeth and the fancy silver
suspender clasps he would wear on his last mission prove he had been
raised in a life of relative opulence, but now he too was slowly emaciating on meager rations, mostly corn and rice mush, with rarely any meat.
He had high hopes for the infernal machine he commanded, but he was
waiting for the right time to take the submarine out, waiting for the seas
to be smooth enough for an effective attack that could break the ranks
of his enemy. The exasperation of the young officer is evident in a letter
he wrote to a friend just seventeen days before his death in the narrow
metal coffin of the *Hunley*:

> *But there is one thing very evident and that is to catch the At-*
> *lantic Ocean smooth during the winter months is considerable of*
> *an undertaking and one that I never wish to undertake again.*
> *Especially when all parties interested at sitting at home and*
> *wondering and criticizing all of my actions and saying why*

don't he do something. If I have not done any thing "God Knows"
it is not because I have not worked hard enough to do something.
And I shall keep trying until I do something.

Dixon's determined closing lines would also become the mantra for
my blast experiments.

CHAPTER 8

PRESSURE TRACE

My adviser had a saying: You have to believe that Sisyphus was happy. It was a reference to the grind of research— weeks of preparation, building anticipation, and careful execution—that often ended in failure.

—Justin Chen, *Coming to Terms with Six Years in Science: Obsession, Isolation, and Moments of Wonder*

The rubbery tentacles of my bundle of cables stretched down the empty hallway of the Duke blast test building. At the end, the underwater blast gauges were still connected and lying on the floor like the flaccid limbs of a beached giant squid. I sat on the cold concrete staring at them, willing them to speak to me. They stayed stubbornly quiet. They had stayed stubbornly quiet through the second day of testing too, consistently giving me nonsensical readings that were nothing more than hushed, jagged burps of noise.

The unseasonably good weather had left us after the first day, and our spectators with it. My mother had watched from a hiding place, protected by a heated seat inside her car as Luke and I had crouched outside over the perplexing gauges. My dad had stayed huddled in his folding chair across the pond, buried in his coat like a bird trying to compress itself into the smallest, warmest ball possible.

Luke and I had taken apart and checked each connection for water, every time finding nothing. We had carefully painted each junction with a waterproof rubber coating anyway, just in case. They had drip-dried inside the makeshift shelter of a cardboard box that the day before held a bulk-sized stash of snack foods, now dumped unceremoniously in the trunk of my car. I had held my coat open to shield them from the wind that blew unimpeded across the fields, to keep them from clanging together as they dried, and at one point I had watched as the vicious wind blew a Phillips-head screwdriver across the wood planking of the pier. Oklahoma had nothing on Pitt Farm in the early spring.

And still, despite all the love and attention, the highest pressure that the gauges had reported was barely a whisper. Explosions make pressure waves; I was still fairly sure of it. But in science, if you didn't measure it, it didn't happen.

Back in the lab, the gauges perversely insisted upon working flawlessly every time. They measured each and every pressure loudly and clearly, in sharp contrast to the way they had performed for me in the field.

I rebuilt my assembly inside the lab exactly as I had used it at Pitt Farm. I set the generator up outside and routed the cables in through the doors; nothing was connected to the power grid, just as it had operated at the pond. I sat, psychically willing, mentally screaming at the gauges to fail for me with each systematic alteration of every single element of the setup so that I could finally replicate and thereby explain their mysterious lack of performance. I stayed up until three in the morning laser-cutting more and more Mylar membranes to equip the hungry driver of the shock tube, and when nobody else was free to help with the tests I started dragging Nick to the lab with me to serve as my mandatory "second person for safety" in case of unforeseen testing disasters.

Nothing replicated the failure. The navy-built gauges staunchly refused to give up the secret. Now they worked with expected military precision for every single test.

As I sat on the hard floor, wrapped in a down coat with my hands still stiff from the cold, I absentmindedly flicked one gauge with a pen, as I had been taught by navy gauge guru Kent Rye. With each flick, a perfect pressure spike appeared on the laptop screen. Flick. Spike. Flick. Spike. Frustratingly perfect.

I had only one idea left. It involved the long cables underwater. I wasn't sure it would work. And it would have sounded crazy to anyone who was not an engineer.

Stretching thousands of kilometers underwater, the first transatlantic telegraph cable was completed in 1858, years before Hunley, McClintock, and Watson began their mechanical underwater experiments. It allowed communication between Newfoundland and Ireland in seconds rather than weeks, and it signaled a mammoth technological leap forward for humanity.

Laying the cable down through the hostile, turbulent ocean and splicing the various behemoth sections together to complete the connection was a historic feat of engineering. It spanned decades, consumed uncounted thousands (if not millions) of hours of labor, and required the development of dozens of radical engineering and scientific innovations. Engineers had to design ways to deal with waves, with weather, with the crushing pressures of the ocean depths, and with the trials of coordinating the meeting of two boats in the middle of the Atlantic long before the invention of the radio.

They also had to deal with the fact that cables, especially underwater cables, tend to bleed. The lifeblood of a conventional cable is electricity. Electrons travel down the metal wire inside the cable's protective coating, tumbling from a higher-energy state at the source end to a lower-energy state at the far side, and creating an electrical current along the line with their motion. But the cables can bleed electrons. Not as human beings bleed, through a wound or a fissure; rather, as a slow and usually negligible ooze that occurs down the entire length of the cable. The electrons strongly prefer to travel neatly down the highly conductive metal, but nonetheless some deviants manage to seep through the walls of the less-conductive insulation.

Most of the time, this ooze is so minuscule that it can be ignored. But if the cable is long enough, or placed in a highly conductive material like water, or in a cold enough environment, then the seepage of electrons can make a difference. As a result, by the time an electrical signal reaches its goal, that signal is dramatically reduced in magnitude. The voltages, which started out large, get reduced to almost nothing by the time they reach the other end of the line. In my case, this would result in measurements of abnormally tiny pressures.

The transatlantic cable, thousands of kilometers long, buried deep under cold, highly conductive salt water, oozed so substantially that it required the development of new methods of protection against the bleed. The cable was eventually insulated by painting it with layer upon layer of gutta-percha, which is essentially a tree sap that dries into a sort of rubber and is sometimes referred to as "natural latex." The ingenious engineers on the project didn't leave the insulation to chance either; they developed an equation and they mathematically modeled the seepage. They called it the cable equation.

Sitting splayed out near the blue tendrils of my dead pressure-gauge squid, I scribbled my way through the cable equation. When my cables were submerged, with meters upon meters of looping gauge lines drooping just beneath the surface of the frigid pond, I concluded that yes . . . these cables very well could be bleeding out a substantial portion of the pressure signal.*

---

*The cable equation was critical to the neuroscience research of Alan Hodgkin and Andrew Huxley, for which they were awarded the Nobel Prize. The comparison to a squid is not accidental, as they used squid axons in their efforts to model how electrical signals travel down nerves. Today, the cable equation is used in studies of every aspect of the nervous system, ranging from Alzheimer's to spinal-cord injuries.

In the 1800s, engineers painted their cables with gutta-percha. But in 2016, I had the advantage of Styrofoam. Using my favorite long black pieces of foam pipe insulation from the hardware store—once again it didn't matter what diameter, but I will never again say that out loud—I bundled the cables tightly inside and wrapped them generously in bandages of heavy waterproof tape.

———

The thick, black foam sausage floated in a line from the pier to the center of Pitt Pond. We had already failed twice, still measuring almost nothing, and we had pulled the model boat out of the water as a result. I had dubbed her the CSS *Tiny* one late night at the lab, and stenciled the moniker onto her stern. She was sitting back on the shore this time, and the goal of this experiment was simply to measure the waveform from the black powder charge that was floating in the pond water, suspended from a chunk of foam pool noodle.

Brad and Luke huddled on towels in the grass while I crouched at the end of the pier, staring at my equipment. Nick sat with them, having been relieved of his assignment pulling the boat back and forth from the folding chair across the pond.

"THREE!" Brad yelled. "TWO! . . . ONE!" He depressed the second button on his setup box to set off the charge. When I saw the plume, I smacked the key to manually trigger the data recording and held my breath as the acquisition box whirred away, processing numbers.

The waveform on the screen was small. Bigger than before . . . but still far, far smaller than I expected. But this time it was smooth! The wave had a beautiful shape, a clean rise, and a visible decay. Gone were the jagged and unpredictable spasms of signal noise that I had previously measured. It still didn't seem correct, but it was progress.

Brad, Luke, Nick, and I sat together in the grass on the shore to regroup and think through our next steps. Luke snacked on a bag of Cheetos he had fished out of my trunk.

"What if it's the charges?" Brad suggested quietly. "The plumes have been smaller than I expected." I nodded. He had to be right. It made sense. We had carefully eliminated all the other variables.

We had placed the gauges in the water first this time, and I had swum out to tap them, both before and after. They had worked; we were cleanly sending signals from Newfoundland to Ireland.

"You know, I talked to one of the explosives agents at the ATF," he continued, "and he said he wouldn't technically classify our science tubes as bombs if he found them at a crime scene. They would be too weakly confined to do real damage."

I turned my head to look at Brad, slowly. Standing up, I walked toward the water, dropping my towel and heavy coat, and kicking off my flip-flops on the way. I waded until the freezing water reached my hips, then began to swim. The bottom of the pond was smooth; my bribed-with-chicken friends and I had verified it. It was man-made, and mostly free of other debris. I took a breath, squeezed my eyes shut, and inverted, hitting the shallow, even bottom with my hands after one swift kick. Kicking to stay submerged, my fingertips ran over the smooth, soft muck until, eventually, they found what they had been groping for: the jagged edge of a piece of copper. Surfacing, sucking in fresh breath to combat the rising levels of CO_2 burning in my blood, I hurled the metal onto the end of the pier and flipped back down for another dive.

Like the ribbons of peeled-back copper attached to the spar of the *Hunley*, we could tell what happened to our charges based on their remains. And shard after shard, every piece of copper I recovered told the same story. Their bodies had bloomed open cleanly along their seams, always starting on one side, more than likely the side of the charge that held the triggering squib.

Our charges were peeling open from one side before the black powder had fully deflagrated, so at least some of the moisture-sensitive powder was getting wet before it could burn and contribute to the explosion. Furthermore, we hadn't been measuring the pressure created by black powder ripping open sheets of solid copper. We had been measuring the pressure created by black powder fracturing a much-weaker seam.

Everything always seems so obvious once you finally learn the answer. The confinement-sensitive black powder was breaking open the charges at their weakest point, like a chain with a bad link. The pressures from the slow-burning deflagrating explosive, at least from the fraction of powder that even had a chance to burn, were being released before they could grow to any kind of furor. We were building charges one measly step stronger than sprinkling the powder on the open ground and letting it burn harmlessly.

Former army man Luke nudged the shiny pile of shrapnel gently with his toe, popping another Cheeto into his mouth before he spoke up.

"How far do you think we are from the nearest hardware store?" he asked, licking fluorescent orange dust off his thumb. "I know some tricks from Iraq."

This book is not a bomb-making manual. Even though much of the information can already be found online, Brad, Luke, and I have all agreed that we will never be an active part of its dissemination. Just like I omitted or was vague about some key steps in the manufacture of black powder, so too will I leave out the most effective methods for building weapons of destruction.

Instead, because I am a gear head, I choose to describe our "science tubes" as cars. The *Hunley* packed a Ferrari. Its relatively thick-walled copper torpedo was a stock Ferrari, one that still had to obey emissions laws and street-driving regulations, but a Ferrari nonetheless. Our sad little tubes, so willing to split open and vomit out their partially burned contents, did not even merit car metaphor status. They were ancient, neglected Schwinn bicycles, with flat tires and rusty chains. To make this project work, our test team needed to upgrade its ride.

Luke and I jumped in my car, all too comfortable with the idea of walking into a reputable place of business smelling like runoff water and algae. Farmer Pitt pointed us toward a local hardware store, one much closer than any of the major chains that would show up on our phones, and we took off.

The hardware store had one visible room, and only a few feet inward from the door was a broad, high counter that blocked access to the rest of the building. On the left was a pegboard with what seemed to be the most commonly purchased items: an assortment of rolls of different types of tapes and the equipment most often needed for fishing. As we entered, a large, well-cared-for German shepherd with a jet-black face and a glossy coat lifted his head from his dog bed behind the counter and let out a single authoritative *woof.*

The proprietor of the shop appeared in response, a gray-haired North Carolina native. He asked us for our list, then disappeared into the back of the store. The shepherd stared at us alertly the whole time he was gone, never once shifting a muscle, never once breaking eye contact. The dog was the real owner of the store. We paid for our bag of supplies with cash, made sure we were extra polite to the human being who fed the owner, and then went back to the pond.

The Confederates too went through multiple design iterations when crafting their torpedoes. And naturally, it was "bomb brother" Gabriel Rains who led the charge for them, pun intended. He became the master of tinkering to optimize each design for its purpose, balancing the needs of buoyancy, method of placement, and trigger design to maximize both reliability and destructive potential. Living as the Charlestonians were, with restricted supplies, Rains and his stable of roughly thirty-five torpedo-makers became masters of repurposing, often retooling wooden beer barrels, copper turpentine stills, and even tin soda-water fountains to build a potpourri of weapons for the defense of Charleston Harbor.

Everyday wooden barrels were converted into silent warriors that hid just beneath the surface of the water, floating on long lines connected to anchors, waiting for the keel of an unsuspecting Union vessel to scrape over them. The metal-banded wood structures provided positive buoyancy, ensuring they would stretch to the end of their tethers. Rains knew that to maximize destruction, the torpedo should be just below but in direct contact with the bottom of the target's hull.

The experimenters even took advantage of repurposed chunks of one of the aborted transatlantic cables, having somehow squirreled it down south before the war. It was used to run long lines out to an electrically triggered torpedo 2 miles from shore so that a spotter could initiate the explosion at the exact right moment to destroy a ship. But the cabling proved an unreliable method, and Rains warned against that tactic in the future. It may have failed because the cable was damaged or because it was from an earlier generation of insulation attempts, but for whatever reason the electrical signal bled out into the water and was too weak to trigger the bomb when the button was pushed. In Rains's words, the voltage "had passed through the gutta percha coating rather than go the distance required."

Rains and his crew also built some explosive charges with casings of iron, similar to the land mines he was churning out by the thousands, some of which had 2-inch-thick walls. But these proved too heavy to be practical in water, requiring an air space above the powder inside to make them float. The blast experts of the time, aware of the needs of confinement, knew this would result in less power: "When powder was burned in a space occupied by itself it gave a pressure four times as great as when burned in double its own space."

Tin torpedoes were lighter than iron but stronger than wood, good for deeper immersion, and careful attention was paid to their construction in order to resist the crushing pressures of water. The conical shape and rounded ends of the most common torpedo designs were important, claimed Rains, and even though materials were scarce, "the thicker the tin the better to resist the pressure of water."

The same was true of the thickness of copper torpedoes. And copper had the distinct advantage of being resistant to marine growth. Barnacles and sea life find it difficult to penetrate to create a foothold, and copper is still frequently utilized as a component in modern paints and coatings for the underbellies of ships. Rains was aware of this material property and used copper for torpedoes that were going to spend long periods of time underwater, so that marine growth would not interfere with the sensitivity of their triggers.

Rains made no effort to hide his distaste for the torpedo boats. He famously refused to be involved with them. He seemed tired of seeing new but always-unsuccessful attempts, writing that he had watched ambitious men build a "thousand and one" failed designs, and referring to submarines in general as "abortions of inventive genius."

The boats, he thought, often suffered from one fatal flaw: "much danger from their proximity of destructiveness viz the exploding torpedoes." The spars were suicide, he was convinced, and the only way to use a torpedo boat "safely is by detached torpedoes."

To cause structural damage to an enemy ship, he was repeatedly insistent that the torpedo had to be immediately below and in direct contact with the hull; off by a few feet, and he asserted it was unlikely to cause any damage at all. In the detailed handwritten textbook he left behind to document his knowledge, he wrote clearly that this insistence on direct contact was "the secret of my great success with torpedoes," and then he underlined the words. However, for submarines to be safe, he stated that they should be not just a few feet away from their torpedoes, but a few dozen feet away. Rains believed the spars needed to be much longer than the short poles planned for use by the submarine crews, a minimum of 40 or 50 feet long to ensure safety.

Trying to advocate for submarine safety, Rains performed careful calculations on the shape and type of charge that could be attached to such a long spar without being too positively buoyant and pulling the bow of the boat upward, or too negatively buoyant and pulling it down. Despite the fact that he was the Confederacy's premier expert on underwater explosions, despite the fact that he was the one responsible for peppering Charleston Harbor with 123 infernal torpedoes, his ideas were rejected. The *Hunley* was fitted with a 16-foot spar, less than half of Rains's minimum recommended length.

It is tempting to read Rains's concerns about the spars and eagerly assume he was agreeing with the theory that the blast propagated through the hull. Unfortunately, Rains did not write down why he was concerned. There are many things to be concerned about when a person is too close to a bomb, and blast transmission is only one of them. Therefore, while his statements are consistent with the theory of blast transmission, from the perspective of an objective scientist it is impossible to conclude exactly why he so feared the use of spar torpedoes. Again . . . scientists are the reason that gravity is only a theory.

The *Hunley* received a thick-walled copper torpedo. Metal so that the torpedo would not be too positively buoyant. Iron was avoided so the powder could be packed tightly. Copper to resist marine growth. Thick metal walls with robustly sealed seams to resist the crushing pressures and water intrusion of ocean life. A torpedo designed to survive until the final journey, but also, accidentally, a torpedo designed to maximize the ripples of pressure that it would send backward through the salty ocean toward the belly of her carrier.

O ur trip to the hardware store yielded some glorious pressure traces. We very, very safely and carefully worked our way through Luke's bag of tricks, starting out small with the modifications that converted our busted-bicycle charges into rusty 1980s Yugos, and working our way up slowly to the modifications that gave us base-model, four-cylinder, harshly used Mustangs with scratched-up plastic wheel covers.

With each charge modification, the pressures in the water increased. And the rise time, that crucial measurement of the amount of time that it took to get to that maximum pressure, shortened. We watched the pressure waves develop one step at a time from harmless, low-amplitude, gently sloping hills into aggressively steep, lethal mountains. We were proving what had already been reported in dozens if not hundreds of academic papers on black powder: Confinement works. But this time, it was our experiment. We made it work. We had finally fixed this part of our experimental setup.

We had to wait almost another month before we could put the boat back in the water with our new-and-improved charges. We had burned all the daylight allotted to Pitt Pond for that day, and Brad had a long line of heroin dealers that he needed to chase before he could come back to volunteer more of his time.

D uring the break between test days Nick insisted that he and I have a rare night out, to celebrate my upcoming birthday. We showered off the pond smell and put on clean clothes. I mustered the energy for makeup and jewelry. We ate expensive steak. He suggested a beer to round out the night, and we wound up at the local brewery where we had first met. Our friends were there, a surprise, and we laughed together over rich chocolate birthday cake. Nick stood to make a speech.

He kneeled. He had a ring. I cried. My strongest memory of any of the words spoken is the "HOLY SHIT!" yelled in surprise by the lab mate seated next to where I stood. We were happy, and our shocked friends snapped pictures of our tear-streaked smiles.

The next day, my birthday, I took a day off work. We sat together on a bench in the warm sunshine. An arm close around my shoulders, Nick explained happily that he had been thinking about this for a while. He had picked now to show me that he was with me through anything. Through fourteen-hour or longer workdays with uncertain access to food. Through hundreds of workdays straight with no breaks. Through hearing a noise at three or four a.m. to come out and find me in the family room, sitting on the floor, cloaked in blankets, hunched over my laptop. He had already ordered me an inexpensive rubber ring, a thin purple band of silicone that I could wear in the pond. I smiled and said thank you. It was thoughtful, and he meant it with love.

Graduate school is notorious for killing relationships; he was a good man, and it had somehow strengthened ours. But inwardly I cringed, mortified and shredded by how thoroughly this soul-consuming project had crept its tendrils into even the most private features of my life.

By the time we could resume testing we were well into June. The South had remembered it was supposed to be a hot climate, and the weather finally agreed with spending all day wet and unsheltered.

I optimistically put the CSS *Tiny* back in the pond at Pitt Farm when we finally returned, complete with a modified charge. Nick, taking the station across the lake, hauled it into the center of the water. Just beforehand, Luke and I tested it as we always did, by giving it a good solid *thwack* with a rubber mallet, square on the bow near the internal pressure gauge. I watched the squiggly line of the gauge jump in response.

Brad gave his countdown as usual. I saw the plume of water first, then felt the wood of the little pier shudder beneath my feet in response, before hearing the explosive rumble last of all. I listened to the data acquisition box whir as it processed.

The pressure wave in the water was beautiful, exactly as predicted. And this time, there was a small, jagged jump on the pressure gauge inside the boat. It didn't look like a normal blast wave. It lasted less than a millisecond, a fraction of a moment. It was barely there. The same nearly negligible squiggle kept happening over and over again, with every test. After the charge modifications, the plumes of water were much larger, more consistent with what I had been expecting. The in-water pressures were finally making more sense. My entire theory might be wrong. Or . . . maybe my setup was still wrong?

I offered to drive back from Pitt Farm so that Nick could nap after the long day of helping me, but he was atypically insistent on taking the wheel. As I settled into the passenger seat of his black Jeep, cocooned in dry towels and prepared for a cozy ride home, he shoved his cell phone toward me.

"Call your mom," he insisted.

"Why?" I was confused. I wanted to relax a minute first, and we had a long drive back.

"I don't know. She said to make sure I drove and to have you call her right away." He looked concerned. All of the alarms simultaneously sounded in my head.

When she picked up, I could hear the tears in her hello. I could hear her stammered breath as she struggled to find her next word, but through the uneven silence I could already guess what happened. My mother does not cry easily.

"Did Grandma die?"

"Yeah," she responded slowly. Then, immediately, with the concern of a mother: "You're not driving, are you? I told Nick not to let you drive because I knew you would be upset." She had known it was a test day, but she hadn't wanted to distract me from my experiment. My father was out of town. She had spent the day at home, sitting alone in the empty house, waiting for me to finish so I could call.

Nick and I spent the rest of the drive back in silence. My grandmother had been a constant in my life, an unwaveringly warm and happy presence. An immigrant from northern Italy, she had lovingly taught me the best parts of that half of my heritage, pointing out buildings around Detroit that had terrazzo floors laid by my cousins—every relative is a cousin when you're Italian—and showing me how to hand-shape fluffy gnocchi with perfect ridges.

When we pulled into the crunchy gravel drive at Duke, though, the equipment still had to take priority. There was no time for emotion until later. These tools, now dirty and sopping wet, were my only engines to keep moving forward toward graduation. Before I could go home and pack to leave for the funeral, Nick and I had to sit on the grimy linoleum of the Duke blast test building and carefully hand-dry then lay out every gauge, tool, and cable.

———

The long trips to Pitt Farm were becoming a problem. Each morning began with loading at least two vehicles, an hour-and-a-half drive, then unpacking and setting up the roughly 600 pounds of equipment. It cut into the day. I needed to be able to complete more testing, and faster, to try to work out the rest of the kinks in my setup. I wanted to find a location on campus where I could set up and use a shock tube underwater to execute more trials rapid-fire, to blast my scale model repeatedly but without investing the time necessary to safely and properly use live explosives.

When I returned to campus, I found myself staring across a featureless wood-veneer desk at the second man I needed to give me access to a body of water, just like Bert Pitt before him.

Darin Smith looked back at me. He worked on campus at Duke's Chilled Water Plant 2, or CHWP2 to those in the know, a facility that accomplishes a surprising amount more than its mundane name reveals. Duke's campus hosts a picturesque reclaimed water pond that fills with rain runoff from around campus, complete with carefully planned plant life and well-manicured walking trails. I had been eyeballing it for weeks, hopeful that Duke would let me put my shock-tube driver and boat in there among their fancy wooden bridges and piers.

The pond was not just decorative; its water was the source of cool air for a substantial part of campus, and the plant where Darin resided— this is not a joke—turned the pond water into air-conditioning using a massive, glittering indoor waterfall. The Willy Wonka jokes practically wrote themselves. Luckily, Darin turned out to be just as amazing as his facility.

"This is awesome," he said. "I need you to write me up a one-page explanation of what you want to do that I can take to my bosses. I can't promise you anything yet. But I think they should be all right with it. . . . Leave out the word 'explosion.'"

The powers-that-be acquiesced. They had two conditions. The first was that life jackets must be worn at all times by personnel swimming in the deep, opaque water. The second was a noise test: setting off a shock tube in the water to measure the decibels heard in the air. They wanted assurance that the sound levels would be safe. The tank tests and blasts at Pitt Farm had been relatively muted, so I eagerly agreed.

I built a metal frame to hold the shock tube in place, and my plan was to sink it in the pond and use the noise test as a trial run to see how well the frame braced the shock tube. A small gaggle came to witness the excitement. The project had apparently generated some buzz, which, combined with the gorgeous sunny weather, meant that a crowd of roughly eight guys had wandered down to the pond to stare at me while I struggled to get this experimental setup to work perfectly on the very first try. One of the lab's undergrads, Matt Udelhofen, had volunteered to sacrifice himself and jump into the murky pond water with me.

The moment I took my first small step into the water I knew Matt and I were in trouble. The toe of my neoprene boot plunged through the deceptively solid-looking pond bottom like an arrow, and with a pathetic squelch, first my foot and then my entire calf got swallowed by the spongy, greedy mud. I watched Matt struggle futilely beside me while I also continued to sink, my legs soon jailed in place by mud shackles, both of us hunching over to avoid being buried above the waist. The life jackets mandated by Duke Safety saved us, and painfully we forward-clawed our way through the putrescent green-filmed molasses until we reached water deep enough to flip on our backs, strap on fins, and kick while keeping clear of the mire. The group watched our comic flail from start to finish while standing on the dry, clean perch of a wooden platform.

The metal frame would—in theory—sit on the bottom of the pond, allowing me to lower the shock tube down onto it with ropes for each test. Since I could not see through the water, I could then set off the shock-tube driver with reasonable certainty that the frame had kept the driver in the correct location. I had given it a broad base on long struts, anticipating some degree of mud, but in this watery sludge not even the most well-designed base would keep it from sinking. Matt and I used an air-filled float to keep it at the surface until we moved it into position.

The frame, as predicted, plummeted unceremoniously with nothing more than a sad burble the moment we let it loose from our hands. With my feet, I could reach down and feel the top few aluminum bars protruding helplessly out of their muddy grave, like the stubbornly upright rigging of a dying shipwreck. I would pull it out eventually at a later date, dangling from the underside of the wooden bridge that marked its gravesite and hooking it with my feet to help the float heave it free from the mud, but for now it was lost.

While we swam, the fish of the Duke pond began to make their presence known for the first time. The introductory nibbles seemed innocuous, but those cautious pioneering fish summoned a swarm of their more aggressive brethren, and soon they tried to consume Matt and me. While struggling with the frame we could not stop moving, or we would risk losing our legs to the bass. I tried not to think about how they coincidentally shared a name with my adviser, Dale Bass.

Matt and I finally gave up. We crawled our way back out of the ooze, abandoning the buried metal frame to the mud gods. We simply dropped the shock-tube driver into the water on a rope and set off the blast. It swung wildly, in a way that would not work for the actual testing, but we were able to get a noise measurement. As the thoroughly entertained but amiable crowd removed their earplugs and took their hands off their ears, the man holding the sound gauge started chuckling. The sound from the blast, he explained, had been three decibels *quieter* than the rumble of a bus that passed by the pond moments before.

The frame may have been lost, but we got approval to conduct the tests. Overall, it was a victory. Matt and I scraped off as much of the greenish-gray mud as we could and, squelching in our neoprene boots with every step, walked triumphantly back to the lab.

The torpedo of the *Hunley* too was surprisingly quiet. "There was no sharp report," stated one USS *Housatonic* crewman of the blast that sank his ship, with another saying, "I heard a report, not very loud, a low stunning crash, a smothered sound." A third crewman, presumably belowdecks, only learned of the explosion when he noticed the rising water sloshing around his ankles.

The interface between the water and the air provides an efficient reflecting surface. Meaning, when the underwater blast wave reaches the surface and hits the air, much of the wave gets reflected back down. The amount transmitted into the air above is therefore much smaller than the amount that was traveling through the water, and as a result the sound heard in the air is surprisingly quiet. The waves can travel for miles underwater, but once they are transmitted into the air they are deadened, muffled by the interface.

We began testing at the reclaimed water pond immediately. I decided to turn the mud into an advantage, and built wooden rails to hold the shock tube in place. At their top ends, the long, almost-vertical rails were braced against the footbridge, where we scattered our test equipment. The bottom ends were sunk deep into the muck that had so strongly encased my legs. They held firm. We could stand on the footbridge and slowly lower the driver down the rails like they were a miniature slide.

The shock tube performed beautifully. The pressure would build up behind the Mylar membranes until they ruptured, creating a sharp boundary between the ambient-pressure water and the high-pressure helium. That boundary propagated outward, pushed by the high-pressure gas, and developed into a shock wave in the water. The driver consistently sent shock wave after perfect, infinitely sharp shock wave into the water and toward the CSS *Tiny*. We could use this setup to figure out what was wrong, why my setup still didn't seem to be working, and then head back to Pitt Farm to repeat the feat with black powder.

After each blast, two undergraduates would haul the heavy driver out of the pond on ropes, remove the bolts with an impact wrench powered by a generator, change out the Mylar membranes, and slide it back smoothly down the wooden rails. The proximity to campus meant that more undergraduates were available to help, and they soon became my soft-spoken saviors. Undergraduates have often been the unsung heroes of science.

And yet, the blasts resulted in nothing but a slight jiggle inside the boat, no matter how I tried the configuration. Each time we would test the gauges by hitting the boat's bow with a mallet, and each time the gauges would work fine beforehand but fail during the test.

I was open to the idea that my theory was wrong, but the readings still didn't make sense. Some degree of pressure transmission through the hull was almost inevitable. Even if the magnitudes were too small to be lethal, and the data didn't support the theory, the internal gauges still should have been measuring pressures *of some kind* that had resulted from the shock waves in the water. Their relative silence told me they weren't yet working as they should.

Slowly, the undergrads began to avoid me in the hallway, rationally more eager to help with projects that left them inside air-conditioning. A small, dedicated team of them became my crutches.

It was a sobering reminder that I wasn't alone in the lab. Other students needed their help too. Each of us got consumed by the pursuit of data. My project wasn't atypical. I wasn't especially beleaguered. This was normal for graduate school.

Years earlier, another student had also been an inadvertent messenger of this same fact. I was spending a lot of time filling air tanks and generally relaxing at a dive shop near Pasadena, California, between my trips to the hyperbaric chamber on Catalina Island. One day at the shop, a PhD student from Caltech had wandered in, looking for help. He wanted water samples from near the underwater bases of the famous tufa towers in Mono Lake in Northern California, and he had concluded that the only way to get them was to jump in. He came to the shop pleading for a dive buddy, asking for someone to accompany him down into the depths of the salty lake where periodic jets of less-dense freshwater would randomly mess with a diver's buoyancy, down near the source of the jets where the water had such a chemically basic pH level that he expected it to burn. We had all declined.

A few days later he came back to return his rental gear. He had gone by himself, breaking the cardinal diving-safety rule of "never dive alone" because he decided he needed the data more than he needed safety. Painful-looking chemical burns formed extensive leopard spots over his face, neck, arms, and hands. But he had gotten his samples. He was happy.

Each time I walked down the now-trampled slope into the pond, I thought of that student. My friends and I had been baffled by his choice at that time, but now I understood him, even though I had long forgotten his name. My DoD-funded scholarship program required that I graduate in five years flat, even though the biomedical engineering PhD program average was roughly six years, and I was unaware of any student who had ever graduated from my lab in less than seven. The scholarship had granted me a few months' extra grace period, but if I couldn't get these gauges to work properly, and soon, I would be expelled from the scholarship program and forced to repay my tuition and salary from the past five years.*

I didn't need my theory to be correct. I could publish the negative results—an "I had a theory, but here's how I proved myself wrong" paper—and still graduate. But I needed to get the test setup working, to get some valid data, before I could solidly declare that I was wrong and write it up as a dissertation. I still thought the theory was plausible, but much more than I wanted to be right, I wanted to be finished, to

---

*This is a feature of the DoD SMART Program that is not found in any other graduate school scholarship, as far as I am aware.

have a final answer. I understood why the Caltech student, eager to finish his work, jumped without hesitation into what was basically a pond full of mildly harmful acid. Every day of testing, I jumped in too.

Perhaps this was a small taste of the desperation that the crew of the *Hunley* felt. They knew how dangerous their boat was, but they were starving, and they were being bombed nightly. A worse situation than mine, definitely, but also one likely to inspire unrealistic optimism.

Sitting on the footbridge, I stared at the laptop monitor. I was under a big black sun tent, but it was mostly there to keep the electronics from overheating. A sunburned stripe on my lower back was itchy. We were almost ready to put the boat back into the water. We just needed to check the internal pressure gauges again. Maybe they would work this time.

I asked one of the undergrads to hit the bow with the rubber mallet. I heard him hit the boat, and it rang out clearly across the pond. But this time, the flat lines of the readings from the pressure gauges inside the hull did not jump in response. They stayed still. I asked him to hit it again. Again, no response.

Fatigued and cranky, I insisted we test anyway, blindly hopeful it was a fluke. Matt Udelhofen and I carried the boat into the water, and I swam out to connect the gas line to the shock-tube driver.

Again, as always, there was the tiniest, most negligible response inside the boat. Frustrated, I insisted we immediately yank the boat out. I wanted to be done dealing with these gauges. I did not know what was happening. They worked perfectly on dry land while in the lab, when measuring pressures in the air, and even when inside my small metal tub in the test tank, but here inside the boat, almost nothing. *Nothing.* It made no sense. I dragged the boat onto the bridge. I was determined that the gauges would at least work during the mallet test. I asked the undergrad to hit the bow again. He brought the mallet down squarely on the stern, directly on the clumsily spray-painted words "CSS *Tiny.*"

I stared at him for a moment, processing the realization that not everybody knew the difference between bow and stern.

Then I had my eureka moment.

I grabbed the mallet and smacked the bow hard. The pressure reading jumped. I hit the stern. Nothing. I understood my mistake, I understood why the internal gauges kept failing: The gauges could only read from one direction. They were facing the bow and wouldn't read pressures coming from any other direction. I needed to put a different gauge inside the boat.

Dripping, still wearing my life jacket, my sun hat soaked with sweat and my neoprene boots still uncomfortably full of pond, I run-sloshed to the toolbox. I pulled out the largest screwdriver I could find, a sturdy Phillips-head beast with rust spots, and I took massive strides back to the boat. Kneeling on the bridge, I lifted the handle of the screwdriver with both hands, and I plunged it straight down like a sacrificial knife through the thick rubber gasket that sealed the top of the boat off from the water.

On the top of the boat was a small removable panel. Each morning I shoved my forearm through the panel opening to place the pressure gauges as far inside as possible. The pressure gauges were toward the bow of the boat, facing forward, so far inside that the procedure to insert them always left a ring of bruises circling my forearm. They were near the bulkhead where Dixon would have sat, and where I expected the blast to most strongly penetrate the hull.

The pressure gauges I was using inside the dry hull of the boat were the go-to gauges for our lab for measuring blasts in air. I wasn't able to use them in the water because they were not waterproof, hence my need for the gauges from the navy to measure the pressure waves *outside* the boat. But these air gauges had served us well for years, reliably providing measurements for all sorts of tests, so when I designed the experiment it had seemed reasonable that they would provide reliable measurements for the pressure waves in the air *inside* the boat.

They were shaped like mushrooms, narrow cylinders topped with slightly wider caps. On the very bottom face of the "stalk" of the mushroom was the part that did the actual pressure sensing, a small circle of mesh. These air gauges were unidirectional, meaning only the mesh panel on the face of the cylinder could sense pressure. If this mesh panel were oriented incorrectly relative to the direction that the pressure wave was traveling, the gauge would not provide a meaningful reading. The mesh panels of the two gauges were facing forward and down, toward the spar and the charge, and they were as far toward the bow as I could place them. Before each test we had hit the bow with the mallet. They read the pressure ripple from hits to the bow. But when the student accidentally hit the boat on the stern they read almost nothing because they were being struck *from the wrong direction*.

I blasted the *Tiny* from the same position as the charge of the *Hunley*: mostly in front of and slightly below the boat. I had assumed, because the charge was off the bow, that much of the pressure would naturally transmit through the bow. The pressures from the charges had been transmitting all along, but I had missed it, because they weren't transmitting in through the bow. They were coming in from another direction.

Luckily, I already had a solution. The underwater gauges that I was using in the water, the gauges that had been loaned to me by the other navy engineers . . . these gauges were omnidirectional. Meaning, they measured waves coming from *any* direction. And even though they were mostly used underwater, they also worked in air. I had confirmed it in the lab dozens of times, when I was testing every configuration I could think of to try to replicate their alleged "failures" out at Pitt Pond.

I slid one of the omnidirectional US Navy gauges into the screwdriver hole I had just mercilessly stabbed in my submarine. I sealed it heavily with waterproof tape. The undergrad hit the boat in both the bow and the stern. It jumped both times. We put the boat back into the water.

The gauge worked like magic. With each test, it showed an internal increase in pressure precisely with the arrival of the shock wave. The initial increase was followed by exactly what I expected: a jagged, erratic waveform of pressure, the initial wave bouncing around inside the small enclosed hull. These waves were small because my shock tube was making small shocks in the water, but their shape was lethal. We knew now that they were getting in, just not through the bow. The next step was to figure out how. And how we had missed it.

Our team began testing furiously, running through every experimental variation we could think of. Each time the driver popped, almost immediately we had it open again, replacing the membrane for another trial. I was running in and out of the pond, trampling ornamental pond grasses with abandon. The excitement of sharing the data and staring at the screen together was palpable.

We changed the orientation of the boat; we changed the orientation of the driver; and we came up with test after test to characterize how the blast was propagating, through which parts of the hull, and by how much. The ultimate goal was to return to testing the boat exactly as the *Hunley* had been blasted, but by methodically changing the setup, we first came up with a full characterization of exactly which parts of the submarine conducted the blast and how well. We knew now that it was going in through her belly, not her bow. No more assumptions.

Inside an enclosed area, the waves bounce. They add to one another. It's a phenomenon called constructive interference. When two positive waves intersect, they combine to form a higher pressure. It can happen with acoustic waves, with ocean waves, and with blast waves. It's why the people hit by explosions inside of buses were killed far more often than the people in open spaces. The constructive interference amplified the pressures inside, increasing their lethality. My original gauges were only reading the initial blip that made it through the bow. I had thought that this would be most of the signal, but I was wrong. Most of the signal came in through the bottom, and then built on itself as it reflected around the interior of the sub.

By the time the sun started to set we had racked up not just the solution to my months of frustration but a tidy handful of invaluable data points. As the light faded and the mosquitoes began to descend, we packed our gear and heaved it with exhausted muscles into the back of my borrowed truck.

I tried to take the undergrads out for milk shakes. It was the only thing I could think of in that moment to say thank you. But tired, sweaty, and utterly depleted from the day, they asked if we could go another time. They wanted to go to bed. I did too. And for the first time in months, I actually slept through the night.

The *Hunley* held her spar on a downward angle. Using historical records, researchers have independently concluded that the depth of the torpedo on the spar could most likely be adjusted, raised or lowered, by pulling on a line attached to a spool on top of the boat. The spar was attached to the recovered boat on a hinge, consistent with the idea. She wanted to get her torpedo as far underneath the bottom of the *Housatonic* as possible, to follow the advice of Gabriel Rains about destroying ships. Contemporary accounts and drawings state that the torpedo was positioned 8 feet below the surface of the water, and therefore a minimum of at least 4 feet below the keel of the *Hunley*.

The *Tiny* transmitted the blast most effectively when the waves were aimed at the central part of her cylindrical body. In our tests to gauge transmission, almost nothing transmitted directly in through the bow; it is likely that the bulkhead and the water in the bilge absorbed most of the pressure waves from that direction. If the torpedo had been on a spar that was horizontally level with the submarine, more like the spar assumed to have been used by the wooden boat *David* that had attacked while on the surface, much smaller fractions of the lethal waves would have been able to transmit inside.

By lowering her spar, the *Hunley* placed herself above the level of the torpedo. By the time the propagating waves reached her underbelly, most would be traveling horizontally, but they would still have a strong vertical component. And that vertical component was ideally positioned to transmit straight through her hull. The crew may have survived if the spar had been fully horizontal, on the surface of the water, but that would likely not have destroyed the *Housatonic*. The *Hunley* was inadvertently designed to kill her own crew.

CHAPTER 9

FROM THE *HOUSATONIC*

This getting blown up by torpedoes is not very good fun.

—Union sailor Adna Bates

Before the citizens of Charleston began to endure thousands of shells lobbed in from their harbor, first the Union forces came for them by land. Like pincers, three flanks of troops wearing blue encircled the last standing major Southern port. Then, slowly, they closed in.

As they marched they left behind swaths of destruction, burning plantation mansions and razing fields of crops, all to reduce the South's ability to produce food and supplies. Gen. William Tecumseh Sherman showed Charleston no mercy on his infamous march through the South, saying, "I doubt any city was ever more terribly punished as Charleston, but as her people had for years been agitating for war and discord, and had finally inaugurated the Civil War, the judgment of the world will be that Charleston deserved the fate that befell her." The blockade would starve the city from the ocean on her southeast, and the land forces would starve her by burning the farms on the other three corners of her map.

And as the Union troops swept through the fields of rice and corn, and their numbers were reduced during combat and in raids, it became common for the now-free former slaves to pick up arms and take the places of the fallen.* The most famous such incident took place on the Combahee River, less than two hours' drive south of Charleston along the modernized coast. Harriet Tubman herself led a band of determined warriors, and together they freed 800 men, women, and children. One hundred and fifty of them immediately signed up. They became part of the Union's 2nd South Carolina Volunteer Infantry, a regiment composed almost entirely of former slaves. Then the 2nd South Carolina marched north, headed straight for Charleston.

To the northwest of Charleston were a scattered number of plantations that had belonged to the estate of the deceased physician Philip Tidyman. Doc Tidyman died in 1850, but not before going to great lengths to ensure that his plantations stayed intact to provide income for his "imbecile" daughter, Susan, as he called her. He drafted a detailed will that stated that the plantations and slaves should stay together as a working unit, with a codicil to clarify that not only did the house servant Judy belong to Susan, but also Judy's recently born son and all her future offspring.

When the Union troops came sweeping through, the overseers of Tidyman's estate became concerned. Their rice fields were in jeopardy, as was their captive labor for working those fields. They moved the slaves into hiding, purportedly for the slaves' own "safe keeping." But the plan failed. The Union forces came. The slaves were freed.

At least four of Tidyman's former slaves ended up on Union ships,

---

*While there is documentation of the willingness of many freed slaves to enlist, there is also historical evidence that at least some were forced to join the Union military against their will. In addition, while the 2nd South Carolina and the 54th Massachusetts (a unit of free African American men from Northern states that later became the subject of the feature film *Glory*) inarguably distinguished themselves honorably according to both the historical combat records and the records left by their immediate officers, there are also deeply conflicting accounts of the type of treatment provided to the African American soldiers by the Union military in general. Both of these complex issues warrant a deeper discussion that is outside the subject matter of this book. For further reading, one starting reference is Wise, 1994.

blockading Charleston from the ocean side, helping to starve out the city close to where they had formerly been put to work.

Reading and writing was previously illegal for them. So, when the freedmen signed up, their last names, the name of their former owner, got respelled phonetically by the Union bookkeepers: Tiddeman. However, one of the men would later change the spelling further, to Teddeman. Of the four Teddemans, William and John found themselves on the payrolls of the USS *Housatonic*. Two young teenagers named Jack and Charles, with Jack the correct age to be Judy's son, would also later formally enlist.

William Teddeman was likely not on board the *Housatonic* during the attack of the *Hunley*. While he was firing at a Confederate vessel the kickback sent the butt of a weapon smashing into his face. Irreversibly blinded by the standards of 1860s medicine, with severe scarring over both his corneas, he was discharged from the Union military prior to February of 1864. William's disability pension was denied because he could not conclusively prove that the gun-related injury, which he was discharged for and which happened while he was on a Union ship, happened during actual combat.

But freedman John Teddeman was almost certainly there. And at least forty-nine other African American men worked alongside him on the *Housatonic*, including a minimum of fifteen other former slaves, many from the plantations around Charleston. A map of the Union's advance toward Charleston Harbor can literally be drawn by the enlistment dates of freedmen from the surrounding plantations. So, on the chilly winter night of February 17, 1864, former plantation laborer John Teddeman stood somewhere on the decks of the USS *Housatonic*, aware of the warnings the crew had received about torpedoes attached to Confederate fish boats.

The numerous African American sailors and soldiers from the North had joined at great risk, even greater than the ubiquitous risk from the war's high body counts. After the Emancipation Proclamation, the Confederate government declared, as retaliation, that any cap-tured black Union soldiers would be treated not as prisoners of war but rather as escaped slaves. They would be imprisoned, tried, possibly hanged . . . but at minimum enslaved. At least 50 of the roughly 160-man crew of the USS *Housatonic*, floating at anchor within eyesight of slave-owning Charleston, would be either hanged or enslaved if cap-tured.

Robert Francis Flemming had joined the Union nonetheless. A marble cutter and stoneworker from near Boston, Massachusetts, he traveled to the enlistment station in New York City to sign up. Flem-ming was made a landsman, a low rate used for new sailors allegedly without any seafaring skills. These sailors would be performing menial or physically hard tasks on their ships because, as the title implied, they were not yet considered to deserve the title of seaman. Landsman Flem-ming found himself first on the decks of the USS *Wyoming*, traveling to see combat in Japan, then later part of the USS *Housatonic* crew and the blockade of Charleston. Soon, he would also find himself giving one of the most hotly contested pieces of eyewitness testimony in American history.

———

The *Housatonic* had lookouts spaced evenly to keep watch all around her perimeter. Six enlisted men and three officers stood at strategic locations along her 205-foot length, peering out at the smooth, brightly moonlit waters on either side of the ship. Flemming's position was on the starboard side of the forecastle, the area at the bow of the boat just above the berthing compartments where at night the rest of the crew slept. His station would have pointed his eyes toward the mouth of Charleston Harbor, and he would have seen the incessant fireworks caused by the shelling.

After sundown on the night of February 17, the *Housatonic* gently tugged at her anchor as the outgoing tide pulled her stern toward the open ocean. Flemming, standing on the starboard side of the ship's wooden deck, had an unobstructed if distant view of Sullivan's Island and Breach Inlet, the gap in the land where the *Hunley* had crept out to the ocean earlier that evening. He unwittingly gazed out at the otherwise blank water where the *Hunley*'s crew cranked, still too far away to be seen.

It made sense that Flemming was the first to notice her, given his watch position, that he was the first to see her sleek black shape moving in an odd direction, and menacingly toward the *Housatonic*. He reported it to the officer nearby, Lewis Cornthwait, but Cornthwait met the report with skepticism.

It was just a log, Cornthwait rebutted. Logs were commonplace, and only a sliver of this dark object could be seen bobbing on the dark, calm surface of that night's gentle waves. But Flemming was unconvinced. Logs do not move across the current of the tide, they float with it, Landsman Flemming explained to his superior officer. In contrast, this odd, long shape was moving with purpose. It was moving perpendicular to the current, not with it, and heading straight for the side of the *Housatonic*. Cornthwait wasted precious minutes listening to Flemming's explanation, precious minutes he would later conveniently forget and deny when he testified whether there was anything else he could have done to save his ship.

Looking through his glass, Cornthwait was finally convinced. This was one of the infernal Confederate threats they had all been on watch for, the reason they had to set up watch shifts from dusk till dawn and keep the ship's engine always at the ready. Cornthwait didn't pause any longer; he ran. He bolted toward the stern of the ship. But the officer of the deck, looking through his own glass at the dark object, had already realized the danger and needed no further convincing. The officer of the deck shouted the order, the quarter gunner smashed a mallet against the gong that would summon all the sailors to their battle stations, and the crew, properly trained and at the ready, immediately responded.

The USS *Housatonic* was no sleeping victim. The crew promptly slipped her tethering chain and summoned her engine into action. Her deck was replete with guns, both large artillery pieces and the small firearms carried by many of the crew. But the men had wasted too many precious minutes squinting out into the darkness, declaring that the slim shape was just a log or a porpoise, and by the time they realized their catastrophic emergency it was too late to aim any of the large weapons downward toward the rapidly approaching *Hunley*. The constructions of the guns and the ship prevented positioning the artillery at the correct downward angle; they would have needed to fire at the submarine when she was still farther away.

A crewman yelled, "Shoot at the boat, it is a torpedo going to blow us up!" Several of the men ran aft, to above where the submarine seemed to be aiming, on the rear quarter of the starboard side. They grabbed their pistols and their rifles and took hurried aim at the approaching mystery vessel. After three futile shots with his pistol, Ensign Charles Craven decided to try with the big guns anyway, working to heave the number-six gun into place at a sharp downward angle.

The captain of the ship, Charles Pickering, had been belowdecks when the first alarm was shouted, seated peacefully at a table, staring at a book of maps spread open in front of him. He heard the yelling and sprang to his feet, grabbing someone else's hat in the confusion, and dashed up above. He clutched his double-barreled gun, loaded full of buckshot, and he jumped up on the horse block right above the spot on the hull where the *Hunley* seemed to be aiming. This position gave him the highest possible angle to fire downward at the black sliver with its two large upward projections that looked like mess kettles. The captain's steward, Landsman John Gough, did not leave any recorded testimony from that night, but based on what happened to him next he must have been standing alongside his captain.

Seeing the imminent doom of the ship, Acting Master John Crosby yelled at the rest of the crew to run forward or they would be blown up. Most of the men headed for the bow and away from the oncoming threat. Pickering considered ordering them back aft to their battle stations, but since the guns were useless anyway, he stayed quiet and let them hurry toward an area of relative safety. He and Gough, however, stayed put.

The *Hunley* pressed her torpedo against the hull of the *Housatonic*. The boulder was shoved off the cliff, and the heat and the fury released began to propagate out into the surrounding black powder.

The explosion sent an immediate and violent shudder through the wooden planks of the condemned *Housatonic*. She gave a massive lurch to port as her right rear flank was blown into flying shards. The running crewmen stumbled and fell, scattered by the forceful stagger of the wounded ship. The ship's lurch caused the hammer of Ensign Craven's gun to come down prematurely and incompletely, damaging the primer but not quite firing the gun, rendering the primer useless and destroying his carefully prepared attempt to shoot. Pickering and Gough, still determinedly at their battle stations, were heaved violently with the exploding deck of the ship. Even the crew enclosed below in the engine room, those who had been stoking the fires to coax the ship to escape the oncoming submarine, knew that something was dramatically wrong: The engine jumped frenetically into too-rapid action, as if her load had been magically removed. As if—an engineer would later testify—her propeller had been blown to pieces.

The crewmen later reported that the blast was surprisingly quiet, "like the distant firing of a Howitzer" or "like a splash of wood in the water." There was no massive, distinct column of water that could be seen by those on deck, as would have been expected from a lone torpedo, because the explosion had occurred immediately against the hull. The force had been properly directed against the hull of the ship, rather than upward into the air as a freely expanding water plume. A burgeoning cloud of dark smoke rolled out from the blast, a roiling and tumultuous haze of burnt black powder that would have reeked strongly of the sulfurous stench of rotten eggs.

Already many of the crew noticed the lapping water rising up around their ankles, even as the fragments of their vessel still rained down around them. It took only moments, they said, before the ship's stern began to sag beneath the surface of the Atlantic. She gave one final lurch, then sank so quickly that most of her small lifeboats were swamped or entangled beyond recovery. Any straggling crewmen who had not yet run to the bow scrabbled there to flee the rising water. They clambered up into the rigging to cling to wooden masts and fabric sails as the body of the ship settled onto the relatively shallow ocean floor, and many of the landsmen simply jumped overboard, plunging into the February-freezing salty water.

Robert F. Flemming became the last person in history to report seeing the *Hunley* afloat. During the mayhem of the attack, as he ran for the safety of the bow of the boat, he carried his gun with him. After the jar of the explosion, he continued to bolt toward the forecastle, and once he got there he paused to look back along the deck of his dying ship. Just off the starboard quarter, where the sub had impacted the side of the *Housatonic*, Flemming saw the long dark line of the *Hunley* jutting above the water, sitting motionless and "apparently stationary." He fired his musket at it in one final parting attempt to sink her, and then he climbed the forward mast to join the rest of the crew.

Captain Pickering found himself suddenly floating in the water below where he had stood, "amongst broken timbers, the debris of panel work and planking." He was bruised and beaten from the hurtling wood planks that had caused him secondary blast trauma, the trauma caused by the impact of objects thrown by the blast.

For a healthy man like Pickering, the greatest obstacle to survival was his own respiratory reflex. Hitting the cold water causes a sharp, uncontrollable, rapidly drawn breath, a rasping suction for air that for many unfortunates means involuntarily pulling the frigid water straight into their lungs. On average, a male plunged into water that cold will forcefully gulp three full liters of whatever is outside his mouth straight into his lungs.

For those who somehow manage to suck in air instead of water, the threat of the initial sharp gulp is then quickly followed by the new danger of uncontrollable hyperventilation, an increase in the rate of respiratory ventilation of up to 1,000 percent. Pickering and all those who jumped overboard would have found themselves unable to suppress the choppy, rapid breaths their bodies forced them to make, irregular gasps that gradually expelled carbon dioxide from their bloodstreams, and slowly raised the pH levels of their blood to values that threatened to render them unconscious.

Plunged unexpectedly into the dark waters of the Atlantic, he and the rest of the men in the ocean would have been subject to the human body's "cold shock" response. Within seconds of immersion his heart began racing, thunking against his chest even faster than during the adrenaline-pumping final approach of the menacing submarine. The veins in his extremities contracted, shrinking down the blood flow to his limbs to reduce the amount of heat lost to the water and to maintain the temperature of the body's core. His skin became pale, clammy, and disturbingly cold to the touch as the surrounding liquid aggressively drained the warmth from his flesh.

Even experienced swimmers can drown when thrown suddenly into cold water. Unable to control the pattern of their breathing, they flail to make forward progress without inhaling the water splashed up by their own movements. Pickering, by his own account, struggled to swim his way to the rigging of the mizzenmast sticking up out of the ocean surface. He was "painfully but not dangerously injured" from the projectiles thrown by the explosion, and also dealing with cold shock. Gough was likely next to Pickering during the blast and struggling alongside him in the water, based on the secondary blast injuries he reported later. Captain Pickering waited in the rigging for rescue, sopping wet and freezing, all the while searching the settling ocean surface in vain for a second glimpse of the victorious torpedo boat.

The crew would have been at low risk for primary blast injuries because the explosion occurred underwater, and the pressure waves from the explosion were therefore unlikely to reach them. The waves decay much more quickly in air. But the forceful heave of the boat, the flying projectiles, and the rapid lurching into the depths of the cold sea were enough to kill five of the *Housatonic* crew.

———————

Two of the small lifeboats survived the attack. Acting Master John Crosby swiftly took charge of his. He plucked sailor after sailor out of the water and off the floating pieces of wooden detritus that used to comprise the starboard stern of the *Housatonic*. Hearing the voice of his captain lodged in the rigging, Crosby ordered the small craft rowed over to Pickering. However, the captain refused to take one of the precious safe spots until everyone floating in the water had been fished out.

With an average water temperature of 50 degrees Fahrenheit in February, the men had less than two hours before they were incapacitated or killed by hypothermia. Even those who had climbed into the rigging or the lifeboats, if they were soaking wet, quickly became susceptible to the pernicious effects of heat loss. They began violently shivering as their bodies vainly tried to produce more heat. Their bodies began to shut down the processes that were not a priority for survival. They gradually lost cognitive and motor functions. Their heart rates slowed, their breathing became increasingly more shallow and faint. If left dangling there, the shivering would eventually be replaced by a full-body, taut, nonstop muscular contraction that would lock their every limb in place. And eventually, they would lose consciousness.

By the time Crosby got back to the drenched Pickering, his little boat now almost full, the captain was in a precarious state. He was "very much exhausted." Crosby would later report that he didn't think the physically depleted and soaking-wet Pickering "could have held out much longer."

Satisfied that everyone who could be saved had been saved, Charles Pickering finally agreed to be plucked from the rigging. With his captain secured, Crosby ordered the two surviving boats to be rowed toward the *Housatonic*'s nearest neighbor in the blockade: the USS *Canandaigua*.

The crew of the *Canandaigua* rushed their vessel into action within minutes of the arrival of these messengers. Like the *Housatonic*, she too had been waiting at a state of readiness, her lookouts on the watch for blockade-runners and other threats. Her crew got her under way almost immediately, but they did not reach the *Housatonic*'s foundered carcass and freezing men until about forty-five minutes after the blast. The captain of the *Canandaigua*, Joseph F. Green, deployed several smaller boats to retrieve the survivors from the wreck site and bring them back to the safety of the larger ship.

Landsman Flemming and the rest of the crew watched the *Canandaigua* and her small boats approach from the rear starboard quarter of their vessel, the quarter the *Hunley* had blown to pieces. One of these little boats finally "picked" Flemming off his perch in the rigging and brought him to safety.

Captain Green and the crew of the *Canandaigua* spread the word of the disaster among the rest of the fleet. In an era long before radios, they used light flashes to communicate. Later accounts from those who had watched from shore that night would reference the "frantic signaling" between the ships as crew after crew in the blockade passed on the word of their compatriots' demise.

Days later, after the planks and splinters and detritus had all drifted off to sea, the US Navy understandably wanted to know exactly what had happened.

"Ascertain the facts," commanded Rear Admiral John Dahlgren in a letter. Dahlgren, now in charge of the South Atlantic Blockading Squadron that was surrounding Charleston, had several years earlier founded the Ordnance Department of the US Navy. Eventually, they would name an entire military base in his honor. And as an ordnance-man, he had some questions about this "Rebel Torpedo."

In response, the key witnesses gathered on the nearby USS *Wabash*. One at a time, the relevant crewmen of the late *Housatonic* testified in front of the three board members of the court of inquiry and the young Marine Corps officer who served as judge advocate. Flemming, Craven, Crosby, Cornthwait, and thirteen others each independently described the details of what they had seen, done, and experienced.

The men were blown up, then they were left clinging in rigging for close to an hour in the winter. To say that the experience may have affected their memories seems reasonable. While the crew agreed on the general story, the specifics are wildly inconsistent. For example, their collective reports of the angle at which the *Hunley* approached contained all of the possible responses. It was at a right angle, declared Crosby, pointed amidships. No, said Cornthwait when he had his turn, it was moving parallel to the ship, and looked like it was only drifting toward the *Housatonic*. Lieutenant Higginson's testimony aligned with Crosby's, but crewman Kelly insisted the same thing as Cornthwait, and still another sailor unintentionally presented a compromise when he testified that the *Hunley* came in at an oblique angle.

The *Hunley*'s speed was also a matter of confusion. The court finally settled on a sort of average of the reports: They agreed the vessel was first sighted when it was at a distance of 75 to 100 yards away, and that it was moving at a speed of 3 to 4 knots. However, they also concluded that the explosion occurred three minutes after the discovery of the object. One knot is equal to 33.8 yards per minute, so if the *Hunley* were moving at those speeds the explosion would have occurred between 33 and 59 seconds after Flemming's first declaration, not even long enough for him to convince Cornthwait the submarine wasn't a log. To match with the times and distances reported by the crewmen, the *Hunley* would have needed either to pause before impacting the *Housatonic*, or been plodding along at a maximum of between 0.5 knots and 1 knot.

But despite these minor inconsistencies, no piece of testimony in the entire record, or perhaps in all of naval history, has been scrutinized so much as some words spoken by sharp-eyed Bostonian lookout Robert Flemming.

"Did you see this object at any time after you fired at it?" the court asked Flemming, referring to his backward shot after the explosion but before he scrambled up a mast to safety.

"I did not," he replied. But then he added, "When the *Canandaigua* got astern, and lying athwart, of the *Housatonic*, about four ships' lengths off, while I was in the fore-rigging, I saw a blue light on the water just ahead of the *Canandaigua* and on the starboard quarter of the *Housatonic*." Meaning: As the *Canandaigua* approached within about 800 feet of the wreck of the *Housatonic*, Flemming stated that he did not see the sub herself, but he did see a light on the stretch of water between the two ships.

This report of a light has become a legend. A blue light was the signal that George Dixon planned to send back to shore to tell the Confederates that the crew of the *Hunley* had been successful in their mission. "Blue light" does not refer to a colored light, but rather a specific mixture of burning chemicals. It was actually bright white in color, not blue, and it was a common tool among both the Union and Confederate Navies for signaling between ships at night.

If Flemming saw this light and it came from the *Hunley*, then it meant the *Hunley*'s crew survived the attack. If Flemming saw this light and it came from the *Hunley*, then for some reason the *Hunley* was still loitering within a few hundred feet of her victim, near a full blockade of heavily armed enemy warships, over forty-five minutes after her successful assault. And she was sending bright, visible signals while in that position. Because of Flemming's testimony about the blue light, even though he overtly stated that he did not see the actual *Hunley*, for a century and a half most people felt they *knew* that the crew of the *Hunley* had survived their attack.

But the surviving records of Capt. Joseph F. Green, the officer in command of the USS *Canandaigua* on that night, provide a tantalizing alternative explanation that has until this writing stayed filed away in the Library of Congress. As part of his duties, Green spent what seems to be an inordinate amount of time dealing with disciplinary squabbles. His handwritten files of letters read almost humorously. They're filled with numerous exclamatory letters from sailors trying to explain away some minor behavioral infraction, and equally vehement letters from other sailors who were tattling, declaring that their shipmates should be punished harshly. Green had to deal with all of them, sorting through which misbehaviors deserved attention and then meting out appropriate punishment.

A few months before the attack of the *Hunley*, Green settled a massive hullabaloo regarding a small boat that had audaciously rowed its way between the imposing ships of the blockade. It had approached without properly displaying the flag with the little boat's assigned number, the number that would announce and identify the boat as a fellow Union vessel. After threats of gunfire and attack if the infraction were repeated, the men of the little boat, trying to avoid punishment, would finally write to Green that they had improperly signaled because they had never been issued such a flag and had no idea what their assigned number was. The conclusion of the incident, and Green's primary concern, it seems, was a warning to the men of the little boat of the importance of signaling their friendly intentions the next time they approached a heavily armed, combat-ready vessel of war. The Union protocol upon seeing a craft without the proper signals was to fire, and to fire immediately. And at night, when flags could not be seen, Green's records contain the preferred signal for such a little boat that was approaching a large ship: "Flash a white light."

So, either the *Hunley*'s crew survived, and inexplicably Dixon kept her positioned for almost an hour within a few hundred feet of the site of her attack and other armed, hostile forces, even as he sent a noticeable, bright signal back to shore . . . or, alternatively, when Captain Green's crew from the *Canandaigua* began to row their small boats toward the large downed ship *Housatonic*, they followed the instructions of their captain, and one of the small boats flashed the correct signal to communicate their amicable approach toward the well-armed vessel: a light on the water. And that light was the one Flemming reported.

About three months after he climbed down from the rigging of the *Housatonic*, Captain's Steward John Gough would be discharged from the Union Navy, and he would later apply for a disability pension. Gough and Pickering had held their positions faithfully, shooting at their attackers right up until the moment of the blast. Gough's right knee had been badly injured in the explosion, and was immobilized by a "thickening of the ligaments." This phrase could be any one—or several—of a cornucopia of injuries that would receive more precise descriptions by modern medical standards, but they are all consistent with secondary blast trauma to the joint. Secondary trauma is the most common injury type for blast survivors, and lower-limb trauma is logically rampant in those exposed to any kind of explosion from below. Gough, like Pickering, was likely brutalized by flying pieces of his own ship. The two were the only *Housatonic* survivors with documented injuries, and both were treated by a physician once safely on board the *Canandaigua*.

When Pickering heard that Gough was applying for a disability pension, he wrote a vehement letter to the pension board on behalf of his former steward. The captain riddled his letter with compliments about Gough's service record. He described the loyal, excellent, stalwart Gough "much injured and crippled" during the attack, and stated that "he deserves & I sincerely hope will succeed in getting a good pension." But the US Navy physicians on the pension board disagreed with the examining physicians who had already documented that Gough's right leg was immobilized from the wound, instead arguing that "claimant is not incapacitated for claiming his subsistence by manual labor from the cause above stated." Landsman Gough, an African American volunteer from the North, was denied the pension.

The rest of the surviving crew of the *Housatonic* found new homes in the Union Navy, and their dispersal among the fleet was indirectly recorded by their reappearance in the pay logbooks of their new vessels. Flemming went on to continue his service on the USS *Wabash*, the ship where he had testified during the court of inquiry. When the war ended, he found his way back home to the Boston area to live out the rest of his life. His headstone now rests there, and is marked as deserving the respect due a veteran.

John Teddeman served on the USS *Canandaigua* alongside the crew that had picked him out of the ocean. In the logbooks of the *Canandaigua*, a few months after the sinking, also appear two new names for the Union cause: Jack and Charles Teddeman. Charles was a young thirteen years old at the time of his enlistment, and while Jack's age was unfortunately not recorded, his height of five-foot-one indicates he was a teenager slightly older than Charles.* There are unfortunately no known documents that trace the journey of Jack and Charles from the Tidyman Plantation to the decks of the *Canandaigua*, but it seems plausible they may have traveled to the *Housatonic* with John and William, been plucked out of the water on February 17, 1864, alongside John, and then signed up to serve with him on the *Canandaigua* as soon as they were deemed old enough.

Capt. Charles Whipple Pickering was promptly cleared of wrongdoing by the Union's court of inquiry. Nothing else could have been done to save the ship, the panel of four decided, and they also determined that everyone including the captain had comported themselves with the discipline and order expected of US Navy sailors. Pickering's injuries and trauma, though severe, eventually healed, and the salty forty-nine-year-old veteran was assigned a new command on the USS *Vanderbilt* until the end of the war. After retiring from the navy he returned home to New Hampshire, where he eventually died from kidney failure near his birthplace in 1888.

The crew of the *Canandaigua* too left behind records of their memories from that night. Young sailor Adna Bates, who would later write home plea after plea to his family to send him his good coat so he would not have to spend another frigid winter without it, also sent his father insider information on the happenings of the Union blockade outside Charleston.

When the small wooden boat *David* had unsuccessfully used a

----

* Charles's height is recorded as four-foot-ten, allowing a rough inference of Jack's age. The 1850 census records from Tidyman's plantation only record one male of that age: Judy's son.

spar torpedo to try to sink the USS *New Ironsides*, Adna Bates wrote to his father all he knew about the attack, including a detailed drawing by an *Ironsides* crewman that was unfortunately not saved with the letter. Then when his father inquired about the differences between ironclads and monitors, Adna once again sent back careful, specific insight. And when his father asked about the "rebel torpedo boats," Adna, who was on the deck of the *Canandaigua* as she plucked the *Housatonic* sailors out of the water, faithfully reported all he knew about the attack, along with a helpful doodle.

Adna Bates's doodle of the *Hunley*.

"[The torpedo boats] are about forty feet long, built of boiler iron & all submerged with the exception of the pilot house & smokepipe, & when first seen look like a log with two half barrels lashed on top. . . . The torpedo is at the end of a long beam with a chain to raise or lower it. . . . The one that blew up the *Housatonic* was seen about 75 yards off & they had slipped the cable & were backing to get clear of their anchor buoy when it struck her.

"She sank in 30 seconds. The Captain was on the quarter deck & was badly hurt with falling splinters. . . . The crew & officers have lost everything." Adna Bates, and therefore most likely some of the sailors of the *Housatonic*, mistakenly assumed that one of the *Hunley*'s conning towers was a smoke pipe, similar to the structure of the wooden *David*. Otherwise, his account is fairly accurate. He seems to be repeating the scuttlebutt he heard directly from the crew, telling his father what he learned from the survivors.

Bates survived the war, but not before he had his own direct experience with the now-legendary Confederate torpedoes. While he was on board the USS *Harvest Moon*, the ship ran over a hidden torpedo and was "blown to atoms."

"One man had his brains blown out," he wrote to his father. After documenting the injuries of a few more members of the crew, he then went on to send home arguably the most massive understatement of the entire war: "This getting blown up by torpedoes is not very good fun."

CHAPTER 10

THE BLAST

One submariner compared the shock wave from a depth charge to tons of gravel being thrown against the hull. Another described the experience as like being in a garbage can while it was beaten with a club.

—Michael Sturma, *The USS* Flier: *Death and Survival on a World War II Submarine*

Confederate troops on watch patrolled Battery Marshall on the clear February night of the *Hunley*'s attack. The battery was an armed fortification on the sandy beaches near the mouth of Charleston Harbor, and it was positioned next to the narrow break in the land that the *Hunley* used as her gateway to the Atlantic. Each time the submarine journeyed out to sea she would thread the waters of this slim inlet, silently passing the soldiers and artillery on shore. Lt. Col. O. M. Dantzler, stationed at Marshall, was well aware of the departing submarine and her ambitious clandestine mission. Late on the night of the seventeenth, he waited in vain for her return.

Two days later, in a letter informing his superiors that she never came back, Dantzler left behind words that have been parsed and analyzed ever since. Words that, like Robert Flemming's intriguing testimony, could be construed as a record of the fabled blue-light signal for victory.

"The signals agreed upon to be given in case the boat wished a light to be exposed at this post as a guide for its return were observed and answered," he wrote. Some modern researchers have interpreted the letter to mean that he saw a blue light on the water after the attack, the signal the crew had planned to use to announce their victory. However, standing at Battery Marshall and spotting a small light near the wreck site of the *Housatonic*, 4 miles away, over twice the length of the Golden Gate Bridge, would have been challenging at best.

Even mammoth objects seem to shrink as they recede into the distance. However, the appearance and visual obviousness of a distant object, like a submarine, can still be described with a little bit of basic geometry. If the world around someone's head forms a full 360-degree circle, each object within that circle occupies a certain fraction of that 360 degrees. The size of the object, as seen by a person at a known distance, can therefore be described in degrees, described by the portion of their visual world that the thing fills.

The moon, for example, takes up 0.52 degrees, just a hair over one-half of 1 degree in the circle. The 40-foot-long *Hunley*, if viewed perfectly broadside from a distance of 4 miles, would occupy only 0.10 degrees. Therefore, as Dantzler stood at Battery Marshall, staring out over the torpedo-filled Atlantic with the nearly full moon glowing down at him, the entire length of the dark *Hunley* would have appeared—at most, if she were perfectly broadside—to be about one-fifth the width of the moon rising above the horizon that he watched. Additionally, only a sliver of the vessel stuck up out of the water, about 2 feet in height, making her an even more difficult target to spot.

Standing at Battery Marshall and spotting the dark-hulled *Hunley* in the moonlit waters outside Charleston would have been mathematically equivalent to standing in the end zone of a football field and locating half of a standard drinking straw nestled in the grass 53 yards away . . . provided the shortened straw was grass-green, you didn't know which yard line it was hidden at, and the experiment took place at night.

The *Hunley* was supposed to light a blue light, though, which should in theory make it more visible. Original recipes contained zinc to add the signature color, but by the Civil War the blue-tinged additions had been largely abandoned and the lights had been reduced back down to burning white balls of saltpeter and sulfur. It was a noticeable signal, but even these dynamic flares had a maximum size.

To an observer standing at a distance, a relatively large blue light will form a spot of brightness that appears at most about 3 meters wide. If lit at the site of the downed *Housatonic*, that 3 meters would have looked like only a pinpoint of white to the searching Dantzler. The light would have also been visually buried by the reflections and rustling waves dancing on the surface of the moonlit ocean. It would not have been easily spotted until the submarine cranked much closer to shore, which most researchers agree never occurred.

Dantzler never said that he saw the blue light that meant success. What he said was that he saw the signal that the *Hunley*'s crew wanted a guiding light that would help direct them in their return. He did not specify *when* he saw this signal, or of what form the signal took.

The *Hunley*'s crew may have signaled to the soldiers on shore as they cranked their vessel out to sea. They could have signaled on their way out of Breach Inlet as they passed the men at the battery, asking that a fire be lit later, after their planned explosion, to help them aim for the narrow passageway and home. The words Dantzler used are, unfortunately, unspecific.

No other witnesses from Marshall reported a blue-light victory signal. No records have ever been found indicating that the Confederate troops built a light or a fire for their submarine. A Charlestonian chronicler of the event would write down, albeit two years later: "The officer in command told Lt. Col. Dantzler when they bid each other good-by, that if he came off safe he would show two blue lights. The lights never appeared."

The brutal reality is that math is more robust than words. Words can be imprecise. Words can be unclear and inaccurately interpreted, and it is common for them to change meaning and subtext based on the interpretations and the biases of the person reading them, especially when hundreds of years have passed since they were first written. Scholars have debated the nuances of texts from Confucius and Aristotle since they were penned millennia ago, and even the blue light itself was long mistakenly thought to be literally blue instead of white in color.

But math can tell only the bare truth. It can provide only the singular, inevitable conclusion that must be reached by the numbers. I finished my calculations of the blue light, of Dantzler's view and how he would have had to spot the *Hunley*. For me, the math screamed its conclusion: I had no reason to believe that the *Hunley*'s crew survived their legendary victory.

Even with that information, the test team and I still had work to do. I needed more blast data before I could draw any positive conclusions. We had achieved a solid start using the shock tubes in the Duke pond, but we needed to repeat the feat with black powder, and then I needed to analyze the numbers. And finally, I needed to defend my dissertation and graduate.

Furthermore, I now had a new ticking clock looming over my head. ATF Brad, the extraordinarily helpful drug dealer–tracking explosives agent who had ensured I kept all my fingers thus far, was moving out of the state. He was being restationed, sent off to fight crime elsewhere in the country. He was set to leave in late August; I had to finish before then.

"The pond is open anytime," Farmer Pitt told me when I asked about scheduling the next day out among his fields. "It's yours whenever you need it."

First, though, we had to get more explosive material. Brad called ahead for me so that I could legally buy it in bulk, giving the supplier some kind of secret ATF password that let me obtain the black powder equivalent of a family pack instead of scrounging for the plastic bottles one or two at a time.

Nick had the day off work and decided he was up for a lengthy drive to a mysterious munitions warehouse deep in the country. It seemed interesting, he said, and the warehouse did not disappoint. It was a nondescript complex of white, high-ceilinged buildings full of industrial shelving stocked to the brim with powder, ammunition, targets, and underground security boxes aimed at helping doomsday preppers bury and hide their gold and bullets. We carefully lodged 20 pounds of freshly purchased black powder in the trunk of my little blue Pontiac, the maximum amount permitted in one vehicle by law.

We were on the highway heading home when the car in front of us decided to start spinning in erratic circles, a crude high-speed parody of a human breakdancing routine. I never saw exactly what caused the accident. Something had sparked the small coupe two cars forward to hit the concrete barrier that divided our left-hand lane from the travelers heading westbound. The car had jumped back off with gusto and begun to turn doughnuts down the highway, catching the front end of the next vehicle in the line and forcing it to join the dance, metal and plastic and glass flying off like whirling shrapnel.

A moment before the chaos began, I had noticed the grille of a massive truck pressed nearly up against my rear windshield, and now my eyes were glued to the rearview mirror despite the rapidly shrinking distance between us and the melee ahead. Nick had the same thought I did, and he calmly but urgently spoke only two words while digging his fingers into the handle of the passenger-side door.

"BEHIND YOU."

I could hear the tires of the truck behind me squealing; the driver had finally looked up and seen what was happening. I tempered my braking force based on how quickly *he* could stop, because I had already decided I would slam into the now-stationary cars in front of me before letting this truck hit my powder-filled rear end. My brain would provide me with only three pieces of information, shrieked rapidly and all at once:

Black powder is impact-sensitive.

Gabriel Rains said 25 pounds will blow the roof off a house.

We are a bomb.

My tires brought us to a heated stop what felt like mere millimeters from the crash, but in reality was probably several feet. The front end of the truck behind me consumed the entire view out my rear window. It was close enough that all I could see were headlights and the wide-eyed state of fear in the driver's eyes. He should have been far more terrified, and he will never know.

The drivers of the formerly spinning cars climbed out and began to walk toward each other over the crunchy trail of plastic and glass. The driver of the front car waved and yelled something that sounded like "I'm so sorry." They both seemed intact. Nick and I shared a moment of profanity, and then glared as the driver of the dark truck proceeded to pushily merge into another lane to continue his trip.

The rest of the trip home was blissfully uneventful.

———

S everal days later, I drove cautiously over the rough, red dirt paths crisscrossing Pitt Farm for what I hoped would be the last time. The long, white shape of the CSS *Tiny* partially filled my sedan, pressed at one end into the outside lip of the trunk, with the bulk of her slim body stretched over the folded-down back row. Once I reached the quiet green shore of the little farm pond, I began to unload the myriad containers, toolboxes, generator, and data-acquisition components that were shoved in beside the tiny submarine. I heard the van of former army med student Luke Stalcup pull in behind me, followed shortly by the rumble of ATF Brad's big black work truck.

We had split the blast equipment up, for safety. Brad had the powder, safe in a secure, reinforced explosives transport box. He climbed down from his driver-seat perch, lowered the tailgate, and began to build the charges on it. By now we were well rehearsed, and each of us knew our roles perfectly.

The Southern summer sun was blazing, and Brad was already sweating through the gray long-sleeved T-shirt he wore as a standard precaution to protect his skin from the dusty black powder. For a moment I watched him, with rivulets of perspiration running down his flushed face, perform cautious measurements of the shiny granules that would go in each charge. In stark contrast, I had shown up in a swimsuit, SPF rash guard, and giant sun hat. For once, I was feeling lucky to be the one whose job was getting in the pond.

It was just the three of us testing this time, plus Luke's wife and their young child, who were prepared with a sun umbrella to sit and watch the blasts. Exhausted from the constant loading and unloading of the equipment, we had stripped down the experimental setup. Between the hard physical labor and the long workdays that somehow magically erased mealtimes off the clock, my weight had dropped 12 pounds during the previous months of testing. So this time, we left behind the high-speed cameras. We didn't have any extra hands with us to operate them anyway. We also left behind the fiber-optic gauges, which only worked sometimes, maybe, if you told them the exact right compliments and said "please" in a soothing tone of voice, because their behemoth acquisition unit was hefty and only erratically coughed up useful data. It was just the three of us, the *Tiny*, the reliable navy gauges, and some black powder.

Crouching in the long grasses at the end of the pier, I tightened the small access panel that shielded the *Tiny*'s interior from splashing water.

An omnidirectional navy gauge was sealed inside. Luke grabbed one of the metal rings protruding above her hull, and I grabbed another. Together we carried the small boat with her lead-covered belly through the mud that ringed the shoreline and set her down in the pond. As she bobbed slowly, I climbed back out to walk barefoot down the sun-warmed wood to the end of the pier, where our tidy pile of electronics was shielded by a big black shade tent. Luke picked up the trusty rubber mallet. When he struck the stern of the floating model, the squiggly digital line on my monitor jumped. The gauge inside was reading, and it was reading perfectly, from all directions.

Brad carried the first charge from his truck to the shore. It was a small contraption with a design that we had perfected and strengthened as much as we could within the permissions given us by the ATF. It was a slightly busted, fifth-owner, four-cylinder Mustang of a charge. Luke attached it to the bow of the boat, which hosted a threaded receptacle that could accept throwaway metal spars. The spar unearthed with the *Hunley* followed a subtly curved shape that implied it had been the recipient of a massive force, and some of our spars had also been similarly deformed by the stronger blasts.

As Luke pulled the *Tiny* into the center of the pond, I was struck once again by how smoothly and easily she glided. Her peaceful wedge barely disturbed the fluid, separating the water on either side with a grace that was jarringly inconsistent with the weapon of death she hid just below the surface. Long dreadlocks of black foam trailed out behind her, the insulation tubes that protected the gauges' wires from the signal-leaching water.

I triple-checked the gauges' signals on my screen and held up a hand to convey my readiness to Brad. He bellowed the countdown. He pushed the second button on the blast box to trigger. First, I saw the plume of the geyser of water, and then I felt the pier vibrate. Last of all, I heard the blast. As always.

Brad yelled from shore that he could feel that charge through the ground. What he meant was: This one was strong. Stronger than any of our previous tests with the boat. I may have grunted in acknowledgment, but I was too consumed by staring at the whirring laptop to respond in any meaningful way. I waited for the screen to display the pressure waves from the charge.

There they were. Both of them. The waveform from the explosion, in the water, with a quick rise that would kill even though it wasn't technically a shock wave, followed by a lovely smooth decay. But even better, there was also a clean waveform from the internal pressure gauge: a squiggly line measuring the jagged, erratic scream of bouncing waves trapped inside the hull of the boat. A squiggly line that had sharp peaks, peaks with rapid rises, peaks that rose to maximum in under the 2-millisecond cutoff for blasts that would hurt human beings.

Before Luke and Brad could begin to set up the second charge, I tossed my hat down on the pier and plunged feetfirst into the warm brown water. It was deeper than before. The pond's bottom now featured a smooth, round crater under the former site of the charge. Once again, I felt around blindly until my fingers contacted what they were groping for, and I pulled out the fragments of the charge casing. The pieces had still separated along the lines of construction between their various parts, so these blasts were still smaller than the one that would have been created by the welded-shut torpedo of the *Hunley*. But this time, the fragments showed that the black powder was reaching some degree of pressure buildup. The blasts were inarguably larger than they had been before.

We set off as many charges as we could before the sun began to set on the pond. Blast after blast, we captured and saved the waveforms. The readings looked blissfully consistent. And like the actual *Hunley*, the scale-model *Tiny* refused to show any damage herself, even after repeated blasts, even as she willingly transmitted the pressures inside.

By the end of that day, the data saved on the laptop was worth more to me than anything I owned. I immediately backed it up in triplicate.

When the sun began to drop in the sky and we were getting low on powder, we realized our testing was finally over. We had blown an additional meter and a half out of the bottom of the pond. But we had gotten what we needed. After cleaning up, I insisted on one final group photo with the *Tiny*. Luke's wife, Alane, obliged, documenting our fatigued, filthy, sweaty, utterly depleted but nonetheless ecstatic faces with my camera. Brad was moving the following week.

The next step was to translate all the squiggly pressure traces into a meaningful description of what happened on that cold, dark night in February 1864. My end goal was not simply to sit in a series of muddy ponds and set off charges for fun. It was to determine, scientifically, whether the crew had been injured or killed by their own massive bomb.

Answering this main question required solving each of its three separate parts. Part one: How strong was the pressure wave in the water from the explosion? Part two: How much of that external pressure wave transmitted inside the boat? And finally, part three: Could the pressures inside the boat have killed the crew?

First, I wanted to tackle question number two on this scientific to-do list: How much of the blast's pressure transmitted inside the submarine? This important question had been the goal of the months of muddy experimentation, after all. And now, with the testing complete, I could finally answer it. I could calculate what percentage of the blast pressures traveling through the water had worked their way inside the hull.

In an explosion, the behaviors of everyday objects can surprise us. Items in the path of the traveling blast wave are hit by that sudden, rapidly rising smack of pressure, which skyrockets from zero to maximum far quicker than any other forces these objects would experience on a normal day. As a result, sometimes even those items that we think of as solid, like steel walls, can ripple and contort like Jell-O for a fraction of a second. This bizarre behavior is what makes high-speed videos so fascinating, and it is also how the blast waves were more than likely getting inside the *Tiny*.

Imagine lying in the grass beneath a trampoline with your eyes closed. Someone climbs onto the stretchy black canvas and jumps. Even if trampoline springs were not infamous for shrieking loudly, you would still be able to tell when each jump occurred without hearing or seeing it. Every downward bounce of the black mat would be felt as a puff of air, a subtle and brief wind caused by the motion of the stretchy surface toward you, pushed downward as if the moving surface were an inefficiently designed fan. The larger the person or the higher the jump, the larger the motion of the trampoline, and the stronger the wind. If the person jumping is small, they get bounced back up without too much drama because they do not have enough momentum to cause a lasting deformation of the surface. But if the wave is more powerful, it is more like a sumo wrestler, with far more momentum. The materials tear, and the wrestler crashes through. Water gets in. The ship sinks.

The same effect occurs when a ship's belly is hit by an underwater explosion. Analogies are never perfect; the reality has some additional complexities, but that's the general idea. The traveling blast wave impacts the hull and for a fraction of a moment the material deforms. Even if the blast causes no permanent damage it will still cause the hull to flex and bend locally at the point of impact. When the hull flexes, it pushes a puff of air inside, just like the moving surface of the trampoline. This puff comes off the back face of the wall as a new, internal pressure wave.

Because I am a scientist—gravity is my favorite theory—here is the fine-print scientific disclaimer that my brain forces me to include: There are some other possible theories to explain the transmission that we measured. This one is just the most likely candidate, given the data that I have right now.

Before testing began, I tracked down the undergraduate student in the lab with the smallest hands, and at my request she reached her slender arm through the access hatch and up into the bow of the *Tiny* to attach a small rosette of strain gauges to the wall. These gauges would measure the amount of "flex" of the wall in response to each blast. And they worked! They showed the hull deforming at the exact time the blast waveforms hit the boat, every time. Unfortunately, the gauges were not positioned on the bottom of the model, where we eventually determined the blast was transmitting the most. As a result, the test team and I cannot say that we have proved exactly how the pressure was getting in. Rather, we have proved only that it was getting in somehow, and that parts of the hull were flexing.

However the pressure wave does get in, once it transmits it can then bounce around within the enclosed narrow walls and build upon itself. The entire goal of the experiments with the *Tiny* was to answer the second critical question, to measure what percentage of the blast wave in the water got passed through to the inside of the boat as this puff, and then hit the crew smack in their chests.

I needed to use knowledge from the decades of studies before mine to analyze the results from my own experiments. Luckily for me, a sunken ship is not very useful, and so with the goal of preserving their vessels, the naval community has studied underwater explosions for quite some time.

One of the first scientists to examine underwater blasts mathematically was G. I. Taylor, the same genius who calculated the atomic bomb's highly classified yield using only photographs published in *LIFE* magazine. To study underwater explosions, he suspended steel plates of varying thicknesses in the ocean and blasted them with TNT, each time measuring the shock wave and noting its effect on the plates. His goal was to predict when World War II–era ships would be fractured and sunk by nearby underwater mines.

Modern scientists are still building upon Taylor's pioneering work.

Each new batch of math wizards slowly contributes their data to the puzzle in a multigenerational group effort to understand how surfaces respond when hit by an explosion.

The advent of computational modeling in the late 1970s changed the game monumentally. The ships and tanks and buildings could suddenly be built artificially, using thousands or millions of tiny data points inside a computer instead of investing the time and expense to make a physical model of each and every setup. Scientists looking to predict the destructive effects of nuclear explosions started plugging the complex equations into elaborate computer simulations, sipping coffee while the machines slogged through the heavy math. Thousands of computers now sit in hundreds of labs, chugging tirelessly through millions of equations without error, overnight and through the weekends.

In a twist of cosmic irony, the modeling work most relevant to the case of the *Hunley* was performed at Clemson University at the same time as, but totally independently from, the conservationists scraping away at concretion in another building. The engineers of the Grujicic Lab built digital slabs of material and calculated how those slabs would respond to shock waves. They used a well-established family tree of equations that traces all the way back through decades of scientific lineage, straight to Taylor himself.

But their model, for the very first time, also carefully examined what happened *behind* the material slabs. Previous papers by other researchers had casually observed that a secondary pressure wave propagated off the back face of the slabs, but they had mostly dismissed it as an interesting side note. The Grujicic Lab modeled it fully. They observed a shock traveling inward off the flexing face of the digital material wall. Their results supported the previously published physical data from a different lab that had measured exactly such a wave propagating inside the body of an armored vehicle. And because the Grujicic model was digital, they could manipulate the variables in multitudinous ways, fully characterize the wall's behavior, and show that their results agreed with the rules and equations explored and outlined by previous researchers.

They still primarily dismissed this secondary shock wave as an interesting side note, just like the group that blasted the armored vehicles. And the fact that they did so was actually quite reasonable and understandable. The rates of transmission were so low that for most situations the secondary wave couldn't be considered a realistic source of potential injury. The shock was interesting, but too minuscule to be harmful. Except, of course, in unusual circumstances that would maximize the exposure. Like if an extremely large bomb were positioned close to a thin-walled structure, such as a historic submarine. Perhaps while immersed in a medium, such as water, that would very efficiently conduct the blast waves toward that structure.

Compared to a normal shock wave, the slow-rising pressure waves created by black powder are the equivalent of the person on the trampoline slowing the speed of their jump. It's as if they hit the trampoline with the same amount of force, but at a slow-motion rate of impact. This key difference makes it difficult to build a computational model to directly examine the effects on a structure from a nearby black powder explosion. Unfortunately, black powder is so profoundly obsolete that there are no published experiments in water—that I could find—to compare a model to. It would therefore be difficult to ensure that a computational model has been built correctly. In other words, the slow rise time tosses something of a wild card into the neat stack of calculations that are normally used to predict the damage from shock waves.

But still, Grujicic and Taylor and all those scientists between them had meticulously puzzled out many of those calculations for how material walls behave when smacked with a shock wave. Structures near a black powder explosion should still follow those same rules and patterns, the same laws of physics, but with the curves shifted because of the slow rise time of the powder. And because of our black powder experiments, our little team now had the data to evaluate how those curves shifted for the unique case of the *HL Hunley*. Together, their rules plus our experimental data could calculate how much pressure got inside the *Hunley*'s hull.

Once processed and plotted, our data turned out to create a stunning little curve, exactly as hoped. Even with the slow rise time of black powder, the measurements of transmission into the hull of the *Tiny* still fit the same smooth, arcing pattern of response as every blast experiment all the way back to Taylor. The curve had shifted, as expected, but it still fit the same rules, and now we had the data to support that assertion.

After some excited emailing back and forth, a friend in the same line of work stuck a gauge inside his underwater model during his next blast test. His structural model was different in form from the *Tiny* and his data point was in a different region of the curve, but nevertheless the single point he provided was neatly in line with the transmission predictions of the *Tiny*'s data. It was an external confirmation that came as a huge relief.

After all the heavy math, the final answer to the question was 8.4 percent. The pressure level inside the crew compartment of the *Hunley* would reach about 8.4 percent of the maximum pressure level of the portion of the blast waveform that slammed against her belly like thunder. At higher pressures, the percent transmitted of that higher pressure would also increase.

If the torpedo had been on an even, level line with the bottom of the hull, with the spar pointing forward rather than downward, almost none of the blast would have transmitted inside through the bow.*

---

*This is a descriptive version of the math and physics and was written to be understandable for general readers. It does not, therefore, go into all the complex details necessary to justify and complete the scientific analysis. The blast physics required to assess this problem does include actual math. For the technical information, please see the original scientific publication, Lance et al., 2017. The paper and all of my experimental data are freely available for download by the public, with no pay wall, through the prestigious open-access journal *PLOS One*.

Question number two was solved. Next, I had to figure out how much pressure was really sent out into the water by the *Hunley*'s massive, copper-encased, black powder torpedo.

———————

Months earlier, I had discovered that the archives of the Hagley Museum were filled with endless stacks of lab notebooks about black powder. Most people in the 1800s resorted to rudimentary approaches for testing the strengths of their powder mixtures, building devices like small pendulums that could measure how far the force from the burning material pushed a swinging weight. But at the du Pont powder mills they insisted upon science, and they were able to generate actual numbers.

The pressure gauges of the time were small, crushable copper devices. There were a few different exact forms, but to measure a test, one of them was screwed into the body of a piece of heavy artillery. Experimenters would load the weapon with the powder to be tested, and fire it. Not only could they measure the distance the projectile traveled, but the little copper devices would deform proportionate to the amount of pressure inside the barrel. The amount of crush could be translated into a numerical measurement of pressure.

Some of those data points were from charges of 135 pounds of powder, just like the minimum size of the *Hunley*'s torpedo. According to the historic data, 135 pounds of Civil War–era black powder, when confined, can create 24,200 pounds per square inch inside the barrel, or 167,000 kilopascals. For reference, that is more than 151 "Rachels standing still" pressing on each and every square inch of the inside of the artillery.

Our charges' construction materials would rupture and shatter at somewhere below their maximum possible internal pressure of 2,600 kilopascals, a number only one sixty-fourth the pressures generated by the du Ponts. Therefore, our little science tubes burst from internal pressures somewhere in the ballpark of a measly one sixty-fourth the internal pressure levels of a fully confined charge. The pressures our charges sent propagating out toward our small boat's hull would have been similarly smaller.

———————

I could also compare the pressures from my mini charges to the large-scale black powder tests conducted by my navy civil service colleagues. I had driven up to watch their actual blasts and been foiled by an ill-timed equipment failure, but the researchers were nonetheless generously willing to share their data. After some careful discussion, we agreed on the exact phrasing that would be used in my dissertation and in the final paper to publish the results. My supervisor from my base in Panama City* signed off on the sentence, and the Public Affairs Office approved it for public release.

"US Navy testing of a full-sized black powder charge designed to measure the output of the *Hunley*'s torpedo showed peak pressure values of approximately 7,600 kilopascals (1,100 psi) at a measurement location comparable to the keel of the *Hunley.*"

The full-sized charge had achieved pressure levels in the water, pressures that would hit along the bottom of the boat, forty-three times as high as mine, despite the fact that this charge was also constructed with limitations that potentially weakened its strength.

The data from the full-sized charge test and the historical data from Hagley told me that the pressures near the submarine's hull in 1864 would have been—at least—in the range of forty-three to sixty-four times stronger than anything I had measured in the pond.

———————

*Naval Surface Warfare Center Panama City Division, also called NSWC PCD.

f the *Hunley* had a charge filled with 135 pounds of black powder, then she would have blasted toward herself a rapidly rising pressure waveform with a peak pressure of, at minimum, the pressure level measured during the full-sized US Navy test: 7,600 kilopascals.

Gabriel Rains cleverly deduced that lowering the torpedo would cause more damage to the enemy ship. So, the torpedo was lowered, inadvertently positioning it so that it would transmit even more of the blast into the *Hunley*. Pressure is technically omnidirectional, but for the type of "trampoline bounce" behavior in this case, the amount transmitted inside is affected by the angle of the blast, and can be calculated as if the pressure is acting at an angle. So, with the torpedo at an estimated downward angle of 11 degrees, the fraction of the 7,600-kilopascal traveling wave that hit the keel perpendicularly would have been 1,460 kilopascals, or about 1.3 Rachels per square inch.

The *Tiny* taught us that 8.4 percent of that peak external pressure would transmit inside the hull. So, using the number of 8.4 percent, the crew sitting at their stations would have been exposed to a minimum of 123 kilopascals of pressure jumping around inside the metal tube. And it would have taken the form of a long scream of a pressure wave, with rapid rise times.

I could now check questions one and two off my to-do list. I knew about how much pressure the charge should have produced, and about how much pressure made its way inside the hull. They were not exact numbers, but they were reasonable estimates of the minimum expected levels.

The only question remaining was whether a minimum of 123 kilopascals of pressure could kill. Luckily, that was the easy part, thanks to the mental giants who came before me.

In the field of injury biomechanics, it's not considered very informative to label threats simply as "fatal" or "safe." The reality is, people can have wildly different physical responses to the same accident. Millions of minor variations, such as body mass, physical fitness, genetics, and the exact position at the time of the event create a spectrum of possible injuries that can result from the same situation. If 100 identical cars traveling at the same speed all crash into 100 identical trees, some of the drivers will walk away while others will not survive. The most useful prediction that we can provide, as a field, is to give each person a percent chance of injury or death.

Blast trauma is no different. The predictive curves, called the "risk curves," calculate the percent chance of injury or death from each explosion. The risk curves for blasts in air are the product of decades of hard labor by hundreds of scientists who laboriously collected and compiled more than 12,000 data points, painstakingly, one at a time. The most common current use for the curves is to help prevent injuries and fatalities to soldiers from IEDs.

At the minimum expected peak pressure of 123 kilopascals, each member of the *Hunley*'s crew would have had a 95 percent risk of immediate, severe pulmonary trauma. The kind that would leave them gasping for air, possibly coughing up blood, and most likely unable to crank. Each man would have also had a 20 percent risk of immediate fatality, of slumping over at his battle station without ever processing the realization of his victory. Because that probability applies to each man, it means that this scenario carries fifty-fifty odds that at least two crewmen dropped dead instantly. With a 95 percent chance of serious pulmonary injury, it seems improbable that any survivors could have done much to help bring the boat to shore. And those are the calculated odds using data from a 135-pound torpedo, tested in an experiment with a casing that was likely underconfined.

S ince the case of the *Hunley*, no other submariners have been shown to have received such injuries, even though many other submarines have experienced underwater explosions. This conspicuous absence is because by the turn of the year 1900, submariners had already unwittingly protected themselves from blast transmission. They began designing their vessels to travel deeper and deeper beneath the surface of the waves, and as they did so they made the hulls of their vessels thicker and thicker. Serendipitously, these thicker hulls also reduced the ability of blast waves to force their way inside. Most submarines beginning around World War I also had two hulls: both an inner and an outer hull, which would have provided further protection. However, to keep the math simple, I will ignore the additionally protective effects of the outer hull.

The inner hull of a typical World War II submarine was shaped out of curved steel with a thickness of ⅞ of an inch, equal to 2.2 centimeters—which is over double the thickness of the *Hunley*'s. Most depth charges were made out of TNT, usually 300 pounds of TNT to be exact, and the submariners knew these bombs could split open their vessels anywhere inside a range of about 100 feet. Using the curves generated during the *Tiny* testing, a hull of this thickness exposed to a 300-pounds-of-TNT explosion that took place just a hair beyond the kill radius would result in a transmission of a measly 0.180 percent of the external pressures to the inside. That is only one forty-seventh of the percentage transmitting into the *Hunley*.

Inside a World War II submarine with its thickened hull, transmitting at a measly 0.180 percent, the pressure levels from an almost-ship-crunching explosion would be only 2.4 kilopascals. This value not only has zero chance of causing any injury or fatality, but it can actually be discussed in terms of sound. It is a pressure level equal to 161 decibels, which is about the same volume level as a nearby gunshot. World War II submariners described the sound of nearby depth charges as "deafening," "abominable," "ear-shattering," and like "someone hitting the hull with a million sledgehammers." A remarkably universal observation is that the barrages of underwater TNT would cause the onboard light-bulbs and other glass items to shatter, a phenomenon that is consistent with low levels of blast waves, which tend to make frangible glass objects their first victims. However, to the submariners, this explosion, even though it was only a tiny fraction of an inch away from crashing through their hull and sinking them, would nonetheless have a zero percent chance of causing injury.

The charge weight of 135 pounds comes from a historical drawing that is nestled away in the US National Archives, in the papers and records of Union officer Quincy Adams Gillmore. General Gillmore was responsible for leading the assault on Charleston, although his ill health meant that he was more frequently absent from the city. The boxes of manila folders holding his papers include a full stack of drawings of Confederate torpedoes, obviously penned by an illustrator with technical expertise. Most of them are drawn to perfect scale, with the goal of documenting the variety of torpedo models that were found in Confederate hands.

The drawings of the torpedo supposedly belonging to the *Hunley* are extraordinary in their detail. A simple, handwritten label at the top of one illustration claims that this is the torpedo "used for blowing up the *Housatonic*." However, no other supporting documentation is attached, and no other information about the torpedo or the attack is present anywhere in Gillmore's files. The drawing floats alone, with absolutely no context besides being buried among other drawings of varied torpedoes.

There are two problems with this claim. First, the drawings are to perfect scale. Because the file folder is filled with miscellaneous Confederate weapons and designs, it seems as if the pile of illustrations was made after the fall of Charleston, long after the attack of the *Hunley*, once Gillmore's staff entered the decimated city and obtained access to the Confederacy's cache of remaining torpedoes. If so, the scale drawing therefore seems to have been made from a second torpedo, one that was declared by someone onsite to be sufficiently similar to the torpedo used by the *Hunley* to justify adding that note at the top.

Second, as previously mentioned, the illustration is labeled as a "Singer's torpedo," but it does not actually depict one. "Singer's torpedo" was a specific, floating, tethered design commonly used by the Confederacy, and it both looked and functioned differently from the one in the drawing. Singer's design was made of tin and had a trigger mechanism with an external spring and plunger, very different from the internal mechanism shown in the illustration.

A Union-compiled book now resting in the National Archives contains contemporary letters and drawings about Confederate torpedoes, and this book unwittingly contains several drawings of Singer's design. None of them are correctly labeled as Singer's torpedoes, indicating that the Union did not in fact know what that design looked like. The labeling discrepancy is therefore critical enough to raise this question: How reliable was this person who declared the two torpedoes were similar or the same?

A different, previously undiscussed historical record states that the "submerged and slumbering thunderbolt" was much larger. It states that the torpedoes being built for the Confederate fish boats were filled with 200 pounds of black powder, not 135. And that record comes with both context and established reliability.

Edmund Ruffin considered himself the chronicler of the Civil War. He wrote down every detail he could, carrying on with ink he made himself once the Confederacy's supplies began to run low. His profound emotional investment in the increasingly futile war did make some sense. After all, he had helped start it.

Long before the 1860 presidential election, the Virginian plantation

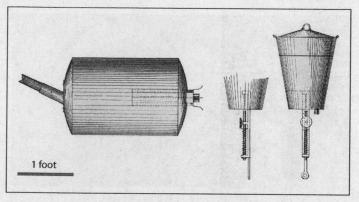

The purported drawing of the *Hunley*'s torpedo (*left*) and a drawing of Singer's torpedo (*right*).

owner and noted agricultural pioneer spent years writing passionately about the South's need to preserve slavery in order to keep the plantations running. So, when abolitionist Abraham Lincoln was elected, Ruffin began to argue even more fervently that secession was the only possible path forward.

Ruffin decided to travel to wherever the action was, so that he could observe and record. At sixty-seven he was considered beyond the ideal combat age, but he insisted on joining the burgeoning Confederate military nonetheless. He had himself photographed proudly in his gray uniform, seated with his long rifle propped between his legs, shoulder-length silver hair swept back to reveal a stern, resolute, increasingly toothless face.

As a sign of gratitude for his influence pushing toward the decision to secede, Ruffin was given an honor he described as a "highly appreciated compliment." He was asked to fire one of the first artillery shots to spark the entire war, at the start of the assault on then Union-occupied Fort Sumter. This privilege permanently secured him as a Confederate hero.

His status as a sort of founding father granted him an all-access

Diarist Edmund Ruffin.

pass to the inner machinations of the Confederate military, and he used this proverbial pass to witness and document as much as he could in tight, tiny handwriting, in the form of a diary that would eventually consume thousands of pages.* Despite his obvious political extremism, historians now consider Edmund Ruffin's diary to be one of the most

---

*Here's an example of Ruffin's unusual level of access: He wanted to attend the hanging of John Brown after Brown's failed raid on Harpers Ferry and attempt to lead a slave insurrection. The hanging was not open to the public, but because of his stature, Ruffin alone was granted an exception. He was given a uniform and permitted to stand among the cadets in formation at the Virginia Military Institute to witness the execution.

important firsthand accounts of the events of the war. More valuably, while he did sometimes record inaccurate information that he had received secondhand from newspaper articles, his actual observations have proven to be largely correct.

In the fall of 1863, when he heard that the city of Charleston was under siege, he journeyed back down to watch and document the fighting. He was treated, as usual, as a VIP. General Beauregard himself heard of Ruffin's arrival and provided him with a personal letter that let him go wherever he wanted to go, and see whatever he wanted to see, always with a hero's accommodation and often with the use of Confederate vessels and troops as personal transport. Luckily for history, among the things he chose to observe and document were the submarine *HL Hunley*, the Confederacy's other fish boats, and perhaps most important, their torpedoes.

Nestled in alongside his profoundly racist rants about the importance of slavery, Ruffin's diary entries about the *Hunley* provide some of the only accurate contemporary descriptions of the boat. He carefully observed her length shortly after her arrival in Charleston, correctly declaring it to be "from 36 to 40 feet." He went on to describe her shape, her dimensions, her bow and stern, her conning towers. Everything he said about the vessel has since been proven correct. He knew her strategic plan, and he knew that the original desired target for all the fish-boat privateers was the highly valued USS *Ironsides*. He wrote what is perhaps the only record that correctly recounted that there were eight men to her crew—most records, even historical ones, incorrectly claim there were nine—and he also saw her torpedo.

"The torpedo, in a copper case, cylindrical, with conical ends . . . It is more than double the size of the torpedo carried by the 'David,' which contained 75 lbs. of powder." The conical ends precisely match the drawings and descriptions of Gabriel Rains about the pointy-ended torpedoes being built for the fish boats, but they stand in contrast to the rounded caps on the drawing from Gillmore's files.

Ruffin later directly interviewed the men working on the torpedo boats, and asked them about the weapons they planned to use. This too he recorded diligently: "The torpedoes will also strike lower [in the water], & the charges of powder will be increased from 75 lbs to 200."

Using basic scaling laws for explosions, increasing the charge weight from 135 to 200 pounds of powder should result in peak pressures in the water that are about 16 percent higher. Applying that increase to the full-sized 135-pound data point would yield 8,816 kilopascals in the water around the keel of the *Hunley*, and 143 inside hitting the crew. Those pressures would give each man a 98 percent chance of serious trauma, and a 42 percent chance of immediate death.

At the end of the war, depressed, lonely, and fraught with physical illness, Edmund Ruffin could not stand the thought of a Union victory and the inevitable end of slavery. He made one last diary entry vehemently declaring his inability to tolerate oppressive "Yankee rule." Then he went upstairs, inserted the end of his long firearm into his mouth, propped the butt of the weapon on the ground, and used a forked stick to press the trigger.

––––––––––

Even though they are severe, the pressures I've calculated may still potentially be lower than what really happened. Blast scientists often use a concept called TNT equivalency, sometimes known as "relative effectiveness," which gets abbreviated as "RE." Through RE, all explosive types can be roughly compared to the common yardstick of TNT. For example, if a nuclear bomb has an RE of 4,500, that means that you would need 4,500 kilos of TNT to create the same amount of "boom" as one kilo of the nuclear-bomb material.

Higher numbers mean a stronger explosive material, and values below 1.0 mean that the explosive is weaker than TNT. It's an unrefined and imperfect yardstick for many reasons—it does not inherently account for the slow rise times of black powder, or the long, drawn-out pressure waves of nuclear weaponry—but it still enables a rough kind of comparison.

RE values for black powder vary even more than for other explosives because of its highly fickle nature. The values can change because of the exact powder composition and method of manufacture, and they definitely change with varying levels of charge confinement. Underconfined charges will, unsurprisingly, underperform. For charges in air with a moderate level of confinement, such as a thick copper casing, the majority of the reported RE values in the scientific literature cluster just above 0.40. It is not perfect to apply these values to in-water tests, but they can still be used to calculate a rough theoretical estimate for the purpose of curiosity. Using an RE value of 0.40, the 200-pound charge would, in theory, have output the same maximum pressure levels as 80 pounds of TNT.

The peak pressures put out by an 80-pound charge would result in a 99.9 percent chance of serious injury, and a 92 percent chance of immediate death for each man inside the submarine. The crew would have also experienced at least a 46 percent chance of death from blast-induced traumatic brain injury, even if their lungs somehow escaped damage. As discussed earlier, blast-induced traumatic brain injury is subtle in its presentation, and it leaves the skull and the structure of the brain intact. Even in fatal cases, the only trace is a diffuse patch of blood that may or may not spread across the outer surface of the brain.

Several of the skulls of the recovered *Hunley* crewmen still, miraculously, held their intact brains. The soft tissues were severely damaged and shrunk by long-term exposure to salt water, but they were nonetheless carefully examined by medical personnel. Some of the brains had patterns of diffuse staining on their surfaces, and those stains appeared to be consistent with blood.

---

had one measly hour in which I had to explain the last several years of my labor. A panel of five academic experts, including my adviser, each wielding a PhD and decades of experience in related fields, would sit in an auditorium and listen to me speak—and then judge whether I would receive a doctorate of my own. Pass or fail. Worthy or not worthy.

I did not need to convince them that the crew died from blast trauma in order to graduate. I just needed to convince them that my methods and analysis had been sufficiently thorough.

I coped with the stress-induced insomnia by baking thematically. I set up a table on one side of the room with a lemon cake from a recipe originating with Robert E. Lee's wife, and an almond cake made famous by Mary Todd Lincoln. I also provided a large bowl of peanuts, a favored snack for both sides in the war during the lean times on the march.

My parents drove down from Michigan to sit near the front, in lecture-hall swivel chairs next to Nick. Friends from the hyperbaric chamber made the walk over from the hospital, giving me a wave and a smile as they climbed the stairs of the lecture hall to find seats of their own. My lab mates took the right-hand side of the room, there for support as always. Two of my coworkers on the naval base in Florida were streaming the defense live via webcam.

"If you pass, touch your shoulder," one had emailed me beforehand. "I'll be watching." Before I began, I looked around at the friendly, familiar faces and had a moment of mental clarity. This room was filled with the people who had carried me through the project, supported me, helped me find the right resources, made sure I had food and clean clothes. They were here to see the results of their hard work too.

After the presentation is over, the committee takes a private moment to themselves to discuss their thoughts. As is normal, I was asked to wait outside, closing the heavy wooden double doors behind me to secure them alone in the lecture hall. My lab mates joined me, and we sat together in awkward, silent suspense. When the doors reopened, I was invited back in, and one of my committee members stuck out his right hand.

"Dr. Lance," he said, "good work." After the firm shake, I brought my hand up to my shoulder for my friend on the webcam.

———————

S tanding on the wrong side of the footbridge's handrail, balanced on a crossbeam, I waved awkwardly at some Duke campus pedestrians who were too polite to ask questions. I wrapped a worn yellow ratchet strap around a solid metal part of the structure, and used every ounce of force I could muster to extricate the long wooden rails from the muck. After struggling to maneuver them over the handrails of the footbridge without falling in, I thought I was finally done with the project. But then a gust of wind blew my sun hat off my head and, before I could drop the rails to grab it, it flew away to land softly on the brown, still surface of the pond. Setting down the wooden planks, I kicked off my sneakers, swung my leg back over the handrail, and plunged feetfirst into the water one final time.

CHAPTER 11

FEBRUARY 17, 1864

Think of the destruction this infernal machine effected. . . . The successes of the Confederates have made the torpedo, which before was looked on with loathing—a name not to be spoken except contemptuously—a recognized factor in modern naval warfare.

—Unnamed Union reporter

A gentle breeze ran over the damaged rooftops of Charleston, carrying the sounds and smells of the war zone out to sea as the sun began to set behind her crumbling skyline. She was "the most bombarded mainland city in US history," and the scope of her destruction meant that she would hold the title, without question, for centuries to come.

The soldiers and sailors on the long, sandy island north of her harbor mouth had watched and felt the same destruction. They had patiently endured thousands of bombs lobbed into their forts and encampments, and they had shared in the mass starvation that was occurring slowly because warships were blockading the harbor entrance. Not even the officers or the wealthy had been spared.

One small group of sailors had a plan, though. They had a dark metal submarine, built by hand, and they would use it to break this blockade. The complete and abject fear that such a weapon of stealth and power would instill would be too great, they believed, for the crew of any Union ship to suppress the panicked urge to flee in terror. They would have to take their ships and run back home to the North, opening Charleston to receive fresh supplies. This "infernal machine" would help the submariners summon the horrors of hell and visit them upon their enemies.

The cigar-shaped sub bobbed peacefully in the protected waters behind Sullivan's Island. Her crew had been waiting for the Atlantic to grow sufficiently smooth so that waves and chop would not swamp their little boat. And on February 17, 1864, the water was finally calm. The crew assembled.

The men in the middle of the boat would have filed in first, with six-foot-one Virginian Frank Collins folding himself into the third crank spot, and Europeans Carlsen and Miller taking their places at handles four and five. Next to the three of them slid arthritic Lumpkin at the second handle, who'd walked to the dock with a slouch but would have conformed nicely to the curved interior of the submarine. European Arnold Becker, also a young man, had nonetheless already lived a hard life of physical activity by his fresh age of twenty. He was now fully trained in the duties of the first crank position as well.

Wicks climbed in the rear conning tower, wrapped in his warm coat, to sit at position six, and he was followed by Joseph Ridgaway at crank location seven, sporting a slouch hat. The men tucked their canteens of water under the bench near their feet, among the various metal blocks arranged in the bilge for ballast weight. They were prepared for the long journey out to the nearest Union ship.

George Dixon dropped into the front conning tower last, taking his seat on the small personal bench reserved for the captain. He was in his mid-twenties, with a full head of blond hair.

The crew knew all about the previous sinkings. They knew about the accidental triggering of the dive planes, and they knew about the incident that got the boat rechristened *Hunley*. They knew that the bloated bodies of previous sailors in their seats had been removed in pieces, their rotted flesh scrubbed off the interior walls by slaves. They knew that Horace Hunley himself had died curled in the conning tower, clutching a candle and trying to escape. But this crew needed the blockade to be lifted, and they were being paid well to do it, and so they climbed through the hatches anyway.

They all carried items in their pockets that spoke deeply of their belief that they would continue living after this night, that they would return home instead of sinking forever into a watery grave. The smokers brought their pipes. Dixon brought with him his pocket watch and several pieces of expensive diamond jewelry. Most notably, secured in Dixon's left pants pocket, right above his old wound, was his lucky gold coin. At his signal, the crew began to crank.

They had timed their departure with the outgoing tide. The waters of nearby Breach Inlet were notoriously swift during ebb tide, and the men would use this current to boost their speed and propel them toward their floating target. They were aiming for the USS *Housatonic*, the nearest ship offshore and one of the few without protective chains or nets dangling in the water to entrap them. As they threaded the little inlet to reach the ocean beyond the protection of Sullivan's Island, they signaled to the men at Battery Marshall, who would spend the night waiting for their return.

After long hours of cranking, Dixon looked out the small glass windows of the fore conning tower over the dark waters ahead of him and saw that they were in range of their target. The lower corner of the wedge-shaped, cast-iron bow boasted a hefty bolt, which served as a pivot for the submarine's 16-foot narwhal tusk of a spar. Someone in the crew slowly, carefully let loose the line that controlled the spar. The line spooled out, and the spar pivoted down. As the spar rotated, the massive orange cylinder at the far end dipped below the surface of the water.

This torpedo was the end result of the sweat and labor of dozens if not hundreds of Confederates all working with the same goal of breaking the blockade. Gabriel Rains first drafted the design, with a trigger modified by one of his crew after his departure from Charleston. It was filled with 200 pounds of black powder that had been made and shipped by younger brother George Washington Rains to replenish the city after a recent battle. The copper had ensured the torpedo stayed barnacle-free during long nights of bobbing in the salt water, and the thick metal wall with its welded seams would ensure proper confinement. The pressure-sensitive trigger would control the bomb so that it would explode only once it was in the perfect position, lowered in the water, well beneath the target's hull. When it was in the worst possible position for the safety of both crews.

Her torpedo now lowered like the lance of a knight, the *Hunley* charged forward. Cranking at full speed, the submariners propelled their vessel to slice through the cold ocean waters, hurtling headlong for the wooden hull of the Union sloop before them.

The scene on the deck of the *Housatonic* was sedate at first, nothing in comparison to the furious cranking happening inside the submarine. This crew had not yet spotted the oncoming threat. Robert F. Flemming patrolled the starboard bow, inspecting the waters that separated his ship from the Confederate lands. John Teddeman performed his regular duties on board. Beneath the deck, Capt. Charles Pickering pored over documents.

Flemming spotted the smooth black sliver moving swiftly against the current of the outgoing tide, and raised the alarm. The gong was sounded. The crew of well over 100 men simultaneously bolted to their battle stations. Pickering dashed upstairs, into the chilly night air. He grabbed a rifle, jumped onto the horse block to get a better downward angle, and began to fire. The men trying to train the heavy artillery all failed to hit the rapidly approaching menace.

The submarine reached her target. The torpedo, buried from view by the water and the waves, jammed into the wooden hull of the *Housa-*

tonic. A retaining wire holding a firing pin in place snapped. The pin, now free, was pushed backward by the spring wrapped around it. Its blunt end smashed into a mercury fulminate cap. The mercury fulminate began to react from the heat generated by the force of the impact. Its flame began to spread.

The fine granules of black powder nearest the cap began to burn first. The grains were consumed from the outside in, each disappearing in a flash, generating a small amount of heat and spewing flaming particles out toward its neighbors. The neighbors began to catch. The fire continued to spread. The heat was enough to start the larger particles burning, the coarser grains that filled the rest of the bomb. The burning front of the growing flame raged through the length of the torpedo, starting at the end near the trigger and moving backward toward the spar of the *Hunley.* Each granule turned into gas. The hot gas began to shove against the walls of the torpedo, trying to break free.

The first split began to form in the copper at the end brushing against the hull of the *Housatonic.* The crack began to grow. Now the gas had an escape route, and it blasted out of its prison with abandon, shredding the copper casing into ribbons and forcing it backward in curls over the tip of the spar. The massive, superheated ball of gas erupted free. It was not enough to create a shock wave, but it was enough to send a terrifying spike of pressure hurtling out through the water in every direction.

The downward angle of the spar ensured that the blast occurred several feet below the underbelly of the submarine. The pressure wave traveled up and toward it. When the wave hit, the hull material flexed, quickly, much more quickly than the submarine as a whole could bounce and respond to jostle the crew inside, and this rapid little jounce of the hull wall forced a second pressure wave inside the boat. Trapped inside the enclosed hull, this second pressure wave began to reflect. It built on itself like a scream in an echo chamber, amplifying the effects of its own destruction.

Also inside the chamber were the crew, hunched over the handles of their cranks. The reflections hit them from all sides and sped rapidly through their flesh. The waves came to a nearly dead stop once they hit bubbly lung, and the blood vessels in the lung walls, unable to absorb the energy, burst wide open. Blood sprayed inward. Breathing stopped. Vessels may have ruptured on the surfaces of their brains. Some may have had minor fractures in the fragile bones surrounding their sinuses. Some simply slumped over, no damage to any tissue but the lungs, dead where they sat.

Those who died immediately would not have even had time to realize the twinned truths of their victory and demise.

A part inside Dixon's gold watch snapped, locking the hands forever at 8:23. Dixon's head dropped against the side of the hull. His ankles were lightly crossed, and one hand fell to his thigh. His body was propped up by the hull wall and his small captain's bench. He never knew that he made history.

If any still lived, they lived only minutes more. Those who survived struggled to breathe, gasping for air against the stabbing compressive pain in their chests. Unable to move from the pain, they would have quickly entered a state of shock. Their heart rates dropped. Their blood pressures plummeted. Their brains and extremities stopped receiving the life-saving oxygen normally sent by the heart. Their breathing slowed . . . then stopped. They too collapsed into the bilge.

The deck of the *Housatonic* had sprayed into a million shards of wood and metal hurtling into the air, deadly projectiles that then rained down onto the crew. Pickering was hit and injured by the thunderstorm of detritus, as was steward John Gough. Most of the crew had already run for the bow and safety, but as the ship gave a mighty heave to port, the few remaining joined in the mad dash forward. A cloud with the noxious stench of rotten eggs drifted off across the smooth surface of the calming ocean.

Some of the crew clambered into small boats, heading for the nearby USS *Canandaigua* to get help. Robert Flemming looked back along the length of his fatally wounded ship and saw the black line of the *Hunley* still floating nearby. The rest worked their way carefully into the rigging. Pickering was fished out of the water and draped among the rigging, soaked and injured. As they waited for rescue, the effects of the cold began to set in. Five had been killed.

The submarine, now filled with silent ghosts, drifted untended on the outgoing tide. A small wave hit her, splashing some water in through a broken window or the unlatched front conning tower, and as a result she dropped slightly lower in the water. A second wave hit as she floated farther, and a third, each contributing a small volume of salt water to slosh in her interior. With no one alive to operate the bilge pumps, the water level slowly began to rise around the ankles of the corpses. Eventually, it became too much. She started to sink. Water rushed through the forward conning tower, bringing the little boat to the sand but leaving an air space inside for stalactites to grow. The *HL Hunley* and her dead crew settled to a quiet grave 30 feet beneath the dark-blue waves.

EPILOGUE

Undoubtedly the concussion produced by the explosion of the torpedo destroyed instantly the lives of Dixon and his crew.

—Unnamed reporter, *The Times-Picayune,*
New Orleans, 1877

The *Hunley*'s feat was not again repeated until World War I. By then, submarines had morphed into sleek, military-funded juggernauts, and torpedoes into vicious, self-propelled projectiles. Fifty years after the death of the USS *Housatonic*, a prowling German U-boat sent a British vessel to her grave, and this second victory further cemented the previously "infernal" submarine as a necessary and deadly new tool of combat.

Even though the *Hunley* victoriously sank her target, she failed in the grander scheme of her mission. Instead of running home in the hoped-for terror, the Union sailors remained undeterred, the fleet stayed put, and the blockade remained unbroken. The citizens of Charleston continued to starve. Columbia, the capital of South Carolina, fell precisely one year after the *Hunley*'s Pyrrhic victory, and the mayor of Charleston surrendered his city the day after that. The former Confederate officers, previously so loath to remain part of America, began one by one to pledge their loyalty to the US government so that they could regain their citizenship.

The *Hunley* was gone, but not forgotten. The mouth of Charleston's harbor was replete with the ravaged, sunken hulks of dozens of combat-damaged ships. Even though they were the final homes of human remains, they were also riddled with hundreds of thousands of dollars' worth of metal and equipment, so salvage companies promptly got to work scrambling for the rights to the wrecks. By 1870 hard-hat divers touched their heavily weighted boots to the sands around the *Housatonic*. They sifted through the debris and muck, raising first the hefty propeller before moving on to other sundry chunks of metal and relics that could be sold at auction. An intact, corked bottle of wine, newly overgrown with seashells and subaquatic moss, made its way into the private collection of one of the divers.

With these dives came reports of the missing *Hunley*. The fish boat, apparently less financially valuable than the massive bulk quantities of scrap metal that could be recovered from the larger ship, was still a point of curiosity and fascination. Some accounts were clear fabrications, claiming that the little sub had been sucked into the hole her own torpedo blew in the side of the *Housatonic*, and that the two lay tangled together "in grim dead lock" on the ocean floor. Many more reports got the distance between the wrecks wrong, a potentially easy mistake to make in the turbid waters where visibility was only a few feet and in an area littered with unlabeled marker buoys, including one near the final location of the submarine and potentially even attached to it.

But some of these reports also contain eerily accurate details, details that we now know to be true. One diver provides a description that the sub seemed to be upside down because her propeller was "now uppermost," which is actually how the unusually constructed vessel would have looked when right-side up, as she was found. One said that her bow was pointing back toward the wreck of the *Housatonic*. Some reported that even in death "all of her men were at their stations."

After the divers left, she sat unperturbed for another hundred years. The turn of the century saw improvements in shipping, and with them the mouth of Charleston Harbor was opened and deepened. The construction of jetties shifted the sands of the area, and the rapid change in topography provides one theory for how the *Hunley* was buried quickly enough to keep her in such pristine condition.

But in the 1970s, archaeologist and diver E. Lee Spence kicked his way nearly 30 feet underwater to help pluck some snagged fishing equipment off an obstruction. Pulling marine growth from the hard surface, he noticed it had the sloping curve of a long, unusually smooth body that seemed atypical for a creation of nature. Spence knew the history of the area and of the *Hunley*, and he marked the location.

Since the site was over 3 nautical miles from land, not including the man-made jetties, it was in federal waters. Spence, who considered the submarine "part of our national heritage," wanted it to be recovered, conserved, and publicly displayed for educational purposes. At the time, Sen. Strom Thurmond was heavily involved in the development and construction of the museum that would eventually become Patriots Point Naval and Maritime Museum in Charleston, and Spence thought this museum would be a suitable location for the artifact. He began to write letters, including to Thurmond, trying to advocate for the boat's recovery and permanent location in Charleston.

He received enthusiastic permissions to perform the recovery from the state and local agencies and the museum personnel, as well as from the local branch of the US Army Corps of Engineers. He provided the army a map depicting the broad area he thought needed further archaeological investigation, but also containing a small, carefully drawn circle nearly centered over the location that would eventually be verified as the final resting place of the *Hunley*. The circle correctly indicated that the *Hunley* had drifted out to sea after her victory and was not located between the *Housatonic* and shore, as most other explorers mistakenly believed at the time. However, the General Services Administration (the GSA), which was most likely the legal owner of the federally located wreck, wrote back vaguely in April 1974 that before they could grant him contractual rights to recover the submarine, they needed to "complete certain internal requirements."

After months of deliberation, the GSA finally responded. They said they still had unresolved questions about the legal requirements of the Antiquities Act and therefore were "holding in abeyance the issuance of any contracts covering the raising of sunken vessels." They did not specify what those questions were.

Spence's claim may have been the accidental victim of an unrelated discovery: He began writing to the GSA in January 1974 and at first they seemed receptive, keeping the personal check he wrote for them to process the claim paperwork. However, by September they had changed their minds. In between, in March 1974, another private team announced that they had found the wreck of the famous ironclad USS *Monitor*. It was also located in federal waters. Any method for granting salvage rights that the GSA applied to the *Hunley* would likely set a precedent for how rights should be granted to the USS *Monitor*.

The government would eventually decide to keep the *Monitor*. Her site would be declared a National Marine Sanctuary, and portions of her wreck would be salvaged by US Navy divers for preservation and display in a museum. The GSA returned Spence's check but made no moves to salvage the *Hunley* themselves as they had the *Monitor*, and the news of the discovery fizzled.

In 1995, Clive Cussler's announcement to the media revived the name of the *Hunley* in spectacular fashion, causing immediate sensational news coverage around the world. The famous author had used his personal funds to partially sponsor the search, and this time the divers brought back video footage as proof. The GSA did not seem interested in being involved, and quickly passed control of the relic to the Department of the Navy.

Following this announcement, the government of South Carolina was more coordinated in its approach than it had been the first time. State senator Glenn McConnell was a prominent member of the Sons of Confederate Veterans and the co-owner of a store dedicated to the sale of Confederate memorabilia, so he immediately designated himself the submarine's fiercest advocate. He assembled the Hunley Commission, a group of state senators, representatives, gubernatorial appointees from the Sons of Confederate Veterans, and a retired rear admiral. Together, the group decided to "be as aggressive as possible" in obtaining "control of this piece of southern history."

Senator Thurmond leapt into action, quickly quashing language in a federal bill that would send the *Hunley* to Alabama, her place of construction. Then on October 24, 1995, the members of the Hunley Commission assembled in DC. With them in the meeting was Strom Thurmond, and across the table were the representatives of the Naval History and Heritage Command, the NHHC, which was called the NHC at that time. Prior to this meeting, the navy had been largely unresponsive to the demands of the Hunley Commission, seeming to push them off with polite but noncommittal language. After this meeting, all parties agreed unanimously that South Carolina would have full control of the *Hunley* in perpetuity.

Interestingly, nobody from South Carolina or the Hunley Commission seems to have any record of exactly what took place in that meeting on October 24, 1995. Thurmond's schedule shows an hour and a half budgeted for the conversation, a lengthy period of time for a man who provided the Dalai Lama with only minutes. Documents obtained from the Hunley Commission via a Freedom of Information Act (FOIA) request explicitly state that Thurmond had at least one aide in the meeting taking notes for the group, but FOIA requests and research in Strom Thurmond's archived documents failed to turn up any record of the notes themselves. Whatever it was that did happen, it got South Carolina the boat. Later, Friends of the *Hunley*–affiliated writer Brian Hicks referred to it as "blackmail."

In the fall of 1995, Strom Thurmond was the newly minted chair of the Senate Armed Services Committee. The US military had an overseas presence in the still-tense situation in Bosnia, but the procurement budget for the Department of Defense was at its lowest point since 1950.

Many weeks that fall, Thurmond had taken to the Senate floor to argue against bills that would further cut the military's funds. It seems plausible that, to win for his state the submarine that they craved, Thurmond might have threatened to simply switch sides in the budget argument.

Before the navy acquiesced in late October, the Hunley Commission had hatched a plan to use E. Lee Spence's information and guidance to go find the boat for themselves. However, they also seemed to want legal assurances from Spence that he did not want to keep the submarine for himself. According to the Hunley Commission meeting minutes, based on what read like thin verbal promises of involvement in the project, with little debate and no lawyer present, Spence signed over all of his rights to the claim. After reaching the agreement of possession with the navy, the Hunley Commission decided that Spence was no longer needed, and that he should be excluded.

The title for the *Hunley* never officially transferred to South Carolina, and it still resides with the US Navy. The important thing, the primary thing that the members of the commission wanted, was control over the display. They wanted to ensure "proper exhibition" "and interpretation" of the submarine, with legal ownership a secondary issue. They seemed especially worried about the changing currents of American political correctness—by then people were already protesting the Confederate battle flag flying over the South Carolina Statehouse. One member of the commission "expressed his concern that 10 or 15 years from now, there might be certain provisions on how the *Hunley* should be displayed." The commission members made a repeated habit of referring to the Civil War as "the War Between the States."

The *Enola Gay*, the plane that dropped the atomic bomb on Hiroshima, was at that time proverbially buried by controversy because of its planned display in the Smithsonian Institution. Some protesters thought the airplane's display needed more focus on the atrocities of nuclear warfare, while other protesters countered that the display should downplay that subject and focus instead on the suffering of American military personnel in the Pacific. Glenn McConnell, during a meeting of the Hunley Commission, "expressed his strong feelings about the presentation of the [*Hunley's*] exhibit—in not wanting to see the *Hunley* become the new *Enola Gay*." Before the agreement of October 24, the Smithsonian was a leading candidate for the permanent placement of the sub.

The *Hunley's* advocates often wrote to one another, and these documents shed further light on the motivation behind their concerns over the display of the Confederate relic. In one letter, Glenn McConnell had the Hunley Commission's attorney send a newspaper clipping to Strom Thurmond along with a letter on McConnell's behalf. The clipping was about a "minority employee [who] 'angrily protested' the use of the Confederate battle flag." The state flag of Georgia, which at that time heavily featured the image of the Confederate battle flag, was removed from a display as a result of that protest. "According to Senator McConnell," the attorney wrote, "this is the type of action which necessitates that the State insist on control over the presentation of the *Hunley*."

The commission members got their way. While early drafts of the agreement between the Hunley Commission and the US Navy included provisions for neutral third-party arbitration in the event of any disagreement over the display, the commission resisted these arrangements vehemently. The final contract provides for some preliminary arbitration over display conflicts, but ultimately the Hunley Commission has full control. However, they do pledge to think carefully about the opinions of all people concerned when making their final decision. In July 2000, South Carolina lowered the Confederate battle flag from the top of the Statehouse Building. In August 2000, the *Hunley* was raised from the ocean floor and carried to North Charleston.

The *Hunley* is on display at the Warren Lasch Conservation Center, a facility owned by Clemson University. The Friends of the *Hunley*, the nonprofit organization charged with fund-raising efforts for the *Hunley* project group, was heavily involved in the museum's curation and is considered legally separate from the university but is based out of the same building. When I last toured the museum I was unable to find, even in the sections dedicated to general Civil War history, a single mention of slavery.

As for me, I tried to move on to other scientific pursuits after the *Hunley* research and my defense, but like the U-Haul emblazoned with the image of the *Hunley* that kept showing up in my apartment complex parking lot, the story of the submarine kept following me around. I was surprised and humbled by the amount of press attention surrounding the paper, especially because I never thought my theory was anything revolutionary. It was one seriously massive bomb, but other people had published the same idea before; I had simply been the first to provide data. The earliest reference I could find was written by a newspaper reporter in 1877, even though he used the now-obsolete terminology of referring to a blast waveform as a "concussion," a term edged out of use because it was too easily confused with the head injury called concussion, which is instead caused by blunt force trauma.

Nick and I were married in April 2017 at the Museum of Life and Science in Durham, wearing Converse sneakers instead of dress shoes. I left my job with the US Navy a few weeks before the release of the final paper in August 2017, but for unrelated reasons. The small project I was pursuing out of Duke Hyperbarics on the side of my doctoral work had blossomed, developing into a feasible safety device that could save the lives of rebreather divers. I already had funding in hand to continue the research when logistical issues on base meant I was asked to abandon the project and return to Florida. I baked and ate an entire small cake while thinking about it, and by the time I queasily scraped the last melted chocolate chip off the plate, I had decided to save the project at the expense of my job.

Leaving the navy meant I had pledged some of my workweek to completing my project as an employee of Duke, which thankfully provided me a scientific home, but that my time was otherwise uncommitted. I realized . . . blast trauma might make a good book subject. And the story of the *Hunley* might provide the perfect way to explain all that science.

Both of the stories in this book are true, and accompanied by all the science to explain them. The book is a blend of the historical narrative, which I have told as accurately as possible based on the documentation currently known to exist, and the modern story of what it took to work through the puzzle. For a purely historical book that more exhaustively lists the details of the *Hunley*'s genesis and life, I recommend Tom Chaffin's excellent *The H. L. Hunley: The Secret Hope of the Confederacy*.

I have told my story as truthfully and completely as possible without writing thousands of pages of nauseatingly comprehensive text. These narratives are based on my memory, email records, and contemporary notes. However, as with all memories, it is possible that other people may recall things differently. I have shortened the narrative of some of the modern events for brevity and clarity, but where I have done so I have checked with the other people involved to be sure they agreed that I maintained the intent, purpose, and tone. For example, some of the events in the book, such as the lucky-shot testing, included more people than are explicitly mentioned; rather than introducing and providing background on everyone, I focused on the portions of the events that were relevant to the narrative.

The views in this book are my own. They do not necessarily represent the official views or positions of anybody else, especially not any of my past or present employers. This assertion is doubly true for the federal government. Where I have mentioned my employers, it was only to provide context for the broader discussion of the storyline, and it is not meant in any way to imply endorsement of this book or its contents.

————————

This mystery has intrigued uncounted millions of people. And now we finally know the answer.

ACKNOWLEDGMENTS

To write a proper acknowledgments section, one that genuinely gives credit to everyone who deserves it, would require an entire second book—a book that nobody would ever read. Instead, I will have to settle for briefly mentioning people here, and then groveling at their feet in profuse thanks for the rest of my natural life.

First, the more abstract credits: In the sixth grade, I told my mom that I was more interested in the woodworking and tinkering of the "industrial technologies" class than I was in the sewing and baking of "skills for living." When I found out all of the other girls had signed up for sewing I tried to back out of my choice and give in to my peers. She wouldn't let me, and that one lesson has dictated the entire course of my adult life. Thanks, Mom.

When my dad came home to find I had taken apart the hair dryer, instead of getting mad he got me the toaster and a screwdriver. I learned that dolls are boring, and I would much rather figure out how things work. Thanks, Pops.

Nobody in science ever accomplishes anything alone. Ever. A massive number of people were involved in this project, and every one of them was critical to its success. My coauthors on the final academic publication, Brad Wojtylak and Luke Stalcup, are why I still have a complete set of fingers and toes. I could write some nice things, but they'd never let me live it down. Instead, I will just have to buy them beer, which they will probably appreciate more anyway.

Many of my lab mates dedicated their time to the project even though they had massive piles of work of their own, and still others formed the critical support structure of student peers that enabled me to survive until graduation—Allen Yu, Courtney Cox, Hattie Cutcliffe, Maria Ortiz Paparoni, and Brian Bigler especially. The list of undergraduates who sacrificed their time and their physical comfort is also quite extensive: Science rock star Henry Warder, Matt Udelhofen, Edward Hsieh, Maddie Bernstein, Praruj Pant, Reed Cone le Beaumont, and honorary undergrad Charlie Bass were all involved. In addition, our lab tech, Jason Kait, was an important member of the team.

Then, of course, there's the long list of people who had absolutely no need to help me, but did anyway. My parents and Nick Azan had the most transparent motivation of being my family, but they still went absolute galaxies beyond what would be considered normal dedication. My uncle Dave Pagnucco loaned me his generator and supplies literally for years, forgoing many tailgates for my science. My unofficial second mentor, Richard Moon of Duke Hyperbarics, spent many days and emails with me working through the details of oxygen consumption and carbon-dioxide production. Mike Natoli and Eric Schinazi, also of Duke Hyperbarics, helped me out with experimental setup and machined me parts when I physically had no way to do it myself. Although Eric demanded brownies, I suspect he's secretly nice enough to have helped anyway even if I couldn't provide them.

Ashleigh Swingler, Greg Murphy, and Ethan Hada trudged out to a freezing-cold pond to spend hours holding a string and a map while I swam around like an idiot measuring bottom topography. I couldn't remember the real name of the employee at the hardware store who tried to help me with the foam tubing, so I renamed him in honor of my good friend Greg Murphy. Ashleigh will probably never forgive me for the mangled clumps of line she had to untangle—sorry!

The employees of Duke were also critically supportive. The staff of Duke's Chilled Water Plant 2 (CHWP2) was unbelievable. They put a huge amount of care and maintenance into that pond, but they were still willing to advocate for us to use it for science. Darin Smith and Chris Silcott were especially influential and helpful. Similarly, I owe a lot of gratitude to Chip Bobbert and the staff of the Innovation Co-Lab. That group not only patiently showed me the ins and outs of laser cutters and 3-D printers, but when they knew I needed many hours more to laser cut enough membranes to feed the hungry shock-tube driver, they quietly locked up and let me stay behind in peace, without kicking me out. Having that resource and their help took months off the testing timeline and hundreds of dollars off my meager budget. Karl Bates of the Duke Office of News & Communications is the only reason I managed to keep my sanity during the release of the final paper, and was the first person to tell me that other people would care about this story too. Brad Murray of Duke's Nicholas School of the Environment patiently answered every one of my numerous questions about the ocean, and I appreciated his help greatly.

I also want to thank Bert Pitt, Mike Phillips, the entire Pitt family, and Chris Kelley. They were all motivated only by their own fascination with the stories found in history, and their desire to help me find some answers for this one. This paragraph is short because there is simply no thank-you that is sufficient to express how much I appreciate the help of the Pitt and Phillips families. I am genuinely lucky and honored to know them.

Artist Tripp Jarvis provided his extraordinary talent to build the CSS *Tiny*, and I have always suspected that he did so at a steep discount because he knew how limited my budget was. His metalworking skills know no bounds.

I also want to acknowledge Greg Harris and Kent Rye one more time. All the flattering things I wrote about them in this book were actually understatements, because in real life they are even more impressive and brilliant. I have appreciated their collaboration, wisdom, and friendship, and I hope it continues for a long time.

My funding sources also deserve acknowledgment: I returned to school as a student with the Department of Defense SMART Scholarship program. The bulk of the direct funding for the project was provided by the Josiah Charles Trent Memorial Foundation, a group at Duke dedicated to funding medical history projects. The Hagley Museum and Library also provided me with a travel scholarship, which enabled me to drive up to Delaware to dive deep into their mountains of black powder data.

And that's just the list of people who helped with the science project! The book was an entire additional adventure.

Many people provided me help with this text and also deserve my undying gratitude. Tony Booth, author of the fantastic *Thetis Down*, was kind enough to send me copies of the primary source documents he digitized and worked through to write his compelling history of the doomed submarine HMS *Thetis*. Adam Jon Kronegh handed me a veritable gold mine of information about Johan F. Carlsen. Both men must have spent solid weeks if not months of time tracking this information down, and I appreciate their willingness to share.

History lecturer extraordinaire Freddie Kiger was kind enough to provide fact-checking for the historical storylines, and also to let me access his encyclopedic brain so that I could more easily provide references and citations for many of the key points of the Civil War. Michael Crisafulli, in addition to all of the massive favors he did that I discussed in the text, was also willing to provide me with figures from his beautiful model and fact-checking of the storylines related to the *Hunley* herself. Eduardo Bonilla-Silva of the Duke sociology department was generous enough to review portions of the text for me to ensure I was respectfully conveying the stories of African Americans in the Civil War. Ron Carwardine provided much-appreciated translational services from German to English, without which I would have been far more confused about certain events during World War II.

A huge acknowledgment and thanks to my superhero agent, Laurie Abkemeier. Laurie has kindly and gently taken my hand and walked me into the world of publishing, despite some of my more introverted tendencies, and she has always, *always* been right. Her wisdom and insight are almost uncanny, at every turn. Thank you to Laurie for making me see that this story was worth telling, for fixing my inverted sentences, and for hammering it all into a coherent shape with me.

I owe many thanks to my editor, Stephen Morrow, his assistant, Hannah Feeney, and the entire staff at Dutton. My phone calls with Stephen are my favorite, and I have thoroughly enjoyed being able to effuse about both science and history with someone who obviously loves the subjects as much as I do. The Dutton crew has taken my thoughts and ramblings and molded them into this book.

I also want to acknowledge the hard work of all the archivists and librarians. There are too many to list by name, but they are the keepers of the books and documents that were the most critical part of piecing together the truth of February 17, 1864. Without carefully preserved documents like the Ruffin diary, the Shock letter, the Gillmore papers, and the information on black powder, none of this research would have ever happened. I included Lucas Clawson in the text as a representative of their profession and to show how, without them, researchers would be infinitely more lost and unproductive. When people say an old document was "unearthed" in an archive, they ignore the agency and labors of the quiet archivists who spend their days sorting, filing, and creating finding aids so that researchers like me can sweep in later and use their careful work. I want to acknowledge the efforts of the employees, librarians, and archivists of Duke's libraries, the US National Archives, the Library of Congress, the Hagley Museum and Library, the Strom Thurmond Institute at Clemson, the Danish National Archives, and all the others that I am forgetting but that hold untold secrets of their own in identical gray filing boxes.

Finally, I owe so much credit to my now husband, Nick Azan. Thank you for understanding me, and more important, supporting me, even in my more zany goals and obsessions. Thank you for taking care of me and encouraging me throughout this entire project. I firmly believe that without you I would have died of scurvy.

NOTES

A note about the notes: References are cited in short form here and should be cross-referenced with the full publication details provided in the bibliography.

Chapter 1: What About the *Hunley*

7   "Being a scientist is like being an explorer": Quoted in May, TED2015 Conference, 2015.

13 "the first successful submarine": Ragan, "Submarine Pioneer," 2001, 3.

13 The US Navy would own her: SCHC, Hunley Programmatic Agreement, 1996.

14 Based on the pattern of the layering in the sediment: Sharrer et al., "Marine Macrofaunal Analysis," 2001.

14 found resting at their battle stations: Quinn, "Time," 2008.

14 None showed any signs of skeletal trauma: FOTH, "Eight Crew Members," 2001; FOTH, "The Evidence," 2016; Martin and Case, "Secret Weapon," 2011.

14 unlock the firmly secured hatch: FOTH, "Dangers of Light," 2006.

14 bilge pumps were not set to pump out water: FOTH, "New Light," 2008.

14 no efforts to turn the bolts inside the hull: Neyland et al., "Hunley Recovery," 2016, 208.

15 a large gas bubble remained: Hicks, *Sea of Darkness*, 2015, 400.

16 spar was 16 feet long: FOTH, "Evidence of Explosion," 2013.

18 blasts transmitting to the inside of protective "bomb suits": Bass et al., "Assessing Blast Protection," 2005.

19 "I am a blast researcher": Lance, "Hunley Drawings," 2014.

19 "I am extremely interested": Lance, "Re: Hunley Drawings," 2014.

20 "As you can imagine": Scafuri, "Re: Technical Drawings," 2014.

20 "Wonder if there are existing pubs": Bass, "Re: Hunley Drawings," 2014.

23 "from the National Archives": FOTH, "Tale of the Torpedo," 2014.

24 ergometers that measure the work done by cranking hand pedals: Åstrand and Rodahl, *Work Physiology*, 1977, 279–82.

Chapter 2: Suffocation

31 "The question of air supply": Lake, *The Submarine*, 1918, 49.

31 After an avalanche, a buried skier: Boyd et al., "Patterns of Death," 2009; Holhrieder et al., "Avalanche Victims," 2007.

- 32 hull was ⅜ inches thick: FOTH, "FAQ," 2001.

33 publicly available assessment of the submarine's site: Murphy et al., "Hunley Site Assessment," 1998.

34 2 inches shy of 18 feet: FOTH, "Crew Bench," 2005.

34 conning towers, oval-shaped protrusions: Murphy et al., "Hunley Site Assessment," 1998.

34 positioned beneath the fore conning tower: FOTH, "Profile: Dixon," 2004.

35 could all be covered tightly: FOTH, "Blackout Mode," 2006.

35 historical reports that describe it: Alexander, "True Stories," 1902.

37 laser scan of the recovered *Hunley*: Jacobsen, Blouin, and Shirley, "Erosion Corrosion," 2012.

37 "Are you willing": Lance, "Keel Ballast," 2015.

38 "I apologize for being": Scafuri, "Re: Keel Ballast," 2015.

39 "Unfortunately that's not really an option": Lance, "Re: Keel Ballast," 2015.

39 value of 7.61 cubic meters: Lance et al., "Suffocate," 2016.

40 which rates of oxygen consumption were most reasonable: USN, *Diving Gas Manual*, 1971, 12–13; Åstrand and Rodahl, *Work Physiology*, 1977, 282–87.

45 above oxygen levels of 0.10 atm . . . about two minutes at 0.063 atm: Mackenzie et al., "Consciousness," 1945; Hall, "Useful Consciousness," 1949; Wolf, "Physiological Consequences," 2014.

47 June 1939, the newly constructed *Thetis*: Booth, *Thetis Down*, 2008.

48 physician scientists Haldane, Alexander, Duff, Ives, and Renton: Alexander et al., "After-Effects," 1939.

48 until the CO_2 levels reached a disconcerting 5 percent: Haldane and Smith, "Air Vitiated by Respiration," 1892.

48 since 1905 at the age of twelve: Foster, "Inquiry into *Thetis*," 1939, 27.

49 steel hyperbaric chamber one-third this volume: Ibid., 4.

50 final partial pressure of carbon dioxide in the chamber . . . above 0.17 atm the whole time: Alexander et al., "After-Effects," 1939.

50 progression of physical symptoms: Ibid.; Haldane and Smith, "Air Vitiated by Respiration," 1892.

50 "make it impossible to continue the experiment": Haldane and Smith, "Air Vitiated by Respiration," 1892.

50 trapped in a bank vault: Gill, Ely, and Hua, "Gas Displacement," 2002.

51 inhaling CO_2 levels potentially upward of 30 to 60 percent: Kettner et al., "Fatal Case of CO_2," 2013.

51 brain increases the breathing rate: Widmaier, Raff, and Strang, *Human Physiology*, 2004, 496–500.

52 "distracting discomfort," . . . "air hunger." . . . "distracting discomfort": USN, *Diving Gas Manual*, 1971, 8–9.

52 after seven minutes of breathing 7 percent CO_2: Richardson, Wasserman, and Patterson, "Circulatory Responses," 1960.

52 "His breath got shallower": Helm, "Most Hated-On Ice Cream," 2018.

53 ventilation rate for an enclosed gas space: USN, *Diving Gas Manual*, 1971, 9.

54 a standard modern fire hose: Strickland et al., *Fire Fighting*, 2008, 727.

54 the morbid lines of their autopsies: Rainsford, "Condition of Bodies," 1939.

54 markers of carbon-dioxide asphyxiation: Saukko and Knight, *Forensic Pathology*, 2015.

54 Blood stained the normally translucent fluid: Rainsford, "Condition of Bodies," 1939.

54 also a common sign of asphyxia in avalanche victims: Boyd et al., "Patterns of Death," 2009.

54 Haldane's self-experimentations: Alexander et al., "After-Effects," 1939.

54 eyes bulging and red: Rainsford, "Condition of Bodies," 1939.

Chapter 3: Fish Boats

57 "You have to admit": Quoted in Carewe, "Jules Verne," 1902.

57 Aristotle wrote that his student Alexander the Great: Rossi and Russo, *Ancient Engineers*, 2016, 197.

57 Chinese sources from 200 BCE: Joseph, *High Technology*, 2008, 3.

58 Cornelis Drebbel stood: Swinfield, *Sea Devils*, 2014, 23–24; Hutchinson, *Jane's Submarines*, 2001, 8.

58 drawings of inventor William Bourne: Bourne, *Inventions and Devices*, 1578.

58 three hours at a depth of 15 feet: Swinfield, *Sea Devils*, 2014, 25.

59 Mark Edwards constructed a successful small replica: Peck, *First Submarine*, 2002.

59 "Cornelius Debrell [*sic*]": Lake, *The Submarine*, 1918, 77.

59 Wilhelm Bauer looked at his two panting countrymen: Shelford, *Subsunk*, 1960, 18–19.

60 Bauer had expected a graceful and smooth disappearance: Unknown, "Bauer," 1875, 1.

60 *Brandtaucher* ("Fire diver"): Unknown, "Bauer," 1875, 1.

60 into a hole 17 meters deep: Hutchinson, *Jane's Submarines*, 2001, 10

60 For at least five hours: Unknown, "Bauer," 1875, 1.

60 Bauer was growing concerned about the air . . . also a man who understood physics: Shelford, *Subsunk*, 1960, 20.

62 "corks of champagne bottles": Quoted in Unknown, "Bauer," 1875, 2.

62 dubbed "infernal machines": Unknown, "Infernal Machine," 1849; Unknown, "Torpedo Inventor," 1863.

63 fighting population of only 1.3 million: USCB, *1860 Census Tables*, 1864.

63 female soldiers fighting undercover: Blanton and Cook, *Fought Like Demons*, 2002.

63 fleet of ninety fighting ships: Long, *Civil War Day by Day*, 1971, 719.

63 "nonexistent": Boatner, *Civil War Dictionary*, 1988, 583.

63 "Southern Slaveholding States": Virginia, "Ordinance of Secession," 1861.

63 "cardinal principle" of "prohibition of slavery": Georgia, "Ordinance of Secession," 1861.

63 "none but the black race": Mississippi, "Declaration of Secession," 1861.

64 Confederate government decided it was time: Walker, Telegraph to Beauregard, 1865.

64 Many in the South were confident there would be no war: McPherson, *Battle Cry*, 1988, 238.

64 "entered upon unexpectedly": Rains, Memorandum, ca. 1880.

64 offering to drink all the blood: McPherson, *Battle Cry*, 1988, 238.

64 "inviting all those who may desire": Davis, "Proclamation," 2012, 43.

65 value of the ship in addition to $20 per man: Abbott, *Civil War*, 1863, 298.

65 Horace Hunley was born . . . eighty-acre sugar plantation: Chaffin, *H. L. Hunley*, 2008, 15–24.

67 invented a machine to mass-produce bullets: Unknown, "Native Enterprise," 1861, 1.

68 "ATTENTION, ENGINEERS!": Marsh, "Attention, Engineers," 1861, 3.

68 by the following fall: Chaffin, *H. L. Hunley*, 2008, 9.

68 McClintock would later claim: Baird, "Submarine Torpedo Boats," 1902.

69 first confirmed, known boat was the CSS *Pioneer*: Kloeppel, *Danger*, 1987, 6–8.

69 a "CSS" designation: Chaffin, *H. L. Hunley*, 2008, 75.

69 sharpened to conical points: Shock, Letter to Fox, 1864, technical drawing.

69 irredeemably unstable: Baird, "Submarine Torpedo Boats," 1902.

69 McClintock provides one account of the crew: Baird, "Submarine Torpedo Boats," 1902.

70 thirdhand, courtesy of a photographer friend: Lake, *The Submarine*, 1918, 39–40.

70 supplied Lake with a photograph: In Lake's book is a photograph of a submarine now referred to as the Bayou St. John submarine for the loss of its proper name. This submarine was supposedly dredged up from the southern border of Lake Pontchartrain, the known stomping grounds of the *Pioneer*, and so she was long thought to be the *Pioneer* herself. Lake too thought the photograph was a picture

of the CSS *Pioneer*. The two boats have been repeatedly confused throughout history. For example, old newspaper articles show clear illustrations of the Bayou St. John submarine, yet describe the *Pioneer*'s story of being scuttled in 1862 to prevent her from falling into Union hands (e.g., Unknown, "Sold for Junk," 1901a). It is almost impossible to disentangle the lore of the *Pioneer* from the lore of the Bayou St. John submarine, but the additional sources for this story support the idea that it is about the CSS *Pioneer*. An additional source from the Barrow Family Papers (Robert Ruffin Barrow was married to Horace Hunley's sister) asserts that there was an early sinking of the *Pioneer*, but does not describe crew deaths in detail. (Quoted in Chaffin, *H. L. Hunley*, 2008, 271n).

70 "was the conception of a wealthy planter" . . . "but they warn't wuth a damned cent": Lake, *The Submarine*, 1918, 39–40.

70 sitting on the shore of Lake Pontchartrain: Baird, "Submarine Torpedo Boats," 1902.

70 "two contrabands [slaves] . . . were smothered to death": Shock, Letter to Fox, 1864. The insistence of the Confederate States upon treating people as property resulted in Union troops employing the logic that they could therefore legally free the slaves as they swept through the South because it was considered acceptable to take possession of the goods and property of regions defeated in combat. The word "contraband" is originally from the expression "contraband of war," meaning captured goods. The origins and use of the word "contraband" by Union troops to mean "slave" or "former slave" are documented in Siddali, *Property to Person*, 2005, 52–53.

71 location that is known to have been used by Hunley: Baird, "Submarine Torpedo Boats," 1902.

71 plantation owner with slaves: USCB, *Census Slave Schedule*, 1850.

71 "sub marine boat for blowing up ships": Roy, Diary, 1862, entry dated December 3, 1861.

71 frequented the same foundry: Roy, Diary, 1862. Roy describes numerous trips to Leeds Foundry during the years 1860–1862. McClintock was known to be working there at that time: Hicks, *Sea of Darkness*, 2015, 62. Roy's diary entry from May 10, 1862, also describes finding the misuse-damaged remains of the steam boat he previously loaned to a "McClintic." The name is slightly different, but the entry is around the time that McClintock would have been scuttling the *Pioneer* prior to his departure from New Orleans, and no McClintic could be found in the region in any census lists. Misspellings were also frequent in Roy's diary (e.g., "Munday," entry dated May 19, 1862).

71 "under the auspices of the Friends of the *Hunley*": Neyland et al., "Hunley Recovery," 2016, 3.

71 "*Hunley* project historian": Ragan, *The Hunley*, 1999, About the Author section.

71 "historical significance"; "worth reprinting in its entirety": Ragan, *Submarine Warfare*, 1999, 51.

72 Ragan was serving on the board of directors: Lasch, Letter to Harper, 2000. Members of the Board of Directors are listed on the stationery.

72 Ragan altered the word in his transcription to read "men": Ragan, *Submarine Warfare*, 1999, 52.

72 repeated the change in both of his books: The other book with the change is Ragan, *The Hunley*, 1999, 23.

72 Union troops arrested Charles Leeds: Roy, Diary, 1862, entry dated May 13, 1862.

72n an onsite compilation: Neyland et al., "Hunley Recovery," 2016, xxii.

72n "local rumor": Hicks, *Sea of Darkness*, 2015, 426.

73 sunk their boat before heading: Baird, "Submarine Torpedo Boats," 1902; Alexander, "Torpedo Boat Hunley," 1902.

73 "impracticable": Buchanan, Letter to Mallory, 1863.

73 "The boats used by the Navy": Quoted in Gruse-Harris, *Great Lakes' Submarine*, 1982, 24, with original letter cited as Graham, Letter to Phillips, 1852.

73 hammered out of multiple wrought-iron plates: Alexander, "True Stories," 1902.

74 had no knowledge of the submersible boats: Baird, "Submarine Torpedo Boats," 1902.

74 originally designed to tow a torpedo: Alexander, "True Stories," 1902.

74 spar attached to her bow: Beauregard, "Torpedo Service," 1878.

74 like Robert Fulton's submarine *Nautilus*: Swinfield, *Sea Devils*, 2014, 33.

74 submarine finally managed to impress: Buchanan, Letter to Tucker, 1863.

74 never carried the label "CSS": Chaffin, *H. L. Hunley*, 2008, 75.

75 approached her operations in Charleston: Clingman, Letter to Nance, 1863.

75 Confederate Army lost patience: Kloeppel, *Danger*, 1987, 38.

75 public demonstrations: Stanton, "Submarines," 1914.

75 Lt. John Payne stood . . . Hasker escaped for the surface: Stanton, "Submarines," 1914; Fort, "First Submarine," 1918.

77 "so swollen and so offensive": Ruffin, Ruffin diary microfilm, 1865, entry dated October 7, 1863.

77 justifying the expense of extra-large sizes: Payne, Requisition, 1863.

77 exhumed in 1999 . . . took months to find the grave: Hicks, *Sea of Darkness*, 2015, 300.

77 free, black nineteen-year-old grandson: USCB, Census entry "Absolum Williams," 1850; Williams, Find a Grave, 1863.

77 custom-dimensioned coffins . . . hands of several crewmen: Stevens and Leader, "Skeletal Remains," 2006.

77 Horace Hunley audaciously suggested: Hunley, Letter to Beauregard, 1863.

77 Hunley decided it was his turn . . . bash his way through the hatch door: Alexander, "True Stories," 1902; Stanton, "Submarines," 1914; Alexander, "Torpedo Boat Hunley," 1902.

78 many seem to be exaggerations and variations: Stanton, "Submarines," 1914.

78 "the peripatetic coffin": Kloeppel, *Danger*, 1987, 43.

78 "ahead of her time": Hicks, "One-Way Mission," 2014; FOTH, "Pump System," 2008.

Chapter 4: The Fury Beneath the Waves

83 "One should not let": von Maltitz, *Black Powder Manufacturing*, 2003, 20.

88 our system of equations . . . not enough time for her to reach her final resting place: Lance, Warder, and Bass, "Lucky Shot," 2017.

89 group including the Friends of the *Hunley* stated: NHHC, "Science Meets History," 2017.

90 invented by alchemists in China: Akhavan, *Chemistry of Explosives*, 2011, 1.

91 brimstone: *Holy Bible, King James Version*, Isaiah 34:9.

92 "Carbon is at the center of it all": Medak, *Breaking Bad* S02E06, 2009.

92 wood must be carbonized: von Maltitz, *Black Powder Manufacturing*, 2003, 38.

93 "all methods of initiation": Cooper, *Explosives Engineering*, 1996, 299.

93 "only takes one little spark": von Maltitz, *Black Powder Manufacturing*, 2003, 15.

94 water-filled containers: Drewes, "Last of the Breed," 2003.

94 test for the quality of black powder: von Maltitz, *Black Powder Manufacturing*, 2003, 162.

95 gas pressure builds: Black powder produces enough gas to fill 193 times the volume of the original solid granules. von Maltitz, *Black Powder Manufacturing*, 2003, 144 (citing data by Bunsen and Schischkoff).

95 the casing containing the powder reaches its failure point: Confinement is a repeated emphasis in most publications that seek to analyze the performance of black powder. The most notable work measuring and modeling black powder in a diversity of charge configurations was performed in Ermolaev et al., "Nonideal Regimes," 2010, where the authors managed to utilize the confinement provided by a thick-walled metal casing to coax the black powder beyond deflagration and into a proper detonation. Additional references regarding the importance of confinement include DuPont, *Blasters' Handbook*, 1969; DeYong and Campanella, "Blast Characteristics," 1989; and McIntyre and Rindner, "Pyrotechnic Test Data," 1980. Reference NHHC, "Science Meets History," 2017, updated on August 2, 2017, also states that "black powder's explosive reaction is highly sensitive to confinement and grain size."

97 behavior often varies substantially: Sassé, *Black Powder Combustion*, 1981.

100 a 90-plus-mile hike: Benjamin(?), "Walking Excursion," 1844. Note: The name of the author of this handwritten document is uncertain, and based on process of elimination from discussion of other members of the walking party.

100 Born in 1817 in New Bern, North Carolina: UNC, Summary Sheet, 1993.

100 "a primitive wilderness": Unknown, "Rains No. 1113," 1898.

100 promotion after promotion . . . the land mine: Waters, "Deception," 1989, 32.

100 "the quiet and monotony of the Engineer Corps": Unknown, "Rains No. 1113," 1898.

101 became known for writing letters: Rains, "Artillery Circular," 1843.

101 a placid appointment back at West Point: Unknown, "Rains No. 1113," 1898.

101 he immediately clamored: Unknown, "Rains No. 1113," 1898; Rains, Letter to Blifs, 1846.

101 "Give my love": Rains, Letter to Gabriel Rains, 1847.

101 stockpiled at most a few months' supply: Rains, "Powder Works Address," 1882, 1.

101 1.2 million kegs . . . 13 lived in the South: du Pont, Census, 1860.

101 not one former powder-making employee: Rains, "Powder Works Address," 1882, 5.

101 "appalling": Ibid., 1.

101 Rains brothers had already left: Unknown, "Rains No. 1113," 1898; Waters, "Deception," 1989, 32.

102 "the Bomb Brothers": Robbins, "Bomb Brothers," 2002.

102 never made black powder before . . . "carte blanche": Rains, "Powder Works Address," 1882, 2.

102 before he received his official commission . . . save time while on his quest: Rains, "Rains's Appeal," n.d.

102 publication by the Waltham Abbey Gunpowder Works: Baddeley, *Manufacture of Gunpowder*, 1857.

102 former employee of Waltham Abbey named Frederick Wright: Rains, "Powder Works Address," 1882, 5.

102 a strategic, militarily defensible spot . . . with all the powder it could ever need: Bragg et al., *Want of Powder*, 2007, 45, 235; Rains, "Rains's Appeal," n.d.

102 Rains designed his factory to explode: Rains, "Powder Works Address," 1882, 17–18.

103 "so that but slight resistance": Ibid., 17.

103 his mills only ever saw 3: Ibid., 18.

103 "vibrated the air" . . . "the sentinel was killed by the shock": Ibid., 20.

103 cottonwood and willow trees: Gorgas, Letter to Rains, 1861.

104 texts on black powder manufacture: Wilson, "Differing Charcoal Types," 1995; von Maltitz, *Black Powder Manufacturing*, 2003, 42.

104 cottonwood worked just as well: Rains, Memorandum, ca. 1880.

104 the modern data support his statements: Wilson, "Differing Charcoal Types," 1995.

104 potassium nitrate was a constant concern: Pratt, Letter to Rains, 1861–1864.

104 a normal by-product of decomposition: Cressy, *Saltpeter*, 2013, 16.

104 "the individual who makes a pound": Rains, *Making Saltpeter*, 1861, 1.

105 long-term plan for potassium nitrate: Bragg et al., *Want of Powder*, 2007, 9.

105 performance should have been unparalleled in its time: Some historians have pointed out that Confederate soldiers often complained about the quality of their powder by stating that their bullets did not fly far enough (O'Flynn, *Confederate Gunpowder*, 1996). However, an equal number of Union soldiers made similar complaints. (See the Official Records of the Union and Confederate Navies in the War of the Rebellion, available and searchable online through multiple repositories.) It seems that the most likely explanation might be that soldiers in combat, on both sides, frequently yearn for more effective firepower.

106 35 cents per pound: Rains, *Making Saltpeter*, 1861, 1.

106 almost 22,000 pounds of powder: Milgram and Gentieu, *Rains*, 1961.

107 "as abundant as blueberries": Waters, "Deception," 1989.

Chapter 5: Anatomy of an Explosion

109 "Every day we walked into the city": Hayman et al., "Kurt Vonnegut," 1977.

109 "reduced mainly to small fragments" . . . "His body was not otherwise disturbed": Rains, "Powder Works Address," 1882, 20.

110 injuries from an explosion are neatly categorized: Zuckerman, "Blast Injuries," 1941.

112 to understand how a shock wave is born: Cooper, *Explosives Engineering*, 1996, 167–72.

113 sound moves at roughly 1,540 meters per second: Segal, Likoff, and Kingsley, "Echocardiography," 1966.

114 a measly 30 meters per second: Goncharoff, Jacobs, and Cugell, "Wideband Transmission," 1989.

114 "the hot chocolate effect": Crawford, "Hot Chocolate," 1982.

114 This process is called spalling: This is a simplified explanation of how spalling occurs. For a more thorough explanation, please see Cooper, *Explosives Engineering*, 1996, 242.

114 intestines have a higher threshold for injury: Cripps and Cooper, "Distribution of Gut Injury," 1996; Lance et al., "Injury Criteria," 2015.

114 fragile archways around the sinus cavities: Petri et al., "Fatalities," 2001; Dussault, Smith, and Osselton, "Blast and Human Skeleton," 2014.

115 traumatic brain injuries: For more on this subject, please see Kleiven, "Most Traumatic Brain Injuries," 2013; Gennarelli et al., "Directional Dependence," 1987; and Rafaels et al., "Brain Injury Risk," 2012.

115 Fatalities from primary blast occur at lower pressures: Panzer et al., "Primary Blast Survival," 2012.

115 common for blast victims to be found dead: Friedrich, *Brandstätten*, 2003, 130. Note: The author cited, Jörg Friedrich, is considered controversial. He lived

through many of the bombings as a child in Germany, and he has engendered controversy by comparing the atrocities he experienced under the shells of the Allies to the atrocities perpetrated by the German military during the Holocaust. The citations provided to his research are in no way meant to endorse or support this stance. Friedrich did an exceptional job collecting and publishing other primary-source accounts of the blasts besides his own, and for this reason alone his work is used as a reference herein.

115 100 percent fatality rate: Panzer et al., "Primary Blast Survival," 2012.

115 1 square meter of surface area: Haycock, Schwartz, and Wisotsky, "Body Surface Area," 1978.

115 person a maximum of 0.2 meters: This calculation was performed using basic kinematic equations and integrating force over time by assuming an ideal Friedlander wave. The Friedlander equation describes the shape of the pressure curve as a function of time. Please see Dewey, "Shape of Blast Wave," 2010.

116 no skeletal damage from the primary trauma . . . on the surfaces of their brains: Panzer et al., "Primary Blast Survival," 2012; Dussault, Hanson, and Smith, "Blast Injury Prevalence," 2017.

116n Operation Plumbbob: Taborelli, Bowen, and Fletcher, "Operation Plumbbob," 1959.

117 "signature wound": Snell and Halter, "Signature Wound," 2010.

118 Graham Cooper and Susana Mellor, began to track the patterns of the cases: Mellor and Cooper, "Analysis of Servicemen," 1989.

118 Cooper was able to set up an experiment: Cooper et al., "Role of Stress Waves," 1991.

118 eruption of the volcano Krakatoa in 1883: Winchester, *Krakatoa*, 2003, 247, 260, 267.

119 soldiers wearing body armor were at higher risk: Cooper et al., "Role of Stress Waves," 1991.

120 Kevlar protects the lungs: Wood et al., "Attenuation," 2013.

120 invented by chemist Stephanie Kwolek: Rothman, "Kwolek," 2014.

121 maximum in less than 2 milliseconds: Richmond et al., "Response of Mammals," 1968; Richmond and White, *Biological Effects*, 1966.

121 a controlled detonation: Johnson et al., "Blast Overpressure Studies," 1993.

122 just outside a train station bunker: Friedrich, *The Fire*, 2008, 447.

123 the same pattern was revealed: Leibovici et al., "Blast Injuries: Bus," 1996; Singleton et al., "Primary Blast Lung Injury," 2013.

123 this scenario also warranted scientific testing: Champion, Holcomb, and Young, "Injuries from Explosions," 2009.

123 roughly a thousand times higher pressures: Cooper, *Explosives Engineering*, 1996.

124 more than double the limit . . . 4 percent chance of serious blast lung injury: Panzer et al., "Primary Blast Survival," 2012.

125 the physics to describe black powder: Examples of people trying to model black powder behavior include Ermolaev et al., "Nonideal Regimes," 2010; Kosanke and Kosanke, "Pyrotechnic Burn Rate," 2003; Napadensky and Swatosh, "TNT Equivalency," 1972; O'Flynn, *Confederate Gunpowder*, 1996; Sassé, *Black Powder Combustion*, 1981; and Wilson, "Differing Charcoal Types," 1995.

126 "water rocket" . . . Bayou St. John: Roy, Diary, 1862, entry dated January 16, 1862.

126 "part of his head": Unknown, "The City," 1862.

126 Mrs. E. H. Baker: Pinkerton wrote about Mrs. E. H. Baker and the details of her espionage in his 1883 memoir of the Civil War, called *Spy of the Rebellion*. The information she provided about the submarine, he claimed, was used to foil other attacks. It is difficult to validate this claim against any specific historical records, possibly because unsuccessful attacks were not as well recorded. Some of his information seems reliable; the design of the torpedo is generally consistent with the construction of the *Hunley*'s charge. The torpedo in the story was triggered using a long, coiled wire, and such a wire was found inside the *Hunley*'s recovered hull. While the recovered wire does not seem to have been used to trigger the torpedo used in the attack on the *Housatonic*, the Friends of the *Hunley* have stated that the wire was possibly used to trigger earlier torpedo designs (FOTH, "Electrically Detonated," 2005). The prototype submarine observed by Mrs. Baker carried two or three men, and the test took place in November 1861, around the same time McClintock, Watson, and Hunley separately began their testing of the two-man vessels they were building in New Orleans.

128 not in any of Allan Pinkerton's corporate records . . . None of his known female spies used the alias Baker: Pinkerton, Agency Records, 1853–1999.

128 Pinkerton writes affectionately about Atwater: Pinkerton, *Spy*, 1883, 396–97.

128 "The names of any employees": Pinkerton, Letter to Watson, 1862.

128 detailed billing documents: Pinkerton, Billing ledgers, 1862, all ledgers searched dated 1862 (earliest available) to 1865.

129 two Atwaters seemed to have reached the rank of captain: NPS, *Soldiers and Sailors*, 2004.

129 near Richmond at the time: Croom, *Company "C,"* 1879, 12.

129 but his wife died just before: Atwater, *Souvenir History*, 1919, 232–33.

129 "a man of strong convictions" . . . "hated all manner of shams": Atwater, Ibid.

129 experimental boats and spar torpedoes were taken . . . made it safely back to shore: USG, *War of the Rebellion*, 1890.

130 "final disposition": Unknown, "Torpedo Inventor," 1863.

131 Placing the torpedo beneath: Rains, *Torpedo Book*, ca. 1870, 20.

131 *David* had a spar: USG, *War of the Rebellion*, 1890, 734.

131 bomb underwater causes a bubble of gas to form: Cole, *Underwater Explosions*, 1948.

131 experimenters of the Confederacy learned the technique: Rains, *Torpedo Book*, ca. 1870, 20.

131 high density of the water . . . had occurred in air: Arons, "Shock Wave Parameters," 1954; Cooper, *Explosives Engineering*, 1996, 409.

132 Objects near the surface are less vulnerable: In summary, the interface between the air and the water reflects a wave of negative pressure back down into the water. This wave of negative pressure helps alleviate the positive pressure of the blast. For a comprehensive explanation, please see Cole, *Underwater Explosions*, 1948.

132 400 yards away: Buchanan, Letter to Tucker, 1863.

132 *Hunley* carried a much larger charge: FOTH, "Tale of the Torpedo," 2014.

Chapter 6: Preparations

135 "I know damn well": Jahren, *Lab Girl*, 2016, 20.

139 G. I. Taylor performed one of the most famous examples of blast scaling: Deakin, "Trinity Test," 2011. Note: To understand the math behind proper scaling of experiments, start first with Buckingham's Pi theorem and dimensional analysis. A thorough review of these topics should be available in most fluid-mechanics textbooks. Useful references specifically relevant to explosions are Chen et al., "Response of Scaled Model," 2009; Collette and Sielski, "Fluid Structure Interaction," 2017; Grujicic, Snipes, and Chandrasekharan, "Blast-Mitigation Effects," 2013; Kambouchev, Noels, and Radovitzky, "Nonlinear Compressibility," 2006; Kambouchev, Noels, and Radovitzky, "Numerical Simulation," 2007; Kambouchev, Radovitzky, and Noels, "Fluid-Structure Interaction," 2007; NCRE, Scaling Laws, 1948; Neuberger, Peles, and Rittel, "Scaling Response," 2007; Ramu, Raja, and Rhyla, "Similitude," 2013; Taylor, "Pressure and Impulse," 1963. For the scaling analysis specifically related to the *Hunley* project tests, please see the academic publication of the results, Lance et al., "Air Blast Injuries," 2017.

141 "ghastly," . . . "the blackened faces" . . . "contorted into all kinds": Beauregard, "Torpedo Service," 1878.

143 fish are surprisingly robust: Yelverton and Richmond, "Explosion Risk for Fish," 1981.

144 safely lodged on Sullivan's Island: Chaffin, *H. L. Hunley*, 2008, 170.

145 strong, outgoing flow: Parks, "Another Death," 2009.

145 "Breach is notorious for drownings": Petersen, "Treacherous Tides," 2014.

145 Edmund Ruffin frequently traveled: Ruffin, Ruffin diary microfilm, 1865, entries dated October 12, 1863; November 13, 1863; December 3, 1863; December 6, 1863.

145 dropped nets and spars in the water to block: Alexander, "True Stories," 1902; Rowan, Instructions from Rowan, 1890; Scharf, *History of the CSN*, 1887, 760.

146 on the unguarded vessel: Alexander, "True Stories," 1902; Beauregard, "Torpedo Service," 1878, 154.

150 similar to wrought iron in the material properties: The material parameters determined to be the most critical (percent differences in the values between mild steel and wrought iron in parenthesis) were density (2.0%), speed of sound (-0.1%), impedance (2.1%), modulus of elasticity (7.1%), and bulk modulus (-0.6%). For parameter values and citations see Lance et al., "Air Blast Injuries," 2017.

151 describes how cylinders respond: Hoo Fatt, "Rigid-Plastic Deformations," 1997; Hoo Fatt et al., "Rigid-Plastic Approximations," 1996.

154 at least two hours a day: Alexander, "True Stories," 1902.

158 trigger used in the Singer's design: Bell, *Heavy Explosive Ordnance*, 2003, 487, 490; Rains, *Torpedo Book*, ca. 1870, 25–26, 44–45.

158 the technical diagram in the National Archives: Gillmore, *Letters and Drawings*, 1865–1867.

158 "the boat was brought to the wharf": Rains, *Torpedo Book*, ca. 1870, 15.

158 "making & managing": Ibid., 15, 25–26.

158 technical drawing of the pressure trigger designed by Gray: Rains, *Torpedo Book*, ca. 1870, 25–26.

Chapter 7: Apple Pie Without Apples

165 "The great obstacle everywhere": Lee, Letter to Longstreet, 1864.

165 Archaeologist Maria Jacobsen crouched awkwardly: Martin and Case, "Secret Weapon," 2011.

169 the same month as Dixon's wound: Vander Hook, *Louis Pasteur*, 2011.

169 over 620,000 soldiers died: ABT, battlefields.org, 2018; Faust, *Republic of Suffering*, 2009, xi.

169 two-thirds of the fatalities: Faust, *Republic of Suffering*, 2009, 4.

169 amputations performed within twenty-four hours . . . two minutes per amputation: Reilly, "Civil War Surgical Care," 2016.

169 femur of the skeleton: FOTH, "Dixon," 2004.

170n historians have begun to question: Chaffin, *H. L. Hunley*, 2008, 235–37.

171 different plants perform this act differently . . . warmer climates like the American South: Bartelink et al., "Stable Isotope Forensics," 2014.

171 results of the carbon analysis: FOTH, "Profile: Becker," 2004; FOTH, "Profile: Dixon," 2004; FOTH, "Becker," 2004; FOTH, "Dixon," 2004; FOTH, "Lumpkin," 2004; FOTH, "Ridgaway," 2004; FOTH, "Collins," 2004; FOTH, "Miller," 2004; FOTH, "Carlsen," 2004; FOTH, "Wicks," 2004; Walker, *Secrets*, 2005, 89.

172 in the mud by the fourth crank handle: FOTH, "Collins," 2004; FOTH, "Carlsen," 2004.

172 tailor's notch: Ubelaker and Bubniak-Jones, "Human Remains," 2003.

172 historical documents listing the *Hunley*'s crew: M. M. Gray, Letter to Maury, 1865.

172 process of elimination identified him as J. F. Carlsen: Walker, *Secrets*, 2005, 94, 100.

173 "Hi, I work as an archivist": Kronegh, Untitled email, 2018.

173 Johan Frederick Carlsen: DSA, Lægdsrulle, 1850–1870.

173 listed as a seaman in the 1860 census: DSA, Folketælling, 1860.

173 Seaman Carlsen had served aboard . . . by its English translation: Kronegh, "Den ukendte Dansker," 2015; DSA, Lægdsrulle, 1850–1870.

173 took a spot on the privateer *Jefferson Davis*: FOTH, "Carlsen," 2004.

173 a black-hulled ship that until recently: McPherson, *War on the Waters*, 2012, 21.

173 possible that the new market for privateers: Ibid.; Scharf, *History of the CSN*, 1887, 79–80.

174 the *Jefferson Davis* eked past: Tucker, *Blue & Gray Navies*, 2013, ch. 3.

174 Carlsen followed his captain back to Charleston: FOTH, "Carlsen," 2004.

174 the records of the foundered *Jefferson Davis*: Kronegh, "Den ukendte Dansker," 2015.

174 high-ranking officers and officials even packed lunches . . . Confederate victory had reassured the South: Davis, *Bull Run*, 2012.

174 asking for a voluntary one-year commitment: Moore, *Conscription and Conflict*, 1924, 1.

174 Conscription Act, the first compulsory draft: Ibid., 12–13.

175 "secure the proper police of the country": CSA, *Public Laws*, 1862–1864, 79.

175 "horrible insurrection": Pvt. Charles Terrill, 2nd Georgia, quoted in Noe, *Reluctant Rebels*, 2010, 47.

175 estimates of 50,000 to 150,000 substitutes serving: Mehrländer, *Germans of Charleston*, 2011, 154.

175 led many to speculate: Sacher, "Disagreeable Business," 2007.

175 substitution was also allowed beginning October 1861: Moore, *Conscription and Conflict*, 1924, 27.

175 German immigrant Frederick Scheuber: Sacher, "Disagreeable Business," 2007.

176 Johan Carlsen also signed up as a substitute: Mehrländer, *Germans of Charleston*, 2011, 343.

176 draftee would have had to accompany . . . accepted the swap: Ibid., 153.

176 the rank of corporal: Ibid., 343.

176 stationed at Fort Moultrie: Coker, *Port Royal*, 2009.

176 were unable to continue: Alexander, "True Stories," 1902.

176 Carlsen was assigned the seat: FOTH, "Carlsen," 2004.

176 a known volunteer from the crew: FOTH, "Becker," 2004.

176 in the pay logbooks: CSN, "Special Expedition Pay," 1863.

177 "harsh physical activity": FOTH, "Miller," 2004.

177 multiple healed fractures: Walker, *Secrets*, 2005, 100.

177 off the decks of the CSS *Indian Chief*: Alexander, "Torpedo Boat Hunley," 1902; Jacobsen, "H.L. Hunley Project," 2005.

177 all except Becker are listed in the official pay records: CSN, "Special Expedition Pay," 1863; CSN, "CSS *Chicora* Pay," 1863. Note: Dixon's salary is not listed in these logbooks. However, the salaries of officers Charles H. Hasker and John A. Payne, both of whom survived the first sinking of the *Hunley*, are listed at their new duty stations on the CSS *Chicora*. Both men earned $1,500 per year, a number that was common for low-to-middle-ranking officers in this type of duty (CSN, "CSS *Chicora* Pay," 1863).

178 James A. Wicks: FOTH, "Wicks," 2004.

178 repeated mentions of the relentless ice and sleet: e.g., Wescoat, Diary, 1863–1864, multiple entries dated December 1863–January 1864.

178 requested that they send him his heavy winter coat: Bates, *Correspondence, 1862–1865*, letters dated July 30, August 15, and October 14, 1864.

178 average of 50 degrees Fahrenheit: NOAA, Temperature Table, 2018.

178 death from hypothermia in less than two hours: Giesbrecht and Wilkerson, *Cold Injuries*, 2006, 62.

178 about 460 watts per person: Åstrand and Rodahl, *Work Physiology*, 1977, 403.

179 h is about equal to ten: Laguerre et al., "Numerical Simulation," 2007.

179 up to the range of 100,000: Kakaç and Yener, *Heat Transfer*, 1994, 18.

179n 59 W/m*K for wrought iron: Theodore, *Heat Transfer*, 2011, 68.

180 When James Wicks climbed: FOTH, "Wicks," 2004.

180 city of Charleston and its harbor therefore: Wise, *Gate of Hell*, 1994, 23, 25.

180 geography made it resistant to an assault by land: Gillmore, *Letters and Drawings*, 1865–1867.

180 "battered and crumbled almost to shapelessness": Spicer, *Flag on Sumter*, 1885, 23.

181 "Swamp Angel": Wise, *Gate of Hell*, 1994, 148–50.

181 Evacuate Fort Sumter: Ibid., 169–70.

181 third of the downtown had been destroyed by a fire: Spicer, "Diary," 1865.

181 estimated 13,000 shells rained down: Spicer, *Flag on Sumter*, 1885.

181 the bells and sirens of Charleston's fire department: Wise, *Gate of Hell*, 1994, 170.

181 Those who could evacuate did: Jaques, Letter to Jute, 1863–1865; Unknown, "Non-Combatants," 1863.

181 "They like the rest of us are refugees": Wescoat, Diary, 1863–1864, entry dated August 10, 1864.

181 "Early this morning the whole village": Ibid., entry dated July 10, 1863.

181 "We can hear the roar of the artillery": Ibid., entry dated July 11, 1863.

182 "The enemies gun": Greenhow, Letter to Boteler, 1864.

182 "The rapidity of the cannonade while I write": Emery, Letter, 1862.

182 Dixon himself stated that by February: Dixon, Letter to Cothran, 1864.

182 even the supplies of paper: Emery, Letter, 1862.

182 "Sundays are as plenty as there are days": Ibid.

182 rebuilding favorite recipes: Richmond, West, and Johnston, *Confederate Receipt Book*, 1863.

182 often tasking slaves by the thousand: Greenhow, Letter to Davis, 1863; Wise, *Gate of Hell*, 1994, 58, 129–31.

182 "The two gun boats now building here": Lemmons, Letter to Gaffney, 1862.

182 "splendid crew of men": Dixon, Letter to Willey, 1864.

183 silver suspender clasps: Quinn, "Saving History," 2008.

183 slowly emaciating on meager rations: FOTH, "Dixon," 2004; Dixon, Letter to Willey, 1864.

183 "But there is one thing very evident": Dixon, Letter to Willey, 1864.

Chapter 8: Pressure Trace

185 "My adviser had a saying": Chen, "Six Years in Science," 2018.

188 the cable equation: Hayes, "Transatlantic Cables," 2008; Thomson, "Electric Telegraph," 1855.

188n critical to the neuroscience research: Armstrong, "History of Ion Channels," 1999.

193 roughly thirty-five torpedo-makers: Rains, *Torpedo Book*, ca. 1870, 6.

193 became masters of repurposing: Ibid., 6, 24, 26, 48, 104.

193 to maximize destruction: Ibid, 20.

193 "had passed through the gutta percha": Ibid., 51.

193 charges with casings of iron: Michie, *Rebel Torpedoes*, 1865, 114.

193 churning out by the thousands: Rains, *Torpedo Book*, ca. 1870, 27–28.

193 "When powder was burned in a space": Michie, *Rebel Torpedoes*, 1865, 109.

194 careful attention was paid . . . "the thicker the tin the better": Rains, *Torpedo Book*, ca. 1870, 44–45.

194 used copper for torpedoes: Ibid., 48.

194 He famously refused to be involved: Alexander, "True Stories," 1902.

194 "thousand and one": Rains, *Torpedo Book*, ca. 1870, 15.

194 "abortions of inventive genius": Ibid., 19.

194 "much danger from their proximity": Ibid.

194 "safely is by detached torpedoes": Ibid., 20.

194 "the secret of my great success": Ibid.

195 minimum of 40 or 50 feet long: Ibid., 73.

195 123 infernal torpedoes: Ibid., 26.

195 fitted with a 16-foot spar: FOTH, "Evidence of Explosion," 2013.

202 "There was no sharp report," "I heard a report": USN, USS *Housatonic* Inquiry, 1864.

203 waves can travel for miles underwater: Wright, "Subjective Effects," 1947.

210 researchers have independently concluded: Neyland et al., "Hunley Recovery," 2016.

210 8 feet below the surface of the water: Gillmore, *Letters and Drawings*, 1865–1867; Tomb, Notes from Papers, 1865.

Chapter 9: From the *Housatonic*

213 "This getting blown up by torpedoes": Bates, *Correspondence, 1862–1865*, letter dated March 2, 1865.

213 "I doubt any city was ever more terribly punished": Sherman, Official Account, 1865, 130.

214 2nd South Carolina Volunteer Infantry: Robinson, "Raid," 1863; Grigg, Combahee River Raid, 2014.

214 headed straight for Charleston: Wise, *Gate of Hell*, 1994, 51.

214 estate of the deceased physician Philip Tidyman: Drake, Bill for Account, 1853.

214 for the slaves' own "safe keeping": Leiding, *Historic Houses*, 1921, 111.

214 four of Tidyman's former slaves: NPS, *Soldiers and Sailors*, 2004, listed under the names William, John, Jack, and Charles Tiddeman (see note below for explanation of spelling).

215 Jack the correct age to be Judy's son: Drake, Bill for Account, 1853.

215 he was firing at a Confederate vessel . . . happened during actual combat: Teddeman, Disapproved Pension, 1884. Note: In the pension file, William's last name is spelled Teddeman, which is different from Philip Tidyman's spelling. However, it can be linked to the same person because in the disapproved pension file it is specified that William was enslaved on a plantation near Charleston that had been owned by a doctor who died a few years before the war. It was common for this German last name to have many variations based on phonetic pronunciation, including Tiedeman, Teddemann, etc. The relevant dates listed in William Teddeman's pension file align with his listing in the NPS Soldiers and Sailors database, although that database spells the last name as "Tiddeman." The four Tiddemans in the NPS database are likely linked to one another based on commonalities between dates of enlistment, service, and location of service. I chose to use the spelling "Teddeman" because it is how the name was spelled by William's son, who filled out the forms on behalf of his father. Therefore, it is the only version that provides any of the men or their descendants with a degree of agency in choosing a spelling.

215 at least forty-nine other African American men: NPS, *Soldiers and Sailors*, 2004.

216 not as prisoners of war: CSA, "Resolution 1863," 1995.

216 Robert Francis Flemming had joined the Union: NPS, *Soldiers and Sailors*, 2004.

216 *Housatonic* had lookouts spaced evenly: Unless otherwise cited, all the details of the sinking of the USS *Housatonic* from the perspective of her crew are taken from

their own testimonies during the exhaustive US Naval Court of Inquiry that was conducted into the event. The Court of Inquiry started a few days after the sinking, on Friday, February 26, 1864, so the memories of the crew were fresh. The handwritten transcript is preserved on microfilm at the US National Archives (Ref USN, USS Housatonic Inquiry, 1864). However, given the importance of the document, I transcribed the text and Michael Crisafulli of the Vernian Era website has been kind enough to publish it on his site so that everyone can access the full, unedited text of the document and read the verbatim testimonies of the crewmen: www.vernianera.com/Hunley/Housatonic-Inquiry.html.

217 Flemming was the first to notice her: Flemming is generally considered the first to spot the oncoming *Hunley*, but Acting Master John Crosby also spotted the submarine at a similar time.

221 "cold shock" response: Mekjavic, Tipton, and Eiken, *Medicine of Diving*, 2003, 139–41; Golden, "Immersion Hypothermia," 1973; Tipton, "Responses to Cold-Water," 1989.

222 based on the secondary blast injuries: Gough, Disapproved Pension File, 1874.

222 less than two hours: Suominen et al., "Near-Drowning," 2002.

222 the pernicious effects of heat loss: Golden, "Immersion Hypothermia," 1973.

223 until about forty-five minutes after the blast . . . safety of the larger ship: Green, Report to Rowan, 1865.

223 "frantic signaling": McLaurin, "Confederate Twins," 1925.

224 founded the Ordnance Department: Peterson and Dahlgren, *Admiral Dahlgren*, 1945.

225 blue light was the signal that George Dixon planned to send: Cardozo, *Reminiscences*, 1866, 124.

226 people felt they *knew*: Hicks, *Sea of Darkness*, 2015, 401.

226 Green settled a massive hullabaloo: Green, Varied Letters, 1863–1864, letters dated March 15, 1863, through March 17, 1863.

227 Union protocol upon seeing a craft without the proper signals . . . "Flash a white light": Green, Memorandum, 1863.

227 disability pension: Gough, Disapproved Pension File, 1874.

227 Secondary trauma is the most common injury type: Dussault, Smith, and Osselton, "Blast and Human Skeleton," 2014.

228 treated by a physician once safely on board the *Canandaigua* . . . "claimant is not incapacitated": Gough, Disapproved Pension File, 1874.

228 to continue his service on the USS *Wabash*: NPS, *Soldiers and Sailors*, 2004.

228 headstone now rests there: Flemming, Find a Grave, 1919.

228 Teddeman served on the USS *Canandaigua* . . . slightly older than Charles: NPS, *Soldiers and Sailors*, 2004, last names spelled "Tiddeman" (see note above for explanation of spellings).

229 assigned a new command on the USS *Vanderbilt*: Hamersly, Records of Officers, 1870; USCB, Census entry "Charles Pickering," 1860, 83.

229 returned home to New Hampshire: Pickering, Pension Application, 1888; USCB, Census entry "Charles Pickering," 1860.

229 insider information on the happenings: Bates, *Correspondence*, 1862–1865, letter dated May 15 (no year).

230 wrote to his father all he knew about the attack: Ibid., letter dated July 9, 1864.

230 careful, specific insight: Ibid., letter dated May 15 (no year).

230 faithfully reported all he knew about the attack: Ibid., (letter not dated). Note: Adna Bates also misreports the speed of the *Hunley*, citing a dramatic 8 knots that would have had her traveling from the first sighting to the explosion in less than seventeen seconds.

231 "blown to atoms": Ibid., letter dated March 2, 1865.

Chapter 10: The Blast

233 "One submariner compared the shock wave": Sturma, *The USS Flier*, 2009, 50–51.

234 "The signals agreed upon to be given": Dantzler, Report to Wilson, 1864.

234 a small light near the wreck site: Lance, Warder, and Bass, "Lucky Shot," 2017.

234 the moon, for example, takes up 0.52 degrees: Wolfe et al., *Sensation & Perception*, 2018.

234 only a sliver of the vessel: USN, USS *Housatonic* Inquiry, 1864; Alexander, "True Stories," 1902.

235 Original recipes contained zinc: Gray, *Operative Chemist*, 1828, 499.

235 white balls of saltpeter and sulfur: USA, *Ordnance Manual*, 1862, 307–8.

235 at most about 3 meters wide: Modern Civil War enthusiasts have reconstructed the chemical mixture and used it in demonstrations, allowing measurement of the luminous power of the signal (Rucker, "Making Blue Light," 2011). Conservatively, the bright part of the signal is usually about 1.5 meters in diameter, with at most about 3 meters between the very outside edges of the dimmest parts of the beam of light. Three meters is still only one-quarter the length of the *Hunley*, therefore one-twentieth the width of the moon.

235 "The officer in command told Lt. Col. Dantzler": Cardozo, *Reminiscences*, 1866, 124–25.

238 *25 pounds will blow the roof off a house*: Rains, *Torpedo Book*, ca. 1870, 34.

243 Water gets in: If a ship is directly over the charge when it explodes, it can also be destroyed by the gas bubble produced by the bomb, which travels upward while pulsating. The destructive power of this gas bubble is extreme. Underwater surfaces can also be damaged by something called a water jet when the explosion occurs nearby. For further information, please see Cole, *Underwater Explosions*, 1948, and Kedrinskii, *Hydrodynamics of Explosion*, 2005.

244 he suspended steel plates of varying thicknesses: Taylor, "Pressure and Impulse," 1963.

245 digital slabs of material: Grujicic, Snipes, and Chandrasekharan, "Blast-Mitigation Effects," 2013.

245 wave propagating inside the body of an armored vehicle: Champion, Holcomb, and Young, "Injuries from Explosions," 2009.

248 24,200 pounds per square inch: du Pont, Papers, 1885.

249 "US Navy testing of a full-sized black powder charge": Lance et al., "Air Blast Injuries," 2017; Harris et al., "Output of Black Powder," 2016.

250 affected by the angle of the blast: Reid, "Response of Surface Ships," 1996.

251 more than 12,000 data points: Panzer et al., "Primary Blast Survival," 2012.

252 inner hull of a typical World War II submarine: Friedman, *Submarines Through 1945*, 1995, 208.

252 inside a range of about 100 feet: Rowland and Boyd, *Bureau of Ordnance*, 1953.

252 transmission of a measly 0.180 percent: The calculated βs value is 1,589, for those who have read the academic publication about this study. $\rho P=174$, $t_i=0.004$ s, $\rho_s=1000$ kg/m3, $U_s=1540$ m/s.

252 "deafening," "abominable," "ear-shattering": Werner, *Iron Coffins*, 2002, 32, 33, 45, respectively.

252 "someone hitting the hull with a million sledgehammers": Kershaw, *Escape from the Deep*, 2010, 4.

253 onboard lightbulbs and other glass items: Ibid., 4; Werner, *Iron Coffins*, 2002, 45.

253 papers and records of Union officer Quincy Adams Gillmore: Gillmore, *Letters and Drawings*, 1865–1867.

254 "Singer's torpedo": Bell, *Heavy Explosive Ordnance*, 2003, 487, 490; Rains, *Torpedo Book*, ca. 1870, 44–45; Sleeman, *Torpedoes*, 1880, 19–20.

254 Union-compiled book now resting in the National Archives: USN, *Torpedoes*, 1860–1865.

254 "submerged and slumbering thunderbolt": Unknown, "Letter from Charleston," 1863.

254 ink he made himself: Ruffin, Diary, vol. 3, 1977, entry dated July 15, 1863.

254 After all, he had helped start it: Ruffin, Diary, vol. 1, 1977.

255 increasingly toothless face: repeated entries in Ruffin, Diary, vol. 2, 1977, and Ruffin, Diary, vol. 3, 1977, e.g. entry dated July 20, 1861.

255 "highly appreciated compliment": Ruffin, Diary, vol. 1, 1977, entry dated April 12, 1861.

256n He was given a uniform and permitted to stand: Ruffin, Diary, vol. 1, 1977, entries October 1859.

257 proven to be largely correct: For assessment of accuracy, please see the footnotes in the transcribed volumes, Ruffin, Diary, vol. 2, 1977; Ruffin, Diary, vol. 1, 1977; Ruffin, Diary, vol. 3, 1977.

257 provided him with a personal letter: Ruffin, Diary, vol. 3, 1977, entry dated September 24, 1863.

257 observe and document were the submarine *HL Hunley*: Ruffin, Ruffin diary microfilm, 1865: entry dated October 12, 1863.

258 "The torpedoes will also strike lower": Ibid., entry dated December 3, 1863.

258 would yield 8,816 kilopascals: To show the details of some of the math here . . . The weight of the black powder charge used by the US Navy was not cleared for public release. However, a graph published by the Naval History and Heritage Command on their website shows the pressure trace from one experiment along with the time scale of that experiment. Using the information from the time scale along with a little bit of knowledge about blast physics makes it possible to back-calculate the charge weight at about 144 pounds, slightly larger than the charge from the Gillmore drawing. Using this charge weight, 0.114 was the TNT RE for the peak pressure that was at the location most relevant to the *Hunley*. Applying that RE of 0.114 to a 200-pound charge results in 8,601 kPa in the water at the same location outside the hull, and 138 kPa inside the vessel (chances are 98 percent for injury, 37 percent for fatality), a negligible difference from the pressures calculated by directly using the similitude equations. For information on similitude, see Cole, *Underwater Explosions*, 1948; Arons, "Shock Wave Parameters," 1954.

258 oppressive "Yankee rule": Ruffin, Diary, vol. 3, 1977, entry dated June 18, 1865.

258 an unrefined and imperfect yardstick for many reasons: RE values often vary a lot, including based on the exact test methods used to measure them. In addition, an explosive will usually have different RE values depending on exactly what parameter you want to measure. For example, many explosives have a different RE value if you are measuring the peak pressures of the shock wave than if you are measuring the total energy released by the explosion.

259 cluster just above 0.40: Cooper, *Explosives Engineering*, 1996; Napadensky and Swatosh, "TNT Equivalency," 1972; Crocker, *Acoustics*, 1998.

259 a 46 percent chance of death: Rafaels et al., "Brain Injury Risk," 2012.

259 leaves the skull and the structure of the brain intact: Cernak and Noble-Haeusslein, "Traumatic Brain Injury," 2009.

259 the brains had patterns of diffuse staining: Martin and Case, "Secret Weapon," 2011.

Chapter 11: February 17, 1864

Note: Citations are not provided again for the facts in the narrative of this chapter if they have been provided earlier in the book.

263 "Think of the destruction": Unnamed reporter, quoted in Beauregard, "Torpedo Service," 1878.

263 "the most bombarded mainland city": Wilkinson, "Siege of Charleston," 2011.

264 six-foot-one Virginian Frank Collins: FOTH, "Collins," 2004.

264 arthritic Lumpkin at the second handle: FOTH, "Lumpkin," 2004.

264 a hard life of physical activity: FOTH, "Becker," 2004.

264 Joseph Ridgaway at crank location seven: FOTH, "Ridgaway," 2004.

264 tucked their canteens of water under the bench: FOTH, "Excavation Continues," 2001.

264 was in his mid-twenties: FOTH, "Dixon," 2004.

264 crew knew all about the previous sinkings: Beauregard, "Torpedo Service," 1878.

265 had timed their departure with the outgoing tide: Lance, Warder, and Bass, "Lucky Shot," 2017.

268 locking the hands forever at 8:23: The hands of Dixon's watch stopped at 8:23 p.m. (FOTH, "Pocket Watch," 2007). However, because the Union and Confederacy kept time differently, this was equal to 8:53 p.m. according to the Union method. The *Housatonic* crew reported the attack occurred between 8:45 and 9:00 p.m. (USN, USS *Housatonic* Inquiry, 1864).

268 entered a state of shock: Frykberg and Tepas III, "Terrorist Bombings," 1988.

Epilogue

271 "Undoubtedly the concussion produced": Unknown, "Torpedo Device," 1877.

271 a prowling German U-boat: Wynn, *Gravesend*, 2016, 27

271 began one by one to pledge their loyalty: Unknown, "Beauregard," 1876.

271 replete with the ravaged, sunken hulks: Willenbucher and Krebs, *Map of Harbor*, 1865.

272 By 1870 hard-hat divers touched . . . could be sold at auction: Unknown, "Down in the Depths," 1870.

272 corked bottle of wine: Unknown, "Relics," 1870.

272 "in grim dead lock": Unknown, "Submarine Boat," 1886.

272 got the distance between the wrecks wrong: e.g., Unknown, "Housatonic," 1871; Unknown, "Torpedo Device," 1877.

272 visibility was only a few feet: Unknown, "Housatonic," 1871.

272 littered with unlabeled marker buoys: Ibid.

272 one near the final location of the submarine: Unknown, Housatonic, states, "The government has a buoy planted about three hundred yards east south-east of the [*Housatonic*]," which is an accurate description of the location of the *Hunley*.

272 "now uppermost": Unknown, "Housatonic," 1871.

272 bow was pointing back toward the wreck: Unknown, "Braved the Deep," 1890.

272 "all of her men were at their stations": Unknown, "Sold for Junk," 1901a.

272 mouth of Charleston Harbor was opened and deepened: Lance, Warder, and Bass, "Lucky Shot," 2017.

272 the rapid change in topography: Credit for this theory goes to Mark Hansen of the United States Geological Survey (USGS).

273 archaeologist and diver E. Lee Spence: Faust, "Hunley Remains Found," 1975.

273 over 3 nautical miles from land: Lance, Warder, and Bass, "Lucky Shot," 2017.

273 "part of our national heritage": Spence, Letter to Gladding, 1974.

273 Thurmond was heavily involved: Board, Museum Proposal, 1971.

273 Spence thought this museum would be a suitable location: Kossler, Letter to Spence, 1974.

273 He began to write letters: Spence, Letter to Gladding, 1974, Thurmond copied.

273 received enthusiastic permissions: Kossler, Letter to Spence, 1974; Gaillard, Letter to Spence, 1974; Nelson, Letter to Spence, 1974.

273 a map depicting the broad area: Spence, Letter to Nelson, 1974.

273 location that would eventually be verified: 32 degrees, 43 minutes, 15.01 seconds latitude; 79 degrees, 46 minutes, 28.81 second longitude; from Hicks, *Sea of Darkness*, 2015, 227.

273 wrote back vaguely . . . "internal requirements": Gladding, Letter to Spence, 1974.

274 "holding in abeyance the issuance": Herman and Valentic, Letter to Spence, 1974.

274 He began writing to the GSA in January: Spence, Letter to Gladding, 1974.

274 by September they had changed their minds: Herman and Valentic, Letter to Spence, 1974.

274 the famous ironclad USS *Monitor*: Unknown, "Monitor Found," 1974.

274 Clive Cussler's announcement to the media: Reuters, "Rebels' Sub," 1995.

274 GSA . . . quickly passed control: Hunley Commission, Minutes, August 2, 1995, 5.

274 designated himself the submarine's fiercest advocate: McConnell, Letter to Clanton, 1995; McConnell, Letter to Thurmond, May 24, 1995.

275 assembled the Hunley Commission: McConnell et al., Bill S. 844, 1995; Hunley Commission, Minutes, August 2, 1995.

275 "be as aggressive as possible": Ernest L. Passailaigue Jr., quoted in ibid., 6.

275 "control of this piece of southern history": Richard M. Quinn Jr., quoted in ibid.

275 quashing language in a federal bill: Thurmond, "Strike Language," 1995.

275 With them in the meeting: McConnell, Letter to Dudley, 1995; Richardson, Schedule, October 24, 1995.

275 polite but noncommittal language: Attorney John Hazzard was "asked to create a list of memoranda which evidence an attempt by the Department of the Navy to circumvent the Hunley Commission" and responded with an itemized list of these actions in Hazzard, Second Letter to Short, 1995.

275 all parties agreed unanimously: Hunley Commission, Minutes, December 12, 1995; Honigman, Letter to McConnell, 1995.

275 an hour and a half budgeted: Richardson, Schedule, October 24, 1995.

275 provided the Dalai Lama with only minutes: Richardson, Week at a Glance, 1995.

275 at least one aide in the meeting taking notes: Hunley Commission, Minutes, December 12, 1995, 2: "Representative [Harry M.] Hallman continued that he

thought the two groups had an agreeable meeting in Washington. It is his belief that 'everyone has someone he answers to' and with that he made the motion that Chairman McConnell contact Senator Thurmond, Senator Hollings, and Congressman Spence, and have the three of them review the notes which were taken by Senator Thurmond's people during the meeting in Washington."

275 "blackmail": Hicks, *Sea of Darkness*, 2015, 225.

275 procurement budget for the Department of Defense: Thurmond, "Opposition to Divert Funding," 1995.

276 Thurmond had taken to the Senate floor: E.g., Thurmond, Bumpers Amendment, 1995; Thurmond, Kohl Amendment, 1995; Thurmond, S 1026, 1995.

276 Hunley Commission had hatched a plan . . . Spence signed over all of his rights: Hunley Commission, Minutes, September 14, 1995; Hunley Commission, Minutes, October 11, 1995.

276 he should be excluded: "Mr. Hazzard and I have no problem with Mr. Lindehan's request that Dr. Spence and Mr. Newel have no role other than to visit." McConnell, Letter to Dudley, 1996.

276 still resides with the US Navy: Dudley et al., "Management Agreement," 1996.

276 control over the display: McConnell, Letter to Shelby, 1995.

276 "proper exhibition": Hunley Commission, Minutes, August 2, 1995, 8.

276 "and interpretation": Dudley, Memo to Horne, October 27, 1995. Memo reads: "McConnell's principal concerns were that: . . . the state be able to interpret the submarine, when displayed, as the commission feels is appropriate."

276 legal ownership a secondary issue: McConnell, Letter to Shelby, 1995; Hunley Commission, Minutes, August 2, 1995, 2.

276 changing currents of American political correctness: Hunley Commission, Minutes, August 2, 1995; McConnell, Letter to Shelby, 1995.

276 people were already protesting the Confederate battle flag: Tanner, "Leaders Protest," 1995.

276 "expressed his concern that 10 or 15 years": Hunley Commission, Minutes, August 2, 1995, 7.

276 "the War Between the States": E.g., Hunley Commission, Minutes, August 2, 1995, 2; Hunley Commission, Minutes, October 11, 1995, 6, 14; Hunley Commission, Transcript, August 6, 1996.

276 proverbially buried by controversy: Unknown, "Enola Gay," 2016.

277 "expressed his strong feelings": Hunley Commission, Minutes, October 11, 1995, 3.

277 Smithsonian was a leading candidate: Pugliese, Letter to Thurmond, 1995.

277 "minority employee": A full citation for this article unfortunately could not be located. However, the title was "Battle Flag Flap Forces Apology from Navy," by the Associated Press. It would have been published shortly before the writing of the below-cited letter in 1995.

277   "control over the presentation of the *Hunley*": Hazzard, Letter to Short, 1995.

277   commission resisted these arrangements vehemently: McConnell, Letter to Honigman, 1996; final agreement, Dudley et al., "Management Agreement," 1996 compared with previous revisions.

277   final contract provides for . . . when making their final decision: Dudley et al., "Management Agreement," 1996, 8: "If the objection cannot be resolved through consultation, the Hunley Commission will take the views of the other parties into account in rendering a final decision on the issue."

277   July 2000, South Carolina lowered: Baca, "Vanishing Symbols," 2000.

277   a facility owned by Clemson: clemson.edu/centers-institutes/conservation/, last accessed April 26, 2019.

278   based out of the same building: Address at 1250 North Supply Street, North Charleston, hunley.org/about-us/, last accessed April 26, 2019.

278   a feasible safety device that could save the lives: Lance et al., "Dewey Monitor," 2017.

BIBLIOGRAPHY

Abbott, John Stevens Cabot. 1863. *The History of the Civil War in America*. Vol. 1. Indianapolis: Ledyard Bill.

Akhavan, Jacqueline. 2011. *The Chemistry of Explosives*. 3rd ed.: Royal Society of Chemistry.

Alexander, W, P Duff, JBS Haldane, G Ives, and D Renton. 1939. "After-Effects of Exposure of Men to Carbon Dioxide." *Lancet* 234 (6051): 419–20.

Alexander, William A. 1902. "The Confederate Submarine Torpedo Boat Hunley." *The Gulf States Historical* Magazine 1 (2): 81–91.

———. 1902. "The True Stories of the Confederate Submarine Boats." *The Daily Picayune*, Sunday, June 29, 6–7.

American Battlefield Trust (ABT). 2018. American Battlefield Trust. www.battle fields.org. Accessed May 2018.

Armstrong, Clay M. 1999. "A Short History of Ion Channels and Signal Propagation." *Current Topics in Membranes* 48: 283–310.

Arons, AB. 1954. "Underwater Explosion Shock Wave Parameters at Large Distances from the Charge." *J Acoust Soc Am* 26 (3): 343–46.

Åstrand, Per-Olof, and Kaare Rodahl. 1977. *Textbook of Work Physiology*. Edited by Deobold B Van Dalen. United States of America: McGraw-Hill, Inc.

Atwater, Francis. 1919. *Souvenir History: North Carolina Branch of the Atwater Family*. Vol. 3. Meriden, CT: Journal Pub. Co.

Baca, Kim. 2000. "2000: For South Carolina, It Was a Year of Vanishing Signals." *The Times and Democrat*, December 31, 28.

Baddeley, Fraser. 1857. *Manufacture of Gunpowder as Carried On at the Government Factory Waltham Abbey*. Waltham Abbey, E. Littler, Sun Street: Item 08143711, Hagley Museum and Library, Wilmington, DE.

Baird, GW. 1902. "Submarine Torpedo Boats." *Journal of the American Society of Naval Engineers* 14:845–55.

Bartelink, Eric J, Gregory E Berg, Melanie M Beasley, and Lesley A Chesson. 2014. "Application of Stable Isotope Forensics for Predicting Region of Origin of

Human Remains from Past Wars and Conflicts." *Annals of Anthropological Practice* 38 (1): 124–36.

Bass, Cameron R. 2014. "Re: Hunley Technical Drawings." Email correspondence with Rachel M Lance. February 20.

Bass, Cameron R, Martin Davis, Karin Rafaels, Mark Rountree, Robert M Harris, Ellory Sanderson, Walter Andrefsky, Gina DiMaroo, and Michael Zielinksi. 2005. "A Methodology for Assessing Blast Protection in Explosive Ordnance Disposal Bomb Suits." *International Journal of Occupational Safety and Ergonomics* 11 (4): 347–61.

Bates, Adna. 1862–1865. In *Correspondence, 1850–1890* (bulk 1862–1865) [manuscript]. David M. Rubenstein Rare Book and Manuscript Library, RUB Bay 0042:04 items 1–72 c.1: Duke University, Durham, NC.

Beauregard, PGT. 1878. "Torpedo Service in the Harbor and Water Defences of Charleston." *Southern Historical Society Papers* 5 (4): 145–61.

Bell, Jack. 2003. *Civil War Heavy Explosive Ordnance: A Guide to Large Artillery Projectiles*. Denton, TX: University of North Texas Press.

[Benjamin?]. 1844. "Walking Excursion from Fort Monroe to Richmond Proposed by Lt. Rains." George Washington Rains Papers, 1843–1949, Collection 01510-z: Southern Historical Collection, University of North Carolina at Chapel Hill.

Blanton, DeAnne, and Lauren M Cook. 2002. *They Fought Like Demons: Women Soldiers in the American Civil War*. New York: Vintage Books.

Boatner, Mark M. 1988. *The Civil War Dictionary*. Philadelphia: McKay.

Booth, Tony. 2008. *Thetis Down: The Slow Death of a Submarine*. South Yorkshire, England: Pen & Sword Books Ltd.

Bourne, William. 1578. *Inventions and Devices: Very necessary for all generalles and captaines, or leaders of men, as wel be sea as by land*. London, England: [online transcription available via Text Creation Partnership, http://name.umdl.umich.edu /A16509.0001.001].

Boyd, Jeff, Pascal Haegeli, Riyad B Abu-Laban, Michael Shuster, and John C Butt. 2009. "Patterns of Death Among Avalanche Fatalities: A 21-Year Review." *Canadian Medical Association Journal* 180 (5): 507–12.

Bragg, CL, Charles D Ross, Gordon A Blaker, Stephanie AT Jacobe, and Theodore P Savas. 2007. *Never for Want of Powder: the Confederate Powder Works in Augusta, Georgia*. Columbia, SC: University of South Carolina Press.

Buchanan, Franklin. 1863. Letter to Mallory, February 14, 1863. In *Franklin Buchanan Letterbook*. Southern Historical Collection, University of North Carolina at Chapel Hill.

———. 1863. Letter to Tucker, August 1, 1863. In *Franklin Buchanan Letterbook*. Southern Historical Collection, University of North Carolina at Chapel Hill.

Cardozo, Jacob Newton. 1866. *Reminiscences of Charleston*. Charleston, SC: Joseph Walker, Agt., Stationer and Printer.

Carewe, Vere. 1902. "Jules Verne Talks About His 100th Romance." *Pittsburgh Weekly Gazette*, Sunday, December 7, 13.

Cernak, Ibolja, and Linda J Noble-Haeusslein. 2009. "Traumatic Brain Injury: An Overview of Pathobiology with Emphasis on Military Populations." *J Cerebral Blood Flow and Metabolism* 20:255–66.

Chaffin, Tom. 2008. *The H. L. Hunley: The Secret Hope of the Confederacy*. New York: Hill and Wang.

Champion, Howard R, John B Holcomb, and Lee A Young. 2009. "Injuries from Explosions: Physics, Biophysics, Pathology, and Required Research Focus." *J Trauma* 66:1468–77.

Chen, Justin. 2018. "Coming to Terms with Six Years in Science: Obsession, Isolation, and Moments of Wonder." StatNews.com, accessed October 20, 2018. https://www.statnews.com/2018/10/14/phd-six-years-scientific-research/.

Chen, Yong, ZP Tong, HX Hua, Y Wang, and HY Gou. 2009. "Experimental Investigation on the Dynamic Response of Scaled Ship Model with Rubber Sandwich Coatings Subjected to Underwater Explosion." *International Journal of Impact Engineering* 36:318–28.

Clingman, TL. 1863. Letter to Captain WF Nance. In *The War of the Rebellion: A Compilation of the Official Records of the Union and Confederate Armies*, Series 1, Vol. 28, Part 1: Reports: US Government Printing Office [available online via hathitrust.org].

Coker, Michael. 2009. *The Battle of Port Royal*. Mount Pleasant, SC: Arcadia Publishing.

Cole, RH. 1948. *Underwater Explosions*. New York: Dover Publications, Inc.

Collette, Matthew, and Robert Sielski. 2017. "Fluid Structure Interaction: A Community View." Ann Arbor: Marine Structures Design Lab, Department of Naval Architecture and Marine Engineering.

Confederate States of America (CSA). 1862–1864. *Confederate States of America, Public Laws of the Confederate States of America, First Congress, 1862–1864*. Edited by James M Matthews. Richmond, VA: R.M. Smith, printer to Congress.

———. 1995. "Confederate Congress, Joint Resolution, May 1, 1863." In *The Civil War: Opposing Viewpoints*, edited by William Dudley, 231–33. San Diego, CA: Greenhaven Press.

Confederate States Navy (CSN). 1863. "Quarterly, or Half-Yearly, Pay, Receipt, and Muster Role of 'Special Expedition' & Naval Detachment on Special Duty at Charleston, South Carolina." Record Group 45, Record Identifier E653-CSS42. National Archives and Records Administration, Washington, DC.

Cooper, GJ, DJ Townend, SR Cater, and BP Pearce. 1991. "The Role of Stress Waves in Thoracic Visceral Injury from Blast Loading: Modification of Stress Transmission by Foams and High-Density Materials." *J Biomechanics* 24 (5): 273–85.

Cooper, Paul W. 1996. *Explosives Engineering*. New York: VCH.

Crawford, Frank S. 1982. "The Hot Chocolate Effect." *American Journal of Physics* 50 (5): 398–404.

Cressy, David. 2013. *Saltpeter: The Mother of Gunpowder.* Oxford, England: Oxford University Press.

Cripps, NPJ, and GJ Cooper. 1996. "The Influence of Personal Blast Protection on the Distribution and Severity of Primary Blast Gut Injury." *J Trauma* 40 (3S): 206S–211S.

Crocker, Malcolm J. 1998. *Handbook of Acoustics.* Hoboken, NJ: John Wiley & Sons.

Croom, Wendell D. 1879. *The War-History of Company "C," Sixth Georgia Regiment (Infantry): With a Graphic Account of Each Member.* Fort Valley, GA: The Survivors of the Company, printed at the "Advertiser" Office.

———. 1863. "Quarterly, or Half-Yearly, Pay, Receipt, And Muster Role of CS Steamer *Chicora*." Record Group 45, Record Identifier E653-CSS42: National Archives and Records Administration, Washington, DC.

Danish State Archives (DSA). 1850–1870. "Lægdsrulle, Ærøskøbing 1850–1870." Ærø Stads og Landsret; pk. 547—1850–1867. Danish State Archives.

———. 1860. "Folketælling [census] 1860, Slesvig." Statistisk Bureau; pk. 32—Nordborg Amt.: Danish State Archives.

Dantzler, OM. 1864. Report of Lieutenant-Colonel Dantzler, C.S. Army, to Lieutenant John A Wilson. In *Official Records of the Union and Confederate Navies in the War of the Rebellion*, Series 1, Vol. 15: South Atlantic Blocking Squadron from October 1, 1863, to September 30, 1864, edited by Charles A Stewart. Washington, DC: US Government Printing Office [available online via hathitrust.org].

Davis, Jefferson. 2012. "Proclamation of Marque, April 19, 1861. By the President of the Confederate States. A Proclamation." In *A Documentary History of the Civil War Era:* Vol. 1, *Legislative Achievements*, edited by Thomas C Mackey. Knoxville: University of Tennessee Press.

Davis, William C. 2012. *Battle at Bull Run: A History of the First Major Campaign of the Civil War.* New York: Knopf Doubleday Publishing Group.

Deakin, Michael AB. 2011. "G. I. Taylor and the Trinity Test." *International Journal of Mathematical Education in Science and Technology* 42 (8): 1069–79.

Dewey, John M. 2010. "The Shape of the Blast Wave: Studies of the Friedlander Equation." Proceeding of the 21st International Symposium on Military Aspects of Blast and Shock (MABS), Israel.

DeYong, LV, and G Campanella. 1989. "A Study of Blast Characteristics of Several Primary Explosives and Pyrotechnic Compositions." *Journal of Hazardous Materials* 21 (2): 125–33.

Dixon, George E. 1864. Letter to Henry Willey. Mount Pleasant, SC: Transcription provided by the Friends of the *Hunley* [available online at www.hunley.org/george-dixon, last accessed March 2019].

———. 1864. Letter to John F. Cothran. Mount Pleasant, SC: Transcription provided via email by the Historic Mobile Preservation Society.

Drake, James H. 1853. In the Court of Equity, Charleston District: Bill for account and relief: Maria C. Drayton, Frederick A. Ford and Rose B. Ford, his wife, Elizabeth Deas, Susan Deas, Ann Deas, Mary Holmes, and the German Friendly Society, vs. James Rose and Henry A. DeSaussure, Ex'rs of Dr. Philip Tidyman, deceased, Julia Rose, Hester T. Drayton, Susan Tidyman, and Alfred R. Drayton. Charleston, SC: South Carolina Court of Equity.

Drewes, John M. 2003. "Last of the Breed—A Visit to GOEX." In *Black Powder Manufacture, Testing, & Optimizing*, edited by Ian von Maltitz. Dingmans Ferry, PA: American Fireworks News.

du Pont, Lammot. 1860. Census of Gunpowder Manufacturers in the US. In Lammot du Pont Papers. Accession No. 384, Box 28: Hagley Museum and Library, Wilmington, DE.

———. 1885. Lammot du Pont Papers. Accession No. 384, Box 38: Hagley Museum and Library, Wilmington, DE.

Dudley, William S. 1995. Memorandum to Capt. Horne, Subj: Confederate Submarine H.L. Hunley, Oct 27. Obtained via FOIA request to the NHHC.

Dudley, William S, G Martin Wagner, Robert D Bush, Glenn F McConnell, and George Vogt. 1996. "Programmatic Agreement Among the Department of the Navy, the General Services Administration, the Advisory Council on Historic Preservation, the South Carolina Hunley Commission, and the South Carolina State Historic Preservation Officer Concerning Management of the Wreck of the H. L. Hunley [signed June–August]." Obtained via FOIA request to the Hunley Commission.

DuPont. 1969. *DuPont Blasters' Handbook: A Manual Describing Explosives and Practical Methods of Use*. 15th ed. Wilmington, DE: Sales Development Section of the Explosives Department, EI du Pont de Nemours & Co.

Dussault, Marie Christine, Ian Hanson, and Martin J Smith. 2017. "Blast Injury Prevalence in Skeletal Remains: Are There Differences Between Bosnian War Samples and Documented Combat-Related Deaths?" *Science and Justice* 57:439–47.

Dussault, Marie Christine, Martin Smith, and David Osselton. 2014. "Blast Injury and the Human Skeleton: An Important Emerging Aspect of Conflict-Related Trauma." *J Forensic Sci* 59 (3): 606–12.

Elliott, JB. 1861. Scott's Great Snake. Entered according to Act of Congress in the year 1861. Control No. 99447020: Library of Congress Geography and Map Division, Washington, DC.

Emery, Jose R. 1862. Letter, Jose R. Emery to unnamed female recipient. David M. Rubenstein Rare Book and Manuscript Library, Sec. A, Box 41, items 1–2, c.1: Duke University, Durham, NC.

Ermolaev, BS, AA Belyaev, SB Viktorov, KA Sleptsov, and SY Zharikova. 2010. "Nonideal Regimes of Deflagration and Detonation of Black Powder." *Russian Journal of Physical Chemistry* B 4 (3): 428–39.

Faust, Drew Gilpin. 2009. *This Republic of Suffering: Death and the American Civil War.* New York: Vintage Books.

Faust, John W. 1975. "Archeologist Claims Hunley Remains Found." *The Times and Democrat*, June 13, 1, 5.

Flemming, Robert Francis. 1919. "Find a Grave," database and images (findagrave .com: accessed January 14, 2019), memorial page for Robert Francis Flemming (July 4, 1830–February 23, 1919), Find a Grave Memorial no. 25776233, citing Wyoming Cemetery, Melrose, Middlesex County, Massachusetts, USA. Maintained by Rubbings (contributor 47671529).

Fort, WB. 1918. "First Submarine in the Confederate Navy." *Confederate Veteran* 26:459.

Foster, John. 1939. "Tribunal of Inquiry into the Loss of H.M. Submarine 'Thetis': Shorthand Notes of Proceedings, Eleventh to Twentieth Days, TS 32/108" TS 32/108. The National Archives, Kew, London.

Friedman, Norman. 1995. *U.S. Submarines Through 1945.* Annapolis, MD: Naval Institute Press.

Friedrich, Jörg. 2003. *Brandstätten, Der Anblick des Bombenkriegs.* Berlin: Propyläen.

———. 2008. *The Fire: The Bombing of Germany, 1940–1945.* Translated by Allison Brown. New York: Columbia University Press.

Friends of the *Hunley* (FOTH). 2001. "Eight Hunley Crew Members Found." Press Release. Charleston, SC: Friends of the *Hunley.*

———. 2001. "Excavation Continues, So Does the Mystery." Press Release. Charleston, SC: Friends of the *Hunley.*

———. 2001. "Frequently Asked Questions." *The Blue Light* (1): 5.

———. 2004. "Arnold Becker." Press Release. Charleston, SC: Friends of the *Hunley.*

———. 2004. "Corporal J. F. Carlsen." Press Release. Charleston, SC: Friends of the *Hunley.*

———. 2004. "Crewman Profile: Becker." Press Release. Charleston, SC: Friends of the *Hunley.*

———. 2004. "Crewmember Profile: Dixon." Press Release. Charleston, SC: Friends of the *Hunley.*

———. 2004. "Frank Collins." Press Release. Charleston, SC: Friends of the *Hunley.*

———. 2004. "James A. Wicks." Press Release. Charleston, SC: Friends of the *Hunley.*

———. 2004. "Joseph Ridgaway." Press Release. Charleston, SC: Friends of the *Hunley.*

———. 2004. "Lt. George E. Dixon." Press Release. Charleston, SC: Friends of the *Hunley.*

———. 2004. "Lumpkin." Press Release. Charleston, SC: Friends of the *Hunley.*

———. 2004. "Miller." Press Release. Charleston, SC: Friends of the Hunley.

———. 2005. "Crew Bench to Be Removed in Preparation for Hunley Conservation." Press Release. Charleston, SC: Friends of the *Hunley*.

———. 2005. "Was the Hunley's Torpedo Electrically Detonated?" *The Blue Light*, October (17):5.

———. 2006. "The Dangers of Light." *The Blue Light* (April): 6.

———. 2006. "Hunley Could Go into Blackout Mode." *The Blue Light* (April): 5.

———. 2007. "Gold Pocket Watch May Help Solve a Timeless Mystery." Press Release. Charleston, SC: Friends of the *Hunley*.

———. 2008. "Discovery May Shed New Light on Fate of Hunley Crew." *The Blue Light* 30 (Winter): 6–7.

———. 2008. "The Hunley's Pump System: Ahead of Its Time." *The Blue Light* (Spring): 6–7.

———. 2013. "Scientists Uncover Evidence of Explosion." Press Release. Charleston, SC: Friends of the *Hunley*.

———. 2014. "Tale of the Torpedo." *The Blue Light* 44: 8–11.

———. 2016. "The Evidence: Crew Remains." Friends of the *Hunley*. https://www.hunley.org/the-evidence/.

Frykberg, ER, and J J Tepas III. 1988. "Terrorist Bombings. Lessons Learned from Belfast to Beirut." *Ann Surg* 208 (5): 569–76.

Gaillard, J Palmer. 1974. Letter to Edward Lee Spence, January 30. Strom Thurmond Archives (MSS 100), Chief of Staff records, Box 2, Folder 54: Clemson University, Clemson, SC.

Gennarelli, Thomas A, Lawrence E Thibault, G Tomei, R Wiser, D Graham, and J Adams. 1987. "Directional Dependence of Axonal Brain Injury Due to Centroidal and Non-Centroidal Acceleration." *SAE Transactions* 96 (3):1355–59.

Georgia. 1861. "Ordinance of Secession, passed Jan'ry 19, 1861. With the names of the signers. An ordinance to dissolve the Union between the State of Georgia and other states united with her under a compact of government." Augusta, GA: Georgia Republic Convention, January 19.

Giesbrecht, Gordon G, and James A Wilkerson. 2006. *Hypothermia, Frostbite, and Other Cold Injuries: Prevention, Survival, Rescue, and Treatment.* Seattle, WA: The Mountaineer Books.

Gill, James R, Susan F Ely, and Zhongxue Hua. 2002. "Environmental Gas Displacement: Three Deaths in the Workplace." *American Journal of Forensic Medicine and Pathology* 23 (1): 26–30.

Gillmore, Quincy Adams. 1865–1867. Illustration of Torpedo "used for blowing up the *Housatonic*," Gillmore, Quincy Adams (1825–1888), Letters, Telegrams, and Reports, January 1865–December 1867, Photographs and Drawings. In ARC 1182763, Container No. 3, Entry No. PI-17 159-M: Civil War, General's Papers, Record Group 94: Adjutant General's Office, 1780s–1917: National Archives and Records Administration, Washington, DC.

Gladding, Peter T. 1974. Letter to Edward Lee Spence, April 30. Strom Thurmond Archives (MSS 100). Chief of Staff records, Box 2, Folder 54: Clemson University, Clemson, SC.

Golden, F St. C. 1973. "Recognition and Treatment of Immersion Hypothermia." *Proc Roy Soc Med* 66:1058–61.

Goncharoff, V, JE Jacobs, and DW Cugell. 1989. "Wideband Acoustic Transmission of Human Lungs." *Med & Biol Eng & Comput* 27:513–19.

Gorgas, Josiah. 1861. Letter to George Washington Rains. George Washington Rains Papers, 1843–1949, Collection 01510-z: Southern Historical Collection, University of North Carolina at Chapel Hill, Chapel Hill, NC.

Gough, John. 1874. Disapproved Pension Application File for Landsman John Gough, USS *Housatonic* (Application Number 3340). Case Files of Disapproved Pension Applications of Civil War and Later Navy Veterans, ca. 1861–ca. 1910; Records of the Department of Veterans Affairs, 1773–2007, Record Group 15: National Archives at Washington, DC [online version available through the Archival Research Catalog (ARC identifier 90411742) at www.archives.gov; 2018].

Graham, WH. 1852. Letter to L. D. Phillips, Esq. Michigan City, IN. Record Group 45, National Archives, Washington, DC.

Gray, MM. 1865. Letter to Major General Dabney H. Maury, Mobile, Alabama. In *Annual Report of the Secretary of the Navy*, 299. Washington, DC: Government Printing Office.

Gray, Samuel Frederick. 1828. *The Operative Chemist*. St. Paul's Church-Yard: Hurst, Chance, and Company.

Green, Joseph F. 1863. Memorandum for the Government of Monitors, Tugs and Boats on Picket Duty. Joseph F Green Papers, 1828–1960 (bulk 1862–1864). Call number 0516L NHF-021, LCCN mm 70055897: Library of Congress Manuscript Division, Washington, DC.

———. 1863–1864. Varied Letters. Joseph F. Green Papers, 1828–1960 (bulk 1862–1864). Call number 0516L NHF-021, LCCN mm 70055897: Library of Congress Manuscript Division, Washington, DC.

———. 1865. "Report of Captain J. F. Green to Commodore S. C. Rowan, Feb 18, 1864." In Annual Report of the Navy Department in Fifteen Volumes, 1863–1864, edited by William Dudley, 289. Washington, DC: Government Printing Office.

Greenhow, Rose O'Neal. 1863. Letter to Jefferson Davis. Papers, 1860–1952, 1863–1864 (bulk) [manuscript]. David M. Rubenstein Rare Book and Manuscript Library, Sec. A, Box 146, items 1–16, c.1: Duke University, Durham, NC.

———. 1864. Letter to Alexander Robinson Boteler. Papers, 1860–1952, 1863–1864 (bulk) [manuscript]. David M. Rubenstein Rare Book and Manuscript Library, Sec. A, Box 146, items 1–16, c.1: Duke University, Durham, NC.

Grigg, Jeff W. 2014. *The Combahee River Raid: Harriet Tubman & Lowcountry Liberation*. Mount Pleasant, SC: Arcadia Publishing.

Grujicic, M, JS Snipes, and N Chandrasekharan. 2013. "Computational Analysis of Fluid-Structure Interaction Based Blast-Mitigation Effects." *Journal of Materials, Design and Applications* 227 (2): 124–42.

Gruse-Harris, Patricia A. 1982. *Great Lakes' First Submarine: L.D. Phillips' "Fool Killer."* Michigan City, IN: Michigan City Historical Society, Inc.

Haldane, John, and J Lorrain Smith. 1892. "The Physiological Effects of Air Vitiated by Respiration." *J Pathology and Bacteriology* 1 (2): 168–86.

Hall, FG. 1949. "Interval of Useful Consciousness at Various Altitudes." *J Appl Physiol* 1 (7): 490–95.

Hamersly, Lewis Randolph. 1870. *The records of living officers of the U.S. Navy and Marine Corps: with a history of naval operations during the rebellion of 1861–5, and a list of the ships and officers participating in the great battles*. Compiled from official sources by Lewis R. Hamersly. Philadelphia: J. B. Lippincott & Co.

Harris, Greg, Thomas McGrath, William Lewis, Kent Rye, Matt Strawbridge, Sean Wills, and Ken Nahshon. 2016. "Characterization of the Underwater Explosion Output of Black Powder." Naval Surface Warfare Center Indian Head Division, Report IHTR-3505 (June 2016).

Haycock, George B, George J Schwartz, and David H Wisotsky. 1978. "Geometric Method for Measuring Body Surface Area: A Height-Weight Formula Validated in Infants, Children, and Adults." *Journal of Pediatrics* 93 (1): 62–66.

Hayes, Jeremiah. 2008. "A History of Transatlantic Cables." *IEEE Communications*, September: 42–48.

Hayman, David, David Michaelis, George Plimpton, and Richard Rhodes. 1977. "Kurt Vonnegut, the Art of Fiction." *The Paris Review* (Spring), 69.

Hazzard, John P. 1995. Letter to Duke Short, Esq., c/o the Honorable Strom Thurmond's Office, October 31. Obtained via FOIA request to the Hunley Commission.

———. 1995. Second Letter to Duke Short, Esq., c/o the Honorable Strom Thurmond's Office, October 31. Obtained via FOIA request to the Hunley Commission.

Helm, Burt. 2018. "Why the Most Hated-On New Ice Cream Brand in America Is a Booming $100 Million Business." *Inc.*

Herman, Milton L, and John M Valentic. 1974. Letter to Edward Lee Spence, September 9. Strom Thurmond Archives (MSS 100), Chief of Staff records, Box 2, Folder 54: Clemson University, Clemson, SC.

Hicks, Brian. 2014. "One-Way Mission of the H. L. Hunley." *Naval History* 28 (1).

———. 2015. *Sea of Darkness: Unraveling the Mysteries of the H.L. Hunley*. Ann Arbor, MI: Spry Publishing, LLC.

Holhrieder, Matthias, Hermann Brugger, Heinrich M Schubert, Marion Pavlic, John Ellerton, and Peter Mair. 2007. "Pattern and Severity of Injury in Avalanche Victims." *High Altitude Medicine & Biology* 8 (1): 56–61.

Honigman, Steven S. 1995. Letter to the Honorable Glenn F. McConnell, December 18. Obtained via FOIA request to the Hunley Commission.

Hoo Fatt, Michelle S. 1997. "Rigid-Plastic Deformation of a Ring-Stiffened Shell Under Blast Loading." *Journal of Pressure Vessel Technology* 119 (4): 467–74.

Hoo Fatt, Michelle S, T Wierzbicki, M Moussouros, and J Koenig. 1996. "Rigid-Plastic Approximations for Predicting Plastic Deformation of Cylindrical Shells Subject to Dynamic Loading." *Shock and Vibration* 3 (3): 169–81.

Hunley, Horace. 1863. Letter to PGT Beauregard. NARA Record Group 109, Microfilm Publication M346, Confederate Papers Relating to Citizens of Business Firms: US National Archives, Washington, DC.

Hutchinson, Robert. 2001. *Jane's Submarines: War Beneath the Waves*. New York: HarperCollins.

Jacobsen, Maria. 2005. "Project 04-106, H.L. Hunley Project: 2004 Archaeological Findings and Progress Report." Department of Defense Legacy Resource Management Program.

Jacobsen, Maria, Vincent Blouin, and William Shirley. 2012. "Does Erosion Corrosion Account for Intriguing Damage to the Civil War Submarine H.L. Hunley?" *Marine Technology Science Journal* 46 (6): 38–48.

Jahren, Hope. 2016. *Lab Girl*. New York: Alfred A. Knopf.

Jaques, Richard E. 1863–1865. Letter from Jaques to Jute, August 24, 1863. In *Correspondence*, 1863–1865 [manuscript]. David M. Rubenstein Rare Book and Manuscript Library, Sec. A, Box 72, items 1–55, c.1: Duke University, Durham, NC.

Johnson, Daniel L, John T Yelverton, William Hicks, and Roy Doyal. 1993. "Blast Overpressure Studies with Animals and Man: Biological Response to Complex Blast Waves." Albuquerque, NM: EG and G Inc.

Joseph, Frank. 2008. "The High Technology of the Ancients: Have We Forgotten Secrets We Once Knew?" In *Forbidden Science: From Ancient Technologies to Free Energy*, edited by J Douglas Kenyon. New York: Simon & Schuster.

Kakaç, Sadik, and Yaman Yener. 1994. *Convective Heat Transfer*. 2nd ed. Boca Raton, FL: CRC Press.

Kambouchev, Nayden, Ludovic Noels, and Raul A Radovitzky. 2006. "Nonlinear Compressibility Effects in Fluid-Structure Interaction and Their Implications on the Air-Blast Loading of Structures." *Journal of Applied Physics* 100 (6): 063519-1-11.

———. 2007. "Numerical Simulation of the Fluid-Structure Interaction Between Air Blast Waves and Free-Standing Plates." *Computers and Structures* 85: 923–31.

Kambouchev, Nayden, Raul A Radovitzky, and Ludovic Noels. 2007. "Fluid-Structure Interaction Effects in the Dynamic Response of Free-Standing Plates to Uniform Shock Loading." *Journal of Applied Mechanics* 74 (5): 1042–45.

Kedrinskii, VK. 2005. *Hydrodynamics of Explosion: Experiments and Models*. Germany: Springer.

Kershaw, Alex. 2010. *Escape from the Deep: The Epic Story of a Legendary Submarine and Her Courageous Crew*. Cambridge, MA: Da Capo Press.

Kettner, Mattias, Frank Ramsthaler, Christian Juhnke, Roman Bux, and Peter Schmidt. 2013. "A Fatal Case of CO_2 Intoxication in a Fermentation Tank." *Journal of Forensic Sciences* 58 (2): 556–58.

Kleiven, Svein. 2013. "Why Most Traumatic Brain Injuries Are Not Caused by Linear Acceleration but Skull Fractures Are." *Frontiers in Bioengineering and Biotechnology* 1:15.

Kloeppel, James E. 1987. *Danger Beneath the Waves: A History of the Confederate Submarine H. L. Hunley*. College Park, GA: Adele Enterprises.

Kosanke, KL, and BJ Kosanke. 2003. "Pyrotechnic Burn Rate Measurements: Interstitial Flame Spread Rate Testing." In *Selected Pyrotechnic Publications of K. L. and B. J. Kosanke*, 664–69. Whitewater, CO: Journal of Pyrotechnics, Inc.

Kossler, Herman J. 1974. Letter to Edward Lee Spence, February 6. Strom Thurmond Archives (MSS 100), Chief of Staff records, Box 2, Folder 54: Clemson University, Clemson, SC.

Kronegh, Adam Jon. 2015. "Den ukendte Dansker ombord på undervandsbåden *Hunley*."English translation provided by Adam Jon Kronegh." *Siden Saxo* 3:5–15.

———. 2018. "Untitled." Email with author via LinkedIn. May 25.

Laguerre, O, S Ben Amara, H Moureh, and D Flick. 2007. "Numerical Simulation of Air Flow and Heat Transfer in Domestic Refrigerators." *Journal of Food Engineering* 81: 144–56.

Lake, Simon. 1918. *The Submarine in War and Peace: Its Developments and Its Possibilities*. Philadelphia: J. B. Lippincott.

Lance, Rachel M. 2014. "Hunley Technical Drawings." Email to Friends of the *Hunley*. February 12.

———. 2014. "Re: Hunley Technical Drawings." Email to Friends of the *Hunley*. February 17.

———. 2015. "Keel Ballast." Email to Michael Scafuri. June 29.

———. 2015. "Re: Keel Ballast." Email to Michael Scafuri. June 29.

Lance, Rachel M, Bruce Capehart, Omar Kadro, and Cameron R Bass. 2015. "Human Injury Criteria for Underwater Blasts." *PLoS One* 10 (11): 1–18.

Lance, Rachel M, Richard Moon, Michael Crisafulli, and CR Bass. 2016. "Did the Crew of the Submarine H. L. Hunley Suffocate?" *Forensic Science International* 260: 59–65.

Lance, Rachel M, Michael J Natoli, Sophia AS Dunworth, John J Freiberger, and Richard E Moon. 2017. "The Dewey Monitor: Pulse Oximetry Can Independently Detect Hypoxia in a Rebreather Diver." *Undersea & Hyperbaric Med* 44 (6): 569–80.

Lance, Rachel M, Lucas Stalcup, Brad Wojtylak, and Cameron R Bass. 2017. "Air Blast Injuries Killed the Crew of the Submarine H.L. Hunley." *PLoS One* 12 (8).

Lance, Rachel M, Henry Warder, and Cameron R Bass. 2017. "Did a 'Lucky Shot' Sink the Submarine HL Hunley?" *Forensic Science International* 270: 103–10.

Lasch, Warren. 2000. Letter to Kenneth M. Harper, Carolina First, April 11. Strom Thurmond Collection (MSS 100), Chief of Staff files, Box 72, 2000: Pd-Ph, Folder 2248: Clemson University, Clemson, SC.

Lee, Robert E. 1864. Letter from General Robert E. Lee to General James Longstreet. In *The War of the Rebellion: A Compilation of the Official Records of the Union and Confederate Armies*, Series 1, Vol. 52, Part 2: *Confederate Correspondence, Etc.*, edited by George W Davis, Leslie J Perry and Joseph W Kirkley. Washington, DC: Government Printing Office, 1898.

Leibovici, Dan, Ofer N Gofrit, Michael Stein, Shmuel Shapira, Yossi Noga, Rafael J Heruti, and Joshua Shemer. 1996. "Blast Injuries: Bus Versus Open-Air Bombings—A Comparative Study of Injuries in Survivors of Open-Air Versus Confined-Space Explosions." *J Trauma: Injury, Infection, and Critical Care* 41 (6): 1030–35.

Leiding, Harriette Kershaw. 1921. *Historic Houses of South Carolina*. Philadelphia, PA: J. B. Lppincott.

Lemmons, PC. 1862. Letter to H. G. Gaffney. In *Gaffney Family Correspondence, 1862–1866*. David M. Rubenstein Rare Book and Manuscript Library, Sec. A, Box 49, items 1–10, c.1: Duke University, Durham, NC.

Long, EB. 1971. *The Civil War Day by Day: An Almanac, 1861–1869*. New York: Doubleday.

Mackenzie, CG, AH Riesen, JR Bailey, TN Tahmisian, and PL Crocker. 1945. "Duration of Consciousness in Anoxia at High Altitudes." *J Aviation Medicine* 16: 156–74.

Marsh, John C. 1861. "Attention, Engineers." *The Times-Picayune*, Friday, April 26, 3.

Martin, Alan, and Robert G Case. 2011. *Secret Weapon of the Confederacy*. Half Yard Productions, September 15, National Geographic Channel.

May, Kate Torgovnick. 2015. "The TED2015 Conference in 30 Quotes." TED Blog, accessed January 2018. blog.ted.com/the-ted2015-conference-in-30-quotes/comment-page-2/.

McConnell, Glenn F. 1995. Letter to Don M. Clanton, May 24. Obtained via FOIA request to the Hunley Commission.

———. 1995. Letter to Dr. William S. Dudley, Director of Naval History, October 18. Obtained via FOIA request to the Hunley Commission.

————. 1995. Letter to Senator Strom Thurmond, May 24. Obtained via FOIA request to the Hunley Commission.

————. 1995. Letter to the Honorable Richard C. Shelby, December 14. Obtained via FOIA request to the Hunley Commission.

————. 1996. Letter to Dr. William S. Dudley, Naval Historical Center, April 16. Obtained via FOIA request to the Hunley Commission.

————. 1996. Letter to Steven S. Honigman, Esq., January 5. Obtained via FOIA request to the Hunley Commission.

McConnell, Glenn F, Passailaigue, Rose, and Giese. 1995. Bill S. 844, May 24. Strom Thurmond Archives (MSS 100), Chief of Staff records, Box 2, Folder 58: Clemson University, Clemson, SC.

McIntyre, Fred L, and Richard M Rindner. 1980. "A Compilation of Hazard and Test Data for Pyrotechnic Compositions." Computer Sciences Corp.: Stennis Space Center, MS.

McLaurin. 1925. "South Carolina Confederate Twins." *Confederate Veteran* 33:328.

McPherson, James M. 1988. *Battle Cry of Freedom: The Civil War Era*. Oxford, England: Oxford University Press.

————. 2012. *War on the Waters: The Union and Confederate Navies, 1861–1865*. Chapel Hill, NC: University of North Carolina Press.

Medak, Peter. 2009. *Breaking Bad*, Season 2, Episode 6, "Peekaboo."

Mehrländer, Andrea. 2011. *The Germans of Charleston, Richmond and New Orleans During the Civil War Period, 1850–1870: A Study and Research Compendium*. Berlin, NY: De Gruyter.

Mekjavic, Igor B, Michael J Tipton, and Ola Eiken. 2003. "Thermal Considerations in Diving." In *Bennett and Elliott's Physiology and Medicine of Diving*, edited by Alf O Brubakk and Tom S Neuman. Philadelphia: Elsevier Science.

Mellor, SG, and GJ Cooper. 1989. "Analysis of 828 Servicemen Killed or Injured by Explosion in Northern Ireland 1970–84: The Hostile Action Casualty System." *British Journal of Surgery* 76 (October): 1006–10.

Michie, Peter S. 1865. "Notes Explaining Rebel Torpedoes and Ordnance as Shown in Plates Nos. 1 to 21 Inclusive." In *Confederate Torpedoes: Two Illustrated 19th Century Works with New Appendices and Photographs* [work transcribed and published 2011], edited by Herbert M. Schiller. Jefferson, NC: MacFarland & Company, Inc., Publishers.

Milgram, Joseph B, and Norman P Gentieu. 1961. *George Washington Rains: Gunpowdermaker of the Confederacy*. Philadelphia Foote Mineral Company: Item 08026183, Hagley Museum and Library, Wilmington, DE.

Mississippi. 1861. "A Declaration of the immediate causes which induce and justify the secession of the state of Mississippi from the Federal Union." Jackson, MS: January 9.

Moore, Albert Burton. 1924. *Conscription and Conflict in the Confederacy*. New York: The Macmillan Company.

Murphy, Larry E, Daniel J Lenihan, Christopher F Amer, Matthew A Russell, Robert S Neyland, Richard Wills, Scott Harris, Adriane Askins, Timothy G Smith, and Steven M Shope. 1998. "H. L. Hunley Site Assessment." Edited by Larry E Murphy. Santa Fe, NM: Submerged Cultural Resources Unit, Intermountain Region, National Park Service.

Napadensky, Hyla S, and James J Swatosh Jr. 1972. "TNT Equivalency of Black Powder. Volume 1: Management Summary and Technical Discussion." Chicago: IIT Research Institute.

Nasmyth, James. 1853. "Submarine Mortar Frigate." *Scientific American*, 8 (23): 178.

National Oceanic and Atmospheric Administration (NOAA). 2018. "Water Temperature Table of the Southern Atlantic Coast." National Oceanic and Atmospheric Administration, National Centers for Environmental Information. nodc .noaa.gov/dsdt/cwtg/satl.html.

National Park Service (NPS). 2004. "The Civil War Soldiers and Sailors System." National Park Service, accessed Multiple accessions, spring 2018. nps.gov /civilwar/soldiers-and-sailors-database.htm.

Naval Construction Research Establishment (NCRE). 1948. Scaling Laws for Damage by Underwater Explosions, ADM 280/41. UK: Department of Research Programmes and Planning, Admiralty, Naval Construction Research Establishment.

Naval History and Heritage Command (NHHC). 2017. "Science Meets History: Incident Analysis of H. L. Hunley." Last Modified August 2, accessed December 12, 2017. www.history.navy.mil/research/underwater-archaeology/sites-and -projects/ship-wrecksites/hl-hunley/hunley-incident-analysis.html.

Nelson, Colonel Robert C. 1974. Letter to E. Lee Spence, May 10. Strom Thurmond Archives (MSS 100), Chief of Staff records, Box 2, Folder 54: Clemson University, Clemson, SC.

Neuberger, A, S Peles, and D Rittel. 2007. "Scaling the Response of Circular Plates Subjected to Large and Close-Range Spherical Explosions. Part I: Air-Blast Loading." *International Journal of Impact Engineering* 34: 859–73.

Neyland, Robert S, Claire P Peachey, Shea McLean, Harry Pecorelli III, Heather G Brown, M Scott Harris, Maria Jacobsen, Paul Mardikian, Michael P Scafuri, and David L Conlin. 2016. "H. L. Hunley Recovery Operations." Washington, DC: Naval History and Heritage Command.

Noe, Kenneth W. 2010. *Reluctant Rebels: The Confederates Who Joined the Army After 1861*. Chapel Hill, NC: University of North Carolina Press.

O'Flynn, Lt. Brian. 1996. *An Analysis of the Quality of Confederate Gunpowder Produced at Augusta Powder Mills* [Master's Thesis]. University of Alabama: Item 08075545, Hagley Museum and Library, Wilmington, DE.

Panzer, MB, CR Bass, KA Rafaels, J Shridharani, and BP Capehart. 2012. "Primary Blast Survival and Injury Risk Assessment for Repeated Blast Exposure." *J Trauma* 72: 454–66.

Parks, Nadine. 2009. "Another Death. Three Rescued. What's Going On?" *The Post and Courier*, July 10.

Payne, John. 1863. Requisition to Joseph Puolah. NARA Record Group 45, Microfilm Publication M625, Area File of the Naval Records Collection, 1775–1910, Roll 414, Area File, Area 8, Confederate States Navy: National Archives, Washington, DC.

Peck, Danielle. 2002. "The First Submarine." In *Building the Impossible*. London: British Broadcasting Corporation.

Petersen, Bo. 2014. "Treacherous Tides." *The Post and Courier*, July 12. https://www.postandcourier.com/archives/treacherous-tides/article_1d717f67-f98b-5d16-8284-beb809088751.html.

Peterson, Clarence Stewart, and John Adolphus Bernard Dahlgren. 1945. *Admiral John A. Dahlgren: Father of United States Naval Ordnance*. New York: The Hobson Book Press.

Petri, Nadan M, Josip Dujella, Marija Definis-Gojanovic, Lena Vranjkovic-Petri, and Dražen Cuculic. 2001. "Diving-Related Fatalities Caused by Underwater Explosions: A Report of Two Cases." *The American Journal of Forensic Medicine and Pathology* 22 (4): 383–86.

Pickering, Mary. 1888. Approved Pension Application File for Dependents of Charles W. Pickering (Certificate No. 3860). Case Files of Approved Pension Applications of Widows and Other Dependents of Navy Veterans, ca. 1861–ca. 1910; Records of the Department of Veterans Affairs, 1773–2007, Record Group 15: National Archives at Washington, DC [online version available through the Archival Research Catalog (ARC identifier 92174471) at www.archives.gov; 2018].

Pinkerton, Allan. 1853–1999. Pinkerton's National Detective Agency Records. MSS36301 and Microfilm 16,574-3P: Library of Congress, Washington, DC.

———. 1862. Letter to Hon. P. H. Watson, Assistant Secretary of War. In *Reports of Detective Allan Pinkerton*, Identifier 4482961. RG 110, Records of the Provost Marshal General's Bureau (Civil War), 1861–1907: National Archives and Records Administration, Washington, DC.

———. 1862. The United States to Allan Pinkerton (itemized billing ledgers). In *Reports of Detective Allan Pinkerton*, Identifier 4482961. RG 110, Records of the Provost Marshal General's Bureau (Civil War), 1861–1907: National Archives and Records Administration, Washington, DC.

———. 1883. "Chapter XXVI: A Woman's Discoveries—An Infernal Machine—The Shipping in Danger—Discovery and Destruction of the Submarine Battery." In *The Spy of the Rebellion, Being a True History of the Spy System of the United States*

Army During the Late Rebellion, 394–403. New York: G. W. Carleton & Co., Publishers.

Pratt, AA. 1861–1864. Letter to George Washington Rains. George Washington Rains Papers, 1843–1949, Collection 01510-z: Southern Historical Collection, University of North Carolina at Chapel Hill, Chapel Hill, NC.

Pugliese, Frank. 1995. Letter to Honorable Strom Thurmond, June 8. Strom Thurmond Archives (MSS 100), Chief of Staff records, Box 2, Folder 54: Clemson University, Clemson, SC.

Quinn, Raegan. 2008. "Saving History: The Magic of Conservation." *The Blue Light* (Fall): 4–6.

———. 2008. "Surface of Time." *The Blue Light* (Fall): 5–7.

Rafaels, K, CR Bass, M Panzer, R Salzar, WA Woods, S Feldman, T Walilko, R Kent, B Capehart, J Foster, B Derkunt, and A Toman. 2012. "Brain Injury Risk from Primary Blast." *J Trauma* 73: 895–901.

Ragan, Mark K. 1999. *The Hunley: Submarines, Sacrifice, and Success in the Civil War.* Orangeburg, SC: Sandlapper Publishing Company.

———. 1999. *Union and Confederate Submarine Warfare in the Civil War.* Mason City, IA: Savas Publishing Company.

———. 2001. "The Confederate Submarine Pioneer, Forerunner of the H. L. Hunley." *The Blue Light* 2 (Fall): 3.

Rains, Gabriel J. ca. 1870. "*Torpedo Book.*" In *Confederate Torpedoes: Two Illustrated 19th Century Works with New Appendices and Photographs* [works transcribed and published 2011], edited by Herbert M. Schiller. Jefferson, NC: MacFarland & Company, Inc., Publishers.

Rains, George Washington. 1843. Artillery Circular, Fort Monroe. George Washington Rains Papers, 1843–1949, Collection 01510-z: Southern Historical Collection, University of North Carolina at Chapel Hill, Chapel Hill, NC.

———. 1846. Letter to W.W.L. Blifs. George Washington Rains Papers, 1843–1949, Collection 01510-z: Southern Historical Collection, University of North Carolina at Chapel Hill, Chapel Hill, NC.

———. 1847. Letter to Gabriel Rains. George Washington Rains Papers, 1843–1949, Collection 01510-z: Southern Historical Collection, University of North Carolina at Chapel Hill, Chapel Hill, NC.

———. 1861. *Notes on Making Saltpeter from the Earth of the Caves.* Augusta, Georgia, Steam Power Press Chronicle and Sentinel [reprinted 1973]: Item 08032775, Hagley Museum and Library, Wilmington, DE.

———. 1882. "History of the Confederate Powder Works: An Address Delivered by Invitation Before the Confederate Survivors' Association." Newburgh, NY; *Newburgh Daily News*: Item ID 08032772, PAM, Hagley Museum and Library, Wilmington, DE.

———. ca. 1880. Memorandum relative to the establishment of the Gunpowder Works at Augusta and the matter of material under charge of Colon. Geo. W.

Rains Corps of Artillers on Ordnance duty in the years 1861, 1862, 1863, & 1864. Accession 2598: Hagley Museum and Library, Wilmington, DE.

———. n.d. Col. Rains's Appeal for the Powder Works Obelisk. George Washington Rains Papers, 1843–1949, Collection 01510-z: Southern Historical Collection, University of North Carolina at Chapel Hill, Chapel Hill, NC.

Rainsford, SG. 1939. "Report on Probable Condition of Bodies in HMS Thetis, ADM 116/4429." ADM 116/4429. The National Archives, Kew, London: Medical Director General of the Navy.

Ramu, Murugan, V Prabhu Raja, and PR Rhyla. 2013. "Establishment of Structural Similitude for Elastic Models and Validation of Scaling Laws." *KSCE Journal of Civil Engineering* 17 (1): 139–44.

Reid, Warren D. 1996. "The Response of Surface Ships to Underwater Explosions." DSTO-GD-0109. Ship Structures and Materials Division, Aeronautical and Maritime Research Laboratory, Commonwealth of Australia: Department of Defence.

Reilly, Robert F. 2016. "Medical and Surgical Care During the American Civil War, 1861–1865." *Proc Bayl Univ Med Cent* 29 (2): 138–42.

Reuters. 1995. "Rebels' Sub Set to Rise." *The Guardian*, May 13, 14.

Richardson, DW, AJ Wasserman, and JL Patterson. 1960. "General and Regional Circulatory Responses to Change in Blood Ph and Carbon Dioxide Tension." *Journal of Clinical Investigation* 40 (1): 31–43.

Richardson, Holly Johnston. 1995. Engagements for Senator Strom Thurmond Tuesday, October 24, 1995. Strom Thurmond Collection (MSS 100), Personal assistant files (MSS.0100.17.2), Box 27, Folder 490: Clemson University, Clemson, SC.

———. 1995. Week at a Glance for Senator Strom Thurmond Monday, September 11, through Monday, September 18. Strom Thurmond Collection (MSS 100), Personal assistant files (MSS.0100.17.2), Box 27, Folder 490: Clemson University, Clemson, SC.

Richmond, West, and Johnston. 1863. *Confederate Receipt Book: A Compilation of Over One Hundred Receipts, Adapted to the Times*. Richmond, VA: G. W. Gary.

Richmond, Donald R, Edward G Damon, E Royce Fletcher, I Gerald Bowen, and Clayton S White. 1968. "The Relationship Between Selected Blast-Wave Parameters and the Response of Mammals Exposed to Air Blast." *Ann NY Acad Sci*, 152 (1): 103–21.

Richmond, Donald R, and Clayton S White. 1966. *Biological Effects of Blast and Shock*. Technical Progress Report on Contract No. DA-49-146-XZ-055: Lovelace Foundation for Medical Education and Research, Albuquerque, NM.

Robbins, Peggy. 2002. "The Confederacy's Bomb Brothers." *Journal of Conventional Weapons Destruction* 6 (1): Article 31.

Robinson. 1863. "A Raid Among the Rice Plantations." *Harper's Weekly*, July, 427.

Rossi, Cesare, and Flavio Russo. 2016. *Ancient Engineers' Inventions: Precursors of the Present*. New York: Springer.

Rothman, Lily. 2014. "Stephanie Kwolek: The Lifesaving Inventor of Kevlar." *Time*, July 7–14: 21.

Rowan, SC. 1890. "Instructions from Captain Rowan, U.S. Navy, to Acting Master Patterson, U.S. Navy, Regarding Precautions Against a Repetition of the Attack." In *The War of the Rebellion: A Compilation of the Official Records of the Union and Confederate Navies*, Series 1, Vol. 15: *South Atlantic Blockading Squadron from Oct 1, 1863, to Sep 30, 1864*, edited by Charles W Stewart. Washington, DC: US Government Printing Office [available online via hathitrust.org].

Rowland, Buford, and William B Boyd. 1953. *U.S. Navy Bureau of Ordnance in World War II*. Bureau of Ordnance, Department of the Navy.

Roy, John. 1862. John Roy Diary, 1860–1862, 1871, MSS 1531. Louisiana and Lower Mississippi Valley Collections, LSU Libraries, Baton Rouge, LA.

Rucker, Chris. 2011. "Making Civil War-Era 'Blue Light': A Pyrotechnic Night Signal." Accessed 2016. [available online at youtube.com/watch?v=h1yfGuLr1dA].

Ruffin, Edmund. 1865. Edmund Ruffin diaries, 1856–1865, MSS51839 (Microfilm). Library of Congress Manuscript Division, Washington, DC.

———. 1977. *The Diary of Edmund Ruffin: A Dream Shattered*. Vol. 3. Edited by William K Scarborough. Baton Rouge, LA: LSU Press.

———. 1977. *The Diary of Edmund Ruffin: Toward Independence*. Vol. 1. Edited by William K Scarborough. Baton Rouge, LA: LSU Press.

———. 1977. *The Diary of Edmund Ruffin: The Years of Hope*. Vol. 2. Edited by William K Scarborough. Baton Rouge, LA: LSU Press.

Sacher, John M. 2007. "'A Very Disagreeable Business': Confederate Conscription in Louisiana." *Civil War History* 53 (2): 141–69.

Sassé, Ronald A. 1981. *The Influence of Physical Properties on Black Powder Combustion*. Technical Report ARBRL-TR-02308. Aberdeen Proving Ground, MD: US Army Armament Research and Development Command, Ballistic Research Laboratory.

Saukko, Pekka, and Bernard Knight. 2015. *Knight's Forensic Pathology*, 4th ed. Boca Raton, FL: CRC Press.

Scafuri, Michael P. 2014. "Re: Hunley Technical Drawings." Email to Rachel M Lance, February 21.

———. 2015. "Re: Keel Ballast." Email to Rachel M Lance, June 29.

Scharf, John Thomas. 1887. *History of the Confederate States Navy from Its Organization to the Surrender of Its Last Vessel: Its stupendous struggle with the great Navy of the United States; the engagements fought in the rivers and harbors of the South, and upon the High Seas; blockade-running, first use of iron-clads and torpedoes, and privateer history*. n.p.: Rogers & Sherwood.

Segal, Bernard L, William Likoff, and Benedict Kingsley. 1966. "Echocardiography: Clinical Application in Mitral Stenosis." *JAMA* 195 (3): 161–66.

Sharrer, Elizabeth A, Suzanne G Darrah, M Scott Harris, and Maria Jacobsen. 2001. "Marine Macrofaunal Analysis of the Interior Sediments from the H. L. Hunley (38CH1651)." Geological Society of America Annual Meeting, Charleston, South Carolina, November 5–8, 2001.

Shelford, WO. 1960. *Subsunk.* London, United Kingdom: George G. Harrap & Co. Ltd.

Sherman, William Tecumseh. 1865. *General Sherman's Official Account of His Great March Through Georgia and the Carolinas.* New York: Bunce & Huntington.

Shock, William H. 1864. Letter to Gustavus V Fox. NARA Record Group 45, Microfilm publication M148, January 1864, vol. 2, Letters Received by the Secretary of the Navy from Commissioned Officers Below the Rank of Commander ("Officers Letters") 1802–1884. National Archives, Washington, DC.

Siddali, Silvana R. 2005. *From Property to Person: Slavery and the Confiscation Acts, 1861–1862.* Baton Rouge, LA: Louisiana State University Press.

Singleton, James AG, Iain E Gibb, Anthony MJ Bull, Pete F Mahoney, and Jon C Clasper. 2013. "Primary Blast Lung Injury Prevalence and Fatal Injuries from Explosions: Insights from Postmortem Computed Tomographic Analysis of 121 Improvised Explosive Device Fatalities." *J Trauma Acute Care Surg* 75 (2): S269–74.

Sleeman, Charles William. 1880. *Torpedoes and Torpedo Warfare: Containing a complete and concise account of the rise and progress of submarine warfare; Also a detailed description of all matters appertaining thereto, including the latest improvements.* Portsmouth, UK: Griffin & Co.

Snell, FI, and MJ Halter. 2010. "A Signature Wound of War: Mild Traumatic Brain Injury." *J Psychosoc Nurs Ment Health Serv* 48 (2): 22–28.

South Carolina Hunley Commission (SCHC). 1995. "The Hunley Confederate Submarine Study Commission Meeting Minutes, August 2, 1995—10:30 a.m." Columbia, SC: Obtained via FOIA request to the Hunley Commission.

———. 1995. "The Hunley Confederate Submarine Study Commission Meeting Minutes, December 12, 1995—2:30 p.m." Columbia, SC: Obtained via FOIA request to the Hunley Commission.

———. 1995. "The Hunley Confederate Submarine Study Commission Meeting Minutes, October 11, 1995—1:30 p.m." Columbia, SC: Obtained via FOIA request to the Hunley Commission.

———. 1995. "The Hunley Confederate Submarine Study Commission Meeting Minutes, September 14, 1995—1:30 p.m." Columbia, SC: Obtained via FOIA request to the Hunley Commission.

———. 1996. "H.L. Hunley Press Conference—Transcript, Tuesday, August 6, 1996, 10:00 a.m." North Charleston, SC: Obtained via FOIA request to the Hunley Commission.

———. 1996. "Programmatic Agreement Among the Department of the Navy, the General Services Administration, the Advisory Council on Historic Preservation, the South Carolina Hunley Commission, and the South Carolina State Historic Preservation Officer Concerning Management of the Wreck of the H. L. Hunley." Columbia, SC: Obtained via FOIA request to the Hunley Commission.

South Carolina State Development Board. 1971. Letter with Enclosed Proposal. "The South Carolina National Naval Museum (A Proposal)." Sent to Strom Thurmond July 15. Strom Thurmond Collection (MSS 100), Administrative Assistant files, Subject files (subseries A), Box 2, Folder: Charleston Naval Museum, July 1971: Clemson University, Clemson, SC.

Spence, E Lee. 1974. Letter to Peter T. Gladding, Director, Sales Division, General Services Administration, January 16. Strom Thurmond Archives (MSS 100), Chief of Staff records, Box 2, Folder 54: Clemson University, Clemson, SC.

———. 1974. Letter with Map to Colonel Robert C. Nelson, District Engineer, US Army Corps of Engineers. Strom Thurmond Archives (MSS 100), Chief of Staff records, Box 2, Folder 54: Clemson University, Clemson, SC.

Spicer, William A. 1865. Diary. In *Papers*, 1865–1885 [manuscript]. David M. Rubenstein Rare Book and Manuscript Library, Sec. A, Box 123, items 1–2, c.1: Duke University, Durham, NC.

———. 1885. *The Flag Replaced on Sumter: A Personal Narrative*. In *Papers*, 1865–1885 [manuscript]. David M. Rubenstein Rare Book and Manuscript Library, Sec. A, Box 123, items 1–2, c.1: Providence Press Company; Duke University, Durham, NC.

Stanton, CL. 1914. "Submarines and Torpedo Boats." *Confederate Veteran*, 22: 398–99.

Stevens, William D, and Jonathan M Leader. 2006. "Skeletal Remains from the Confederate Naval Sailor and Marines' Cemetery, Charleston, SC." *Historical Archaeology* 40 (3): 74–88.

Strickland, Russell, Wesley Kitchel, Stephen Ashbrock, Paul Boecker, III, Ronald Bowser, John Brunacini, Kenneth Gilliam, Russell Grossman, Jerry Hallbauer, Edward Hartin, Michael Jepeal, Alan E Joos, Richard Karasaki, John Kenyon, John Leete, Dan Madrzykowski, Roy Paige, Harold Richardson, Cary Roccaforte, Anne Wieringa, and Ron Williams. 2008. *Essentials of Fire Fighting and Fire Department Operations*. Edited by Carl Goodson and Lynne Murnane. 5th ed. Stillwater, OK: Fire Protection Publications.

Sturma, Michael. 2009. *The USS Flier: Death and Survival on a World War II Submarine*. Lexington, KY: The University Press of Kentucky.

Suominen, P, C Baillie, R Korpela, S Rautanen, S Ranta, and KT Olkkola. 2002. "Impact of Age, Submersion Time and Water Temperature on Outcome in Near-Drowning." *Resuscitation* 52 (33): 247–54.

Swinfield, John. 2014. *Sea Devils: Pioneer Submariners*. Stroud, Gloucestershire, UK: The History Press.

Taborelli, RV, IG Bowen, and ER Fletcher. 1959. "Operation Plumbbob: Tertiary Effects of Blast-Displacement." Civil Effects Test Group: Lovelace Foundation for Medical Education and Research, Albuquerque, NM.

Tanner, Robert. 1995. "Black Leaders Protest Recent Statehouse Moves." *The Greenville News*, May 23, 17.

Taylor, GI. 1963. "The Pressure and Impulse of Submarine Explosion Waves on Plates." In *The Scientific Papers of Sir Geoffrey Ingram Taylor*, Vol. 3: *Aerodynamics and the Mechanics of Projectiles and Explosions*, edited by G Batchelor, 287–303. Cambridge, UK: Cambridge University Press.

Teddeman, William. 1884. Disapproved Pension Application File for Contraband William Teddeman, USS *Housatonic* (Application Number 9541). Case Files of Disapproved Pension Applications of Civil War and Later Navy Veterans, ca. 1861–ca. 1910; Records of the Department of Veterans Affairs, 1773–2007, Record Group 15: National Archives at Washington, DC [online version available through the Archival Research Catalog (ARC identifier 90460494) at www.archives.gov; 2018].

Theodore, Louis. 2011. *Heat Transfer Applications for the Practicing Engineer*. Los Angeles, CA: John Wiley & Sons.

Thomson, William. 1855. "On the Theory of the Electric Telegraph." *Proceedings of the Royal Society of London* 7: 382–99.

Thurmond, Strom. 1995. Statement by Senator Strom Thurmond (R-SC) on the Floor of the Senate in Opposition to the Amendment to Divert Funding from LHD-7 to Contingency Operations. Strom Thurmond Collection (MSS 100), Speeches, Folder 203, C:Post-1983, Statements on the Senate Floor, June 30, 1995–August 3, 1995.

———. 1995. Statement by Senator Strom Thurmond (R-SC) on the Floor of the Senate Regarding the Bumpers Amendment to S 1026 (August). Strom Thurmond Collection (MSS 100), Speeches, Folder 203, C:Post-1983, Statements on the Senate Floor, June 30, 1995–August 3, 1995.

———. 1995. Statement by Senator Strom Thurmond (R-SC) on the Floor of the Senate Regarding the Kohl Amendment to S 1026. Strom Thurmond Collection (MSS 100), Speeches, Folder 203, C:Post-1983, Statements on the Senate Floor, June 30, 1995–August 3, 1995.

———. 1995. Statement by Senator Strom Thurmond (R-SC), Chairman of the Committee on Armed Services, on the Senate Floor, Introducing S 1026, the National Defense Authorization Bill for Fiscal Year 1996. August 2, 1995. Strom Thurmond Collection (MSS 100), Speeches, Folder 203, C:Post-1983, Statements on the Senate Floor, June 30, 1995–August 3, 1995.

———. 1995. "Thurmond Seeks to Strike Language that Might Move CSS Hunley to Alabama," August 9. Strom Thurmond Collection (MSS 100), Legislative assistant files (MSS.0100.15.1), Box 22, Folder 663.

Tipton, M J. 1989. "The Initial Responses to Cold-Water Immersion in Man." *Clinical Science* 77: 581–88.

Tomb, James H. 1865. "Notes from Papers of First Assistant Engineer Tomb, C.S. Navy, Regarding the Submarine Torpedo Boat, Charleston, SC, January 1864[5]." In *Blue & Gray at Sea: Naval Memoirs of the Civil War*, edited by Brian M Thomsen, 435. New York: Tom Doherty Associates.

Tucker, Spencer. 2013. *Blue & Gray Navies: The Civil War Afloat*. Annapolis, MD: Naval Institute Press.

Ubelaker, Douglas H, and Erica Bubniak-Jones. 2003. *Human Remains from Voegtly Cemetery, Pittsburgh, Pennsylvania, Excavations* (Archaeology). Washington, DC: Smithsonian Institution Press.

University of North Carolina (UNC). 1993. Summary Sheet, George Washington Rains. George Washington Rains Papers, 1843–1949, Collection 01510-z: Southern Historical Collection, University of North Carolina at Chapel Hill, Chapel Hill, NC.

Unknown. 1849. "Infernal Machine Arrest." *Keowee Courier*, June 9, 2.

Unknown. 1861. "Native Enterprise." *Daily Delta*, Saturday, August 17.

Unknown. 1862. "The City: Redivivus." *Times-Picayune*, February 12, 2.

Unknown. 1863. "Letter from Charleston." *Times-Picayune*, March 20, 1.

Unknown. 1863. "Non-Combatants." *Edgefield Adviser*, quoting the *Charleston Mercury*, August 26, 3.

Unknown. 1863. "A Torpedo Inventor Sent to Fort Lafayette in Irons." *The Daily True Delta*, November 5, 1.

Unknown. 1870. "Down in the Depths: Wrecking Operations in Charleston Harbor—The Sunken Monitors—the Sloop-of-War *Housatonic*." Original to the *Charleston Courier* (August 5, 1870), republished in the *Osage Mission Journal*, September 8, 1.

Unknown. 1870. "Interesting Relics." *Daily Phoenix*, July 31, 2.

Unknown. 1871. "The Housatonic." *Yorkville Enquirer*, June 29, 3.

Unknown. 1875. "Wilhelm Bauer." *Scientific American*, August 28, 32–33.

Unknown. 1876. "General Beauregard." *Harrisburg Telegraph*, 21 July, 2.

Unknown. 1877. "The Confederate Torpedo Device." *Times-Picayune*, June 24, 9.

Unknown. 1886. "A Submarine Boat: The Story of a Queer Confederate Craft." *Russell Register*, June 26, 4.

Unknown. 1890. "They Braved the Deep: Risks and Death Roll of an Experimental War Craft." *Wichita Daily Eagle* (publishing an American Press Association article), July 19, 8.

Unknown. 1898. George Washington Rains, No. 1113. Class of 1842. In Annual Reunion, June 9th, 1898, 71–75. George Washington Rains Papers, 1843–1949, Collection 01510-z: Southern Historical Collection, University of North Carolina at Chapel Hill, Chapel Hill, NC.

Unknown. 1901a. "Sold for Junk: First Submarine War Ship Is Now Old Iron." *Evening Star*, July 27, 21.

Unknown. 1901b. "Sold for Junk: First Submarine War Ship Is Now Old Iron." *Evening Star*, Saturday, July 27.

Unknown. 1974. "Wreck of USS Monitor Found off Cape Hatteras." *Baltimore Sun*, March 8, 1–3.

Unknown. 2016. "Controversy over the Enola Gay." www.atomicheritage.org [accessed April 2019], October 17.

United States Army. 1862. *The Ordnance Manual for the Use of the Officers of the United States Army*, 3rd Ed. Philadelphia, PA: J. B. Lippincott & Co.

United States Census Board (USCB). 1850. Database with images. FamilySearch. FamilySearch.org, citing NARA Microfilm Publication M432. Washington, DC: National Archives, n.d.

———. 1860. United States Census, 1860. Database with images. FamilySearch. FamilySearch.org, citing NARA Microfilm Publication M432. Washington DC: National Archives, n.d.

———. 1864. "Recapitulation of the Tables of Population, Nativity, and Occupation, United States Census, 1860." Washington, DC [available online at www2.census.gov/library/publications/decennial/1860/population/1860a-46.pdf]: United States Census Bureau, Government Printing Office.

United States Navy. 1860–1865. *Torpedoes*. RG 45: US National Archives and Records Administration, Washington, DC.

———. 1864. "Proceedings of the Naval Court of Inquiry on the Sinking of the USS Housatonic." NARA Microfilm Publication M 273, Reel 169, Case 4345, Records of the Judge Advocate General (Navy), Record Group 125: National Archives and Records Administration, Washington, DC [transcription available online at www.vernianera.com/Hunley/Housatonic-Inquiry.html].

———. 1971. *U.S. Navy Diving Gas Manual*, 2nd ed., NAVSHIPS 0994-003-7010. U.S. Navy Supervisor of Diving, Naval Ships Systems Command.

United States War Department. 1890. *The War of the Rebellion: A Compilation of the Official Records of the Union and Confederate Armies*, Series 1, Vol. 28, Part 1: *Reports*, edited by Robert N Scott. Washington, DC: US Government Printing Office [available online via hathitrust.org].

Vander Hook, Sue. 2011. *Louis Pasteur: Groundbreaking Chemist & Biologist*. Edina, MN: ABDO Publishing Company.

Virginia. 1861. "Virginia Ordinance of Secession." Virginia Convention, Richmond, VA, June 14.

von Maltitz, Ian. 2003. *Black Powder Manufacturing, Testing, and Optimizing*. Dingmans Ferry, PA: American Fireworks News.

Walker, LP. 1865. "Telegraph from LP Walker to Gen. Beauregard, Charleston, South Carolina, April 10, 1861." In *The Political History of the United States of*

America, During the Great Rebellion, from November 6, 1860, to July 4, 1864, edited by Edward McPherson. Washington, DC: Pilp & Solomons.

Walker, Sally M. 2005. *Secrets of a Civil War Submarine: Solving the Mysteries of the H.L. Hunley*. Minneapolis, MN: Carolrhoda Books.

Waters, W Davis. 1989. "'Deception Is the Art of War': Gabriel J. Rains, Torpedo Specialist of the Confederacy." *The North Carolina Historical Review* 66 (1): 29–60.

Werner, Herbert A. 2002. *Iron Coffins: A Personal Account of the German U-Boat Battles of World War II*. New York: Holt, Rinehart, and Winston.

Wescoat, Artha Brailsford. 1863–1864. Diary [manuscript]. David M. Rubenstein Rare Book and Manuscript Library, Sec. A, Box 139, item 1, c.1: Duke University, Durham, NC.

Widmaier, Eric P, Hershel Raff, and Kevin T Strang. 2004. *Vander, Sherman, and Luciano's Human Physiology*. New York: McGraw-Hill.

Wilkinson, Jeff. 2011. "Siege of Charleston." *The State*, September 25. [Published online].

Willenbucher, E, and CG Krebs. 1865. General Map of Charleston Harbor South Carolina, showing rebel defences and obstructions. In "Reports, Correspondence, and Drawings Relating to Torpedoes, 1855–1867" (Record Group 71, Entry 43A). National Archives and Records Administration, Washington, DC.

Williams, Absolum. 1863. "Find A Grave Index," database, FamilySearch (family search.org/ark:/61903/1:1:QVV4-DYBX: 13 December 2015), Absolum Williams, 1863. Burial, Charleston, South Carolina, United States of America, Magnolia Cemetery; citing record ID 8648203, Find a Grave, www.finda grave.com.

Wilson, Charles. 1995. "Effect of Differing Charcoal Types upon Handmade Lift Powder." *Journal of Pyrotechnics* (10): 49–55.

Winchester, Simon. 2003. *Krakatoa: The Day the World Exploded*. New York: HarperCollins Publishers, Inc.

Wise, Stephen R. 1994. *Gate of Hell: Campaign for Charleston Harbor, 1863*. Columbia, SC: University of South Carolina Press.

Wolf, Matthew. 2014. "Physiological Consequences of Rapid or Prolonged Aircraft Decompression: Evaluation Using a Human Respiratory Model." *Aviat Space Environ Medicine* 85 (4): 466–72.

Wolfe, Jeremy M, Keith R Kluender, Dennis M Levi, Linda M Bartoshuk, Rachel S Herz, Roberta Klatzky, Susan J Lederman, and Daniel M Merfeld. 2018. Sensation & Perception, 4th Ed., Companion Website. Sinauer Associates. https://wolfe4e.sinauer.com/.

Wood, GW, MB Panzer, JK Shridharani, Matthews KA, and CR Bass. 2013. "Attenuation of Blast Overpressure Behind Ballistic Protective Vests." *Injury Prevention* 19: 19–25.

Wright, HC. 1947. *Subjective Effects of Distant Underwater Explosions*, RNPL3/47. Alverstoke, Hants, UK: Medical Research Council, Royal Naval Personnel Research Committee, Underwater Blast Sub-Committee.

Wynn, Stephen. 2016. *Gravesend in the Great War*. Barnsley, UK: Pen and Sword.

Yelverton, JT, and DR Richmond. 1981. "Underwater Explosion Damage Risk Criteria for Fish, Birds, And Mammals." *J Acout Soc Am* 70 (1): 84.

Zuckerman, S. 1941. "Discussion on the Problem of Blast Injuries." *Proc R Soc Med* 34: 171–92.

CREDITS

255 Illustration of Singer's torpedo: USN, Torpedoes, ca. 1864. Purported drawing of *Hunley*'s torpedo: Gillmore, *Letters and Drawings*, 1865–1867, US Naval Archives.

256 Portrait of diarist Edmund Ruffin: Unknown. Ruffin Portrait, ca. 1861. Image No. 111-BA-1226, National Archives and Records Administration, Washington, DC.

INDEX

Page numbers in *italics* indicate illustrations.